Jesus' Teaching on Repentance

Jesus' Teaching on Repentance

J. D. Choi

International Studies in Formative Christianity and Judaism
Global Publications, Binghamton University
2000

Library of Congress in Publication Data

J. D. Choi, *Jesus' Teaching on Repentance*

ISBN 1-586840-21-5

Published and Distributed by:
International Studies in Formative Christianity and Judaism
Global Publications, Binghamton University
State University of New York at Binghamton
Binghamton, New York, USA 13902-6000
Phone: (607) 777-4495 or 777-6104; Fax: (607) 777-6132
E-mail: pmorewed@binghamton.edu
http://ssips.binghamton.edu

DEDICATION

To my teacher

Professor J. C. O'Neill

TABLE OF CONTENTS

ACKNOWLEDGMENTS

I pay tribute to Professor J. C. O'Neill, a Christian gentleman and scholar of acumen, who supervised my work throughout with great patience and constant care and encouragement. His teachings and guidance are invaluable. I was honoured to learn from him. My debt to him is apparent at every stage in the following pages and my gratitude is everlasting.

I specially thank Dr. D. L. Mealand who acted as second supervisor. His strong interest and acute criticisms have helped me to form a habit, of always being aware of the counter argument. I am particularly grateful for his kind and extensive orientation in the Jewish and Greek texts.

My thanks go to Dr. D. A. Templeton. His encouragement and sympathy embedded in humour and modesty will always remind me of how to uplift the spirit of fellow Christians. I owe thanks to Dr. J. I. H. McDonald for his constant encouragement. He showed a keen interest from the early stages of my research. His refreshing ideas helped me to broaden my perspective. I also thank Dr. P. Hayman who allowed me of his precious time for the discussion of repentance and restitution in Judaism.

I am grateful to Professor D. Forrester, Principal of New College, who kindly supported my application to receive a scholarship from the Archie McIntyre Fund, and also to the Dean of New College, Mr. D. Wright, who kindly supported my application to receive a New College Studentship. I also express my gratitude to the Librarians of New College, Dr. Simpson and Mrs. Norma Henderson and other librarians who kindly helped me to find important books and articles.

I and my family will always remember Rev. and Mrs. McDonald, Rev. and Mrs. Ritchie, Rev. and Mrs. McIntosh, members of the Mayfield Church for their love and timely care for my family. I owe special thanks to the Executive Secretary Chang-Sun Kim, of the Korean

Christian Mission Centre, who support my research with a valued scholarship. Their generous and significant support allowed me to concentrate on research, especially at the later stage.

I express my sincere gratitude to two Professors, Bruce Chilton and Jacob Neusner of Bard College. Professor Chilton kindly recommended my dissertation to Professor Neusner who accepted it to be published under the monograph series of the University of South Florida.

I owe a great debt of Christian love to Mrs. Yoon-Hee Kim and all the members of the Timothy Scholarship Group for their generous help. I render thanks to Dr. Eun-Hwa Lee and his family who have helped my research go on from the beginning to the end with Christian love. The same thanks go to Mr. and Mrs. Chung (Hah-Won), Park (Rae-Chang), Lee (Sang-Jung). I owe great love to many Christian brothers and sisters who help me with their prayers. Their support was enormous.

J. D. Choi
Department of Christian Studies
Seoul Women's University

ABBREVIATIONS

ANRW	Aufstieg und Niedergang der roemischen Welt
AthR	Anglican Theological Review
b.	Babylonian Talmud
BAGD	*Griechish-deutsches Woerterbuch zu den Schriften des Neuen Testaments und der uebrigen urchristlichen Literatur.* By W. Bauer, Berlin: Verlag A. Toepelmann, 5th German ed. (1958) (1st ed. 1928). ET by W. F. Arndt & F. W. Gingrich & F. W. Danker. 2nd ed. *A Greek English Lexicon of the New Testament and early Christian Literature* (1979) (1st ed. 1957). Chicago: The University of Chicago Press.
BDF	Blass, F. & Debrunner, A. *Grammatik des neutestamentlichen Griechisch. Goettingen: Vandenhoeck & Ruprecht*, 1953 ET by R. Funk A *Greek Grammar of the New Testament.* Cambridge: Cambridge University Press, 1961.
Bib	Biblica
BJRL	Bulletin of the John Rylands University Library of Manchester
BZ	Biblische Zeitschrift
CBQ	Catholic Biblical Quarterly
EQ	Evangelical Quarterly
ET	English Translation
ExpTim	Expository Times
HeyJ	Heythrop Journal
HthR	Harvard Theological Review
JBL	Journal of Biblical Literature
JJS	Journal of Jewish Studies
JQR	Jewish Quarterly Review
JSNT	Journal for the Study of the New Testament
JTS	Journal of Theological Studies
m.	Mishnah
NovT	Novum Testamentum

NTS	New Testament Studies
REB	Revised English Bible
RSV	Revised Standard Version
SBL	Society of Biblical Literature
SE	Studia Evangelica
SJT	Scottish Journal of Theology
ST	Studia Theologica
t.	Tosephta
T.	Testament [e.g. of the Twelve Patriarchs]
TDNT	*Theologisches Woerterbuch zum Neuen Testament.* vol. 1-10 (1933-1979). ed. by G. Kittel and G. Fridrich. Stuttgart: W. Kohlhammer Verlag. ET by G. Bromiley. *Theological Dictionary of the New Testament.* Eerdmanns Publishing Company. vols. 1-10 (1963-1976)
TU	Texte und Untersuchungen.
TynBul	Tyndale Bulletin
TZ	Theologische Zeitschrift
ZNW	Zeitschrift fuer die neutestamentliche Wissenschaft
ZThK	Zeitschrift fuer Theologie und Kirche
y.	Jerusalem Talmud

I follow "Instructions for Contributors" in *JBL* [1976: 331-346], except where specifically stated otherwise. For example, I use Sifra instead of Sipra which is used in the *JBL* instructions.

CHAPTER I

E. P. Sanders' Theses and the General Case against Him

A. E. P. Sanders

Professor Ed Parish Sanders was born in Texas U.S.A. on April 18th, 1937, the son of Mildred and E. T. Sanders.[1] He was educated in Texas Wesleyan College (B.A.) and Perkins School of Theology at Southern Methodist University (B.D.).[2] "When Ed Sanders graduated from Perkins School of Theology he continued his theological education at Union Theological Seminary. There he pursued a Ph.D. in New Testament with W. D. Davies and studied with Louis Martyn and Professor Farmer's own Doktorvater, John Knox".[3] During his research period Sanders was able to have one year of study abroad under venerable scholars: "Farmer worked out a year's study abroad for Ed Sanders. He sent him to David Daube at Oxford. Ed was to establish competence in working with rabbinic texts with Daube. He was also directed to Joachim Jeremias at Goettingen and to the study of Hebrew in Israel as well as topographical study of Palestine."[4] In 1966 Sanders completed his

---

[1] *Who's Who* [1991: 1619].

[2] *Who's Who* [1991: 1619].

[3] Peabody [1987: xvi].

[4] Peabody [1987: xvi].

doctoral dissertation,[5] "*The Tendencies of the Synoptic Tradition*, where he examined the adequacy of previously accepted canons of criticism for distinguishing early and late traditions within the gospels."[6] This was published as number 9 of the Society for New Testament Studies Monograph Series (SNTSM) at Cambridge University Press in 1969.

He began his teaching Career as an Assistant Professor of Religious Studies at McMaster University (Canada) in 1966.[7] Afterwards, he became an Associate Professor in 1970 and Professor in 1974.[8] In 1984 he moved to the University of Oxford as Dean Ireland's Professor of Exegesis of Holy Scripture and remained there until 1990 when he became Professor of Religion at Duke University. He was also a visiting Professor at the Jewish Theological Seminary (1980); held the Chair of Judeo-Christian Studies, Tulane University (1980); W. G. Mason Distinguished Visiting Professor of College of William and Mary in Virginia (1981); Visiting Fellow Commoner, Trinity College, Cambridge (1982), Donnellan Lecturer, Trinity College Dublin (1982).[9]

After ten years of teaching his prolific writings started to come out, beginning from his pioneering work *Paul and Palestinian Judaism* (1977) which immediately caught the attention of New Testament scholars. Between 1980-1982 Sanders with B. F. Meyer and other scholars edited a series of articles significant for the study of *Judaism and Christianity: Jewish and Christian Self Definition* (1980) (vol. 1), *The Shaping of Christianity in the Second and Third Centuries* (vol. 2) (1981), *Aspects of Judaism in the Graeco-Roman World* (1982) (vol. 3). This was

---

[5] Peabody [1987: xvi].

[6] Peabody [1987: xvi].

[7] *Who's Who* [1991: 1619].

[8] His tenure in McMaster University continued until 1988. *Who's Who* [1991: 1619].

[9] *Who's Who* [1991: 1619].

followed by *Paul, the Law and the Jewish People* (1983).[10]

One of the most monumental works on the ministry of Jesus, *Jesus and Judaism*, was published in 1985[11] and immediately caught scholarly attention. After editing *Jesus, the Gospels and Church* (1987) which was dedicated to his mentor W. R. Farmer, he published (with Margaret Davies) a sound introductory text on the synoptic gospels, *Studying the Synoptic Gospels* (1989). A more elaborate piece of research on Jesus within the context of Judaism was published in 1990, *Jewish Law from Jesus to the Mishnah. Paul* (1991) is his most recent work so far. On top of with these significant books he has contributed many articles to various journals. His first article was entitled "The Argument from Order and the Relationship Between Matthew and Luke" published in [1986-1969: 249-261] and followed by "Mark 10:17-31 and Parallels" [1971: 257-270].

Sanders has contributed significantly by editing numerous books besides in addition to those books and journals mentioned above. Sanders became a Fellow of British Academy in 1989. Anything he writes about such a central topic as Jesus' teaching and practice with regard to sinners is worth paying utmost attention.

---

[10] Morgan & Barton describe this book as a "major reorientation in understanding of Paul" [1988: 327].

[11] Morgan & Barton describe this book as having "proposed stimulating theory of Jesus as prophet; (restoration eschatology), 115, 121, 124, 131, 242-244." [1988: 327]

B. A General Review of Sanders' *Jesus and Judaism*

What was the relationship between Jesus and Judaism? There have been numerous attempts to answer this old but essential question in understanding Christianity. Two answers can be given: Jesus within Judaism and Jesus against Judaism. It is unfortunate that some scholars have thought of Christianity as a religion which is totally different from Judaism despite its Palestinian origin. As a result, a guild of scholars have portrayed Jesus as conflicting with Judaism and Jewish leaders in several aspects of his ministry. Originally this prejudice arose due to some parts of the New Testament which depict Jesus as a figure contending with Jewish leaders and with some part of Jewish tradition. But now, some scholars are beginning to understand the relationship between Jesus and Judaism in a different way from the traditional viewpoint. In addition, a new development of Biblical criticism allows readers to grasp the situation of the early Church as reflected in controversial passages. One of the significant results of this new approach of interpreting the episodes of Jesus within Judaism is reaped by E. P. Sanders in his book *Jesus and Judaism*.

Impressively, Sanders begins his argument from the hypothesis that Jesus expected the restoration of Israel [1985: 116-119, 91-115]. Sanders' approach of attempting to define the causal relationship between several key events of Jesus' life and the after effects of his death [1985: 320-325] is exemplary. The headings of each chapter themselves illustrate Sanders' systematic treatment of Jesus' ministry: Temple, miracles, sinners, Gentiles, Kingdom, law, opposition, crucifixion. This link helps readers to form consecution of the life of Jesus.

What is the refreshing about independent argument of Sanders? Traditionally, the "cleansing of the Temple" has been regarded as the decisive reason for crucifying Jesus. However, Sanders regards this action of Jesus as an event symbolizing the imminent destruction of the Temple [1985: 69-76]. This argument sharply differs from the traditional interpretation of this event: Jesus threw the tables over because the offerings and the exchange of money gave the merchants an unrighteous profit. Sanders attempts to validate his thesis by pointing out the fact that the Jewish people expected a new Temple as part of their eschatological aspirations [1985: 77-90].

A unique idea of Sanders lies in his understanding of repentance [106-119]. This concept is closely related to Jesus' goal and method for the "restoration of Israel". For Sanders, Jesus' approach to his goal is closely related to his way of consorting with the Jewish people. Unlike the traditional interpreters, Sanders claims that Jesus never asked for the national repentance of Israel as a whole. He argues that there is very little material which depicts Jesus as calling Israel to repent, and that Jesus may have offered them inclusion in the Kingdom not only while they were still sinners but also without requiring repentance as normally understood in Judaism [106-109, 112-113, 115-119, 206-208]. According to Sanders this is why Jesus was accused of being a friend of people who remained as sinners [200-204, 208, 279-280]. Furthermore, Sanders argues that Jesus did not issue a call for repentance and that it was Luke who emphasized the reform of the wicked who accepted him [112, 113, 175, 203, 206, 277, 322]. Sanders' main argument can be summarized in two points: Jesus never called for national repentance in his public ministry and he forgave sinners without asking for their repentance or for their making restitution.

At this point it would help us to understand Sanders' position better if we examine the traditional concept of this issue. From the time of the Old Testament repentance has been regarded as the essential condition for receiving forgiveness. It is a fundamental concept and the constant presupposition of the prophetic message in the Old Testament. When the Israelites broke the law, prophets and priests exhorted them to repent in various ways. As a sign of repentance sinners were to make restitution; in return, the damaged person could forgive the sinner. In other words, the transgression of commandments governing relations among human beings requires compensation as well as repentance to God. This idea of repentance is well known in Judaism, being one of the basic views of

Judaism at the time of Jesus. In this respect the argument of Sanders has a different meaning altogether.

One of Sanders' most significant contributions is his clarification of the concept of the Pharisees and this result opens a new possibility for the interpretation of "sinners" by defining the groups, the sinners, the wicked and, "the people of land" (*'amme ha-arets*) (Josh 4:24) [174-199]. Sanders disentangles the misunderstanding of traditional interpretation: "The people of land" does not equal "sinners", who can be identified only with "the wicked" [209-210]. This classification calls for a major revision of those who were sinners. "The wicked" is confined only to a limited group who are actually wicked. This limit by itself already reduces Jesus' prophetic role significantly. Sanders uses this definition for his argument that the early church was formed with mainly these wicked people.

Contrary to the interpretations of some scholars, Sanders reads all the scenes of debate between Jesus and the Pharisees as having more than a slight air of artificiality [264-265; 174-211; 275-281, 291-292]. Sanders does not think that Jesus consciously intended to oppose the law in principle [1985: 267-269, 272]. Instead he argues that even though Jesus did not oppose the law itself or reject it, he did not regard the law as absolutely binding ("let the dead bury the dead"; divorce) [267-268]. Sanders also notes that "at least once Jesus was willing to say that following him superseded the requirements of piety and the Torah. This may show that Jesus was prepared, if necessary, to challenge the adequacy of the Mosaic dispensation." [255]. Another of his important arguments is that Jewish material contemporary to Jesus does not reveal the type of externally oriented legal Judaism that had been criticized by Jesus and Paul [275-281]. At this point Sanders' approach goes beyond traditional interpretations to the socio-religious aspects in the study of Jesus and Judaism.

Sanders' explanation on the reason for Jesus' crucifixion plays an important role in his argument. He tries to establish the relationship between Jesus and Judaism by answering the question, why was Jesus crucified? With regards to the death of Jesus, Sanders argues that his attack on the Temple and his message concerning the forgiveness of sinners are important reasons for his crucifixion [1985: 293, cf. 287-288]. These two reasons are complicated by the addition of one other reason: the Jewish leaders would have opposed a charismatic leader who put the security of their own position at risk [1985: 293]. Here Sanders puts forward a thesis which explains Jesus' death as a result of the action of Jewish leaders who attempted to destroy him [1985: 286, 289, 309-318]. They attempted to avoid direct military intervention of Romans [1985: 288]. This interpretation is perhaps plausible. However, Sanders does not explain why they did not do the same to John the Baptist who in a sense was more hostile to the function of the Temple and who attracted a multitude of people into baptism.

Sanders intends to distinguish Jesus and John the Baptist, although he argues that Jesus continued the work of John the Baptist [227]. Sanders concedes the fact that John proclaimed the imminent judgment and sought the repentance of the Jews. However, according to Sanders, Jesus did not stress the same thing [227]. Strangely, he argues that the support of the populace for Jesus was not so great as to restrain the priests and Romans from acting against him [289, 304]. Is this hypothesis convincing? If a charismatic figure proclaimed the forgiveness of the wicked and threw the tables over in the Temple without drawing people's attention, it must have been purposely ignored by the priests. But the case of Jesus was different. He had the ability to draw many people. Further, the Roman soldiers could not have ignored the charismatic leader because they were sensitive to any sort of gathering of the Jewish people. Sanders argues that it is suspicious to categorize Jesus as a "unique" person. He refuses to admit the claim to the Resurrection as a unique claim because of the report concerning the appearance of *Apollonius of Tyana* after his death: what is unique is the effect of that claim [319-320].

Granted his refreshing arguments on the interpretation of the Jesus event, it must be pointed out that his methodology for analyzing the arguments of other scholars should be called into question. Sanders tends to avoid a direct confrontation with other scholars' argument. His logic is sophisticated and every argument can be regarded as the fruit of long reflection. Although his hypothesis shows consistency and coherence, some of his analysis seem to rest on questionable assumptions. For example the meaning of the "New Temple" [1985: 229, 233] remains ambiguous. The mainframe of Sanders' work seems to be based on this proposition: "New ages by definition must alter the present" [1985: 319]. Did the Jews expect the total destruction of the Jerusalem Temple, to be followed by another construction [1985: 75]? Or did they expect a different Temple system which would have forced the Jewish people to recognize the original meaning of offerings, or as Sanders calls it, a renewal of the Temple [326]? This ambivalent position could really bring about an entirely different result, because Sanders assumes the Temple cleansing as one of the most important reasons of Jesus' crucifixion [1985: 287-288].

Despite some significant remaining questions, this book must be regarded as a monumental work of a contemporary theologian who paves a way that leads to closer examination of the life of Jesus who is believed, by Sanders, to have pursued his own program, the restoration of Israel. Sanders' work contributes substantially to the study of the ministry of Jesus.

C. The Position of E. P. Sanders on Repentance: A general criticism on Sanders' five theses.

Professor E. P. Sanders in his book *Jesus and Judaism* [1985] argues five theses. For the clear understanding of the following theses it is necessary to define "sinners". Sanders defines "sinners" as "those who sinned willfully and heinously and who did not repent" [1985: 177], in other words "lawbreakers".[12] Sanders rests his case upon an assumption that this understanding of "the wicked" prevailed also before A.D. 70 [1985: 178; 1977: 243-244; 257, 272, 398-406].

1. Jesus does not ask for national repentance [108, 111, 112, 113, 115, 117, 203, 210, 222, 223, 227, 303, 322, 326]. "He (Jesus) did not make thematic the message that Israel should repent and mend their ways so as to escape punishment at the judgment." [115]. Jesus was more interested in individual forgiveness than in national forgiveness [111-112]. "The situation is this: there is not a significant body of reliable sayings material which *explicitly* attributes to Jesus a call for *national* repentance." [111]. "It is emphasized that Jesus has the power to announce the forgiveness of an individual's sins and thus to heal him (Matt. 9.2-6//Mark 2.3-11//Luke 5.18-24)." [111].

2. Jesus does not deny the need of repentance [112, 326]. "I am not arguing that Jesus did not 'believe in' repentance and turning to God. I

[12] P. S. Alexander uses this term [1986: 103]. Recently D. A. Neale puts forward the argument on the metaphorical, not historical, meaning of "sinners" [1991: 68-97]. This extensive research of the meaning of ἁμαρτωλός throughout the vast amount of texts ranging from the O.T. to Apocrypha, Pseudepigrapha, some Greek texts, to the church fathers is a significant contribution. However, his confinement of search only to ἁμαρτωλός seems to be the reason why his argument remains not entirely convincing. For example, king David's repentance attested in LXX 2 Sam 12:13 ʽημάρτηκα τῳ κυρίῳ...ἁμαρτημά naturally escapes Neale's search. A comprehensive search and interpretation which included many cognate words would have resulted in a different picture.

presume that, as a good Jew, he did so." [112].

3. Jesus does not make repentance according to the law which requires restitution and/or sacrifice a condition for joining his band of disciples [203, 204, 206-207, 210, 227, 255, 267, 271, 277, 280, 282, 301, 307, 326]. "He may have offered them inclusion in the kingdom not only while they were still sinners but also without requiring repentance as normally understood, and therefore he could have been accused of being a friend of people who indefinitely remained sinners." [206].

4. The only requirement was to "follow" him, i.e., to join his band and "accept" his message [207, 210, 227, 255, 271, 326]. They did not have to observe the law. "I propose, then, that the novelty and offence of Jesus' message was that the wicked who heeded him would be included in the kingdom even though they did not repent as it was universally understood what is, even though they did not make restitution, sacrifice, and turn to obedience to the law." [207].

5. Jesus does not give his message on forgiveness an eschatological thrust like John the Baptist [111-112, cf. 259]. "...'forgiveness' in the message of Jesus does not take on the tone of eschatological restoration" [112].

I want to propose five arguments which are against Sanders, or in which my emphasis are different from those of Sanders'.

1.

a. My counter thesis is as follows.

Jesus asks national repentance. All alike were sinners because no group could continue to claim that it alone was the true Israel (4 Ezra 8:35)[13] which did not need repentance [Theissen, 1977: 104 (ET);

---

[13] "For in truth there is no one among those who have been born who has not acted wickedly, and among those who have existed there is no one who has not transgressed."

Trautmann, 1980: 162]. Jesus did expect all to repent,[14] although he did not call all to follow him [Hengel, 1968: 62 (ET)]. Jesus seems to intend to call for repentance by a strategy different from that which Sanders attributes to him.

b. My general argument against Sanders is the following.

Sanders agrees with the fact that Jesus preached the kingdom [1985: 326]. How did the Jewish people accept the coming of the kingdom? On one hand their deep frustration over foreign dominion meant that they accepted the coming of the kingdom with hope and elation. On

---

[14] Dodd, 1971: 86 (ET); Hengel, 1968: 61 (ET); O. Betz, 1965: 28, 32, 35, 39 (ET); Jeremias, 1971: 177 (ET); Westholm, 1978: 132; B. Meyer, 1979: 205; Trautmann, 1981: 162-163; Vermes, 1981: 24. Sanders argues that "The ancients cannot be relied on to give accurate estimates of a crowd", but "Paul's figure is as good as we can do" [1985: 304]. According to Sanders, "'the whole crowd' did not actually hail Jesus as king or marvel at his teaching, nor did the whole populace of Jerusalem subsequently support Peter and the others (Matt 21:8; Mark 11:18, Acts 5:26," [304]. "It is probably not true that the populace support for Jesus was so great that the priests and Romans were afraid to act against him (e.g. Mark 12:12)" [304]. Sanders even suspects the accuracy of Josephus' reference to "the populace" and "the crowd" [303]. Are all these arguments correct? Why does Sanders not suspect the same reference on John the Baptist? The size of crowds seems to have nothing to do with the urging of the priest. Sanders argues how can we believe the accuracy of reference on the number in the N.T. when even the science of estimating crowds is very recent indeed, is still partially unreliable, and in part depends on aerial photography [1985: 304]. Sanders seems not to have paid the due attention to the fact that Jesus commanded them to sit down in groups, by hundreds or fifty (Mark 6:39-40; Luke 9:14-15). Counting the number of groups could result in the fairly correct estimation of the number of a crowd. Sometimes the ancients were as wise as the moderns! Further Sanders believes that Jesus' miracles doubtless contributed greatly to his success in gathering crowds; "he (Jesus) attracted attention and commotion" [1985: 173]. Hence, Jesus could speak before the crowds of the Jewish people after healing the sick. Sanders' argument of Jesus' having drawn small numbers of people seems to be not convincing. Sanders also thinks that "Jesus was a great and challenging teacher" [1985: 129]. How could a great teacher of the last messenger of God calling for the kingdom draw only a small crowd?

the other hand, they knew well that the kingdom is accompanied by judgment (Isa 55:7; Ezek 18:21; 33:11; Ps 51:2, 3, 9, 12; cf. Moore [1927, vol. 1: 501, 509, 520]). Accordingly they would accept the kingdom with repentance; the fact that the "Kingdom of God is near will involve *reparation and calls for preparedness*" [Catchpole, 1978: 570] (italics mine). The nearness of the kingdom is the motivation and wellspring of the new morality [J. Weiss, 1892: 67, 12, 21-22, 86-87, 90, 96-101, 105-106 (ET); Schrage, 1982: 28-29 (ET)]. So the proclamation of "the kingdom" would make the Jewish people feel the threat of judgment. Hence, even without the word μετανοέω or μετάνοια, this expectation had the power to evoke the repentance of the Jews. The preaching of the kingdom was tantamount to preaching repentance.

Jesus felt himself called to associate with the work of John the Baptist. Sanders also assumes that Jesus got his start in close association with a prophet who asked for national repentance with eschatological overtones [1987: 233]. So, Jesus could have continued to ask the Jewish people to repent. But Sanders refuses to follow this line and argues that "...Jesus looked for the coming kingdom, as did John, but gave a different turn to the message, both by what he said and by what he did." [1987: 234]. One of the reasons why Sanders doubts Jesus' proclamation of repentance to the nation of Israel [1985: 115] seems to lie in the following set of assumptions: Jesus made a smaller impact than John the Baptist [226]; Jesus thought of someone else, John, as having called all Israel to repent [326]; Jesus may have seen himself as supplementing and thus completing John's work [227]. Sanders argues that John had called on Israel to repent and had warned of a coming judgment, but too few had responded [227-228] (many repented, [340]). But the kingdom did not come. So Jesus set out to promise inclusion to the most obvious outsiders [227, 340]. Sanders seems to go too far. Where is the evidence that too few had responded to John's call? Mark 1:5 ("all the people" and "all the Judea") and Matt 3:5 ("all Judea", "all the region of the Jordan") clearly state that many had responded to John the Baptist's call. Jesus could have drawn a multitude of people. It is quite possible that Jesus could have continued what John the Baptist initiated (Matt 3:12; Luke 3:17) because he starts under John the Baptist. The fact that Jesus is baptized by John suggests the continuity and consistency of the work of John and Jesus who preach the same message. Sanders argues that probably "He (Jesus) did not emphasize the national character of the kingdom, including judgment by groups and a call for mass repentance, because that had been the task of John the Baptist, whose work he accepted" [326]. But the Jewish people would hardly understand by "the imminence of the kingdom" anything other than "the imminence of God's reign of Israel". Further there seems to be several sayings which could stress the national judgment by groups and a call for mass repentance (e.g. Luke 4:25-30).

Sanders argues that Jesus may not have had a completely worked out plan which would convey his hope and expectation to "all Israel" [226]. "He may not have had a clear programme for making a bridge between the 'little flock', the special recipients of his message, on one hand, and 'all Israel', on the other." [227]. Then how could Sanders argue that Jesus communicated the significance of his message for all Israel well enough [227] with such an inconsistent plan? Sanders' answer is that Jesus did think that he (John the Baptist) himself had to do it all [227]. Contrary to Sanders, Jesus hardly left the basic proclamation to his great predecessor [227]. Jesus himself proclaimed the imminence of the Kingdom, like John the Baptist, which would motivate the Jewish people to repentance.

It is difficult to understand Sanders' distinction between his community and the community (Israel). What is certain is that Sanders does not think that Jesus intends to achieve the restoration of Israel by making his own community grow to the community. Contrary to Sanders, Jesus seems not to distinguish his community from the community (the whole nation of Israel). If Jesus wanted to make his own community, it would not be anything other than the Jewish community because the Jewish people would understand the 'kingdom' as the whole Jewish nation. Sanders also notes that "For Judaism, the kingdom was always the kingdom of Israel."[1985: 26][15] Nonetheless Sanders argues that "that might give his followers a sense of community; but it is not accurate to say that he welcomed those people (the sinners) back into the community" [1985:203]. There seems to be no particular reason to argue that Jesus does not welcome sinners back into the community. It is hard to imagine any Jew turning down the opportunity to be accepted as a Jew of good standing when the chance is given. Further, it is unlikely that the repentant sinners would follow Jesus' community rather than the whole Jewish community because making restitution is extremely difficult; the community and the Temple could help them resolve even their financial difficulties.

We can find other evidence of Jesus' calling for national repentance in his sending of disciples. Jesus could ask his disciples to proclaim the same message to the Jewish people (Matt 10:5-7; Luke 9:2; 10:9, 11. cf. Mark 6:12) as "fishers of men" (Mark 1:17, Luke 5:10). Sanders also confirms the fact that Jesus sent his disciples to Israel [324].[16] Jesus and his disciples could agree with John the Baptist in proclaiming the same message ἤγγικεν ἡ βασιλεία (Matt 3:2; Mark 1:15; Matt 4:17; Matt 10:7; Luke 9:2, 10:9). This consistency of the message would convince the Jewish people about the authority of the message. If Jesus asked for national repentance, Sanders would expect him to make "an emphatic call to all Israel to repent in view of the coming end and the explicit promise that God's forgiving mercy would be extended in saving and restoring his people" [113]. Could not Jesus' public proclamation and his teaching in parables and other sayings be an

---

[15] However he proceeds to an unconvincing argument. "...Jesus was a spokesman for the coming restoration of Israel, for the establishment of God's ideal kingdom *over the nation of Israel as such.*" [1987: 238]. This is one of the main theological assumptions upon which Sanders establishes his whole theory. However Sanders affirms that "But we can answer our basic question in positive terms: *Jesus affirmed the value and permanence of the nation of Israel as a nation.*" [1987: 238].

[16] "I would put these features of the early movement back into the lifetime of Jesus" [324] although he denies the authenticity of Matt 10:6 [104].

emphatic call to all Israel? Is not the disciples' proclamation of the coming of the kingdom an emphatic call to repent? God's saving mercy includes repentance. Jesus calls for repentance to prepare the Jewish people for the forgiving mercy of God. Sanders affirms that Jesus' followers worked within the framework of Jewish eschatological expectation [118]. However Sanders argues that the twelve tribes, the Israel of standard expectation, cannot be assembled by waiting for individual commitment [115]. Nonetheless, he still concedes that it is perfectly possible for Jesus to have talked about both individual change and group redemption [115-116]. It must be noted that in Sanders' restoration plan disciples have no particular role until Jesus' crucifixion. They simply had to wait for the judgment of Israel (Matt 19:28; Luke 22:28-30) [115] which had not materialized. According to Sanders' argument, the disciples started to act only after Jesus' crucifixion [1985: 106, 111, 226, 231]: "The apostles subsequently both preached and performed 'wonders', but that cannot be said with certainty of the disciples in Jesus' lifetime." [103]. Then for what purpose did Jesus choose them? Jesus could intend to renew Israel by calling for the repentance of individuals and groups. Jesus could expect that his disciples' proclamation would spread to all parts of Israel. The legitimacy of the disciples' judgment is probably based upon their preceding proclamation of judgment (Matt 19:28; Luke 22:30). The coming out of the people to Jesus, along with sinners and the sick, could be the result of Jesus and the disciples' proclamation.

The sending of disciples to the lost sheep of Israel could hint that Jesus takes a bold approach, reaching out to the public, rather than remaining within a faction [1985: 106]. Following the O.T. prophetic tradition John and Jesus could preach the apocalyptic prophetic message. "...Jesus did not separate himself from the people with an esoteric group of the elect" [Hengel, 1968: 59 (ET)] but continued to reach out to all parts of Israel. Thus, it is unlikely that Jesus intends to form his community. "He was engaged in a great campaign of repentance, directed towards the 'lost sheep of the house of Israel', and, like other Jewish

Messiah-figures of whom we have record, he thought that the more Jews could be induced to repent, the more the coming of the Kingdom would be confirmed." [Maccoby, 1989a: 102].

c. I will rely on the following passages.
(1) Mark 1:15; Matt 4:17
(2) Matt 6:12; Luke 11:4a
(3) Mark 8:12
(4) Matt 10:5-15; Mark 6:7-13; Luke 10:1-12; cf. 9:1-6
(5) Matt 11:16-19; Luke 7:31-35
(6) Matt 11:20-24; Luke 10:13-15
(7) Luke 13:1-5
(8) Matt 18:12-14; Luke 15:4-7
(9) Matt 12:39; 16:4; Luke 11:29
(10) Matt 12:41-42; Luke 11:31-32
(11) Matt 23:37-38; Luke 13:24-35a

Sanders regard the saying in (8) as authentic. Sanders conceives of (1) (4) (6) (7) (9) (10) as inauthentic. He only partly agrees with the authenticity of (5). Sanders does not deal with the authenticity of (2) (3) (11). Sanders does not deal with the authenticity of Luke 17:20-21, Matt 20:16 and Matt 19:30; Mark 10:31; Luke 13:30. However these passages could imply national repentance.

2.
a. My counter thesis is as follows.

Jesus clearly stressed repentance. Jesus put conditions on redemption.

b. My general argument against Sanders is the following.

Even Sanders agrees that salvation of 'all' and punishment of some are not mutually exclusive, nor are redemption and judgment (Ps. Sol. 17:26-29) [104]. The sayings on judgment and election, the distinction of the righteous from the wicked, coupled with a threat of the destruction of the latter, imply a demand for repentance [Conzelmann, 1968: 108-11] (ET)]. The eschaton brings salvation and judgment simultaneously; Luke 17:31-37 lucidly portrayed the double nature of the coming kingdom [Conzelmann, 1968: 110-111, 114-115 (ET)]. The sudden coming of the end means total disaster to some and total salvation to others. "...the kingdom of God is a cosmic catastrophe depicted in certain events which constitute the eschatological drama of Jewish apocalyptic." [Schmidt, 1933: 585 (ET)] (italics mine). Sanders' argument seems to remain unconvincing. He argues that Jesus did not make thematic the message that Israel should repent and mend her ways to escape punishment at the judgment. However, he concedes that Jesus was not opposed to the idea of final judgment [1985: 115]. More positively sanders argues that "He continued to believe in a judgment" [1985: 322]. Then how could a charismatic leader turn back from the people on the verge of perishing in the absence of repentance? It is much more likely that Jesus, having perceived the impending judgment, did proclaim a thematic message, the repentance of whole Israel.

Further "acceptance of Jesus' message" is also a condition [1985: 210]. If Jesus did not set conditions for joining his band of disciples the early church would not have put "believe in Christ" as a condition for their members. Repentance of Jesus' followers was a condition as much as faith was condition for the early Christians. "Acceptance of Jesus' message" could mean to accept his message asking radical change (cf. Sermon on the Mount). The fact that a former tax-collector Matthew follows Jesus (Matt 10:3; Luke 6:15) illustrates a change in his life tantamount to repentance. A call to ethically and eschatologically defined repentance and the gathering of disciples in the face of judgment are intertwined, as we can see in the case of John the Baptist [Hengel, 1968: 35 (ET)]. So ἀκολουθεῖν could already assume repentance in the followers. Thus, this acceptance could already include radical reformation.

c. I will rely on following passages.
(1) Matt 5:23-24; 6:14; Mark 11:25
(2) Matt 5:25-26; Luke 12:58-59
(3) Matt 6:12; Luke 11:4
(4) Matt 18:12-14; Luke 15:4-7
(5) Matt 18:23-35
(6) Luke 13:6-9

Sanders regards (4) (6) as authentic. Sanders conceives of (1) and (2) as inauthentic. Sanders does not deal with the authenticity of (3) (5). Although I do not include here Matt 13:24-30 (The Wheat and Tares) Matt 13:47-50 (The Parable of the Fishnet), which Sanders regards as authentic [1985: 114-115], they could be taken to stress repentance. Sanders misunderstands John's prediction of Jesus' work (Matt 3:12; Luke 3:17) to be a saying about John's work [1985: 92]. This saying indicates the judgmental character of Jesus' work.

3.
a. My general argument against Sanders is as follows.

Jesus does make repentance a condition for joining his band of disciples who respond to his call.

b. My general argument against Sanders is the following.

Jesus does not teach his followers or repentant sinners what to do; he could assume that they knew what they should do e.g., fast on the day of Atonement [1985: 203, 207].

A question arises. How can Jesus ask his followers to make restitution when he even commands one of his would-be-followers to leave his dead father? To put the question in a more general form. How does the urgency to follow him go along with the necessity of restitution? Although "following Jesus" could include repentance, still one requirement remains: his followers must complete the duty of making restitution. The answer to this question depends on whether the former tax collector Matthew repents and makes restitution before, or even after following Jesus. If he did, it is possible to argue that other disciples or followers also have made restitution if it was necessary.

ἀκολουθεῖν implies "following Jesus as a disciple" in the following passages: Matt 4:20; Mark 1:18 (the call of Peter and Andrew); Matt 8:19 (one scribe who would be his disciple); Matt 8:22; Luke 9:60 (leave the dead); Matt 9:9 (the call of Matthew); mark 2:14 (the call of Levi); Matt 19:21; Mark 10:21; Luke 18:22 (the call of the rich young Man); Matt 19:27-28 (Peter's question on reward). Sanders affirms that Jesus probably did have at least one tax collector among his followers although his name was not securely remembered [1985: 206-207].[17] But Sanders argues that it is noteworthy that the tax collector in Matt 9:9-13; Mark 2:14-17; Luke 5:27-32 "is not said to have repented, repaid those whom he had robbed, and assumed a life conformable to the law. What he did was follow Jesus." [1985: 207]. However the former tax collector's holding of a feast could imply a significant change happened in his life, his fulfillment or resolution to make restitution. Or at least Jesus could have expected this collector to make restitution. His response to Jesus' call could be interpreted as a sign of repentance.

Some accounts depict Jesus' followers as responding promptly when called by Jesus (εὐθέως, Matt 4:20). Matt 9:9 depicts a man called Matthew following Jesus' call without any tangible delay (ἀναστὰς ἠκολούθησεν). Matthew might be seen not to fulfill his obligation of restitution. However, Matthew still invites guests to his

---

[17] Sanders argues that Matt 9:9-11; Mark 2:13-17; Luke 5:27-32 "seems to rest on a kernel." Accordingly it would be not necessary to deal with the authenticity of this passage because Sanders also concurs with its authenticity. The moot point is only whether restitution was required of a former tax collector.

family (Mark 2:14; Matt 9:9-14) in the following verses. Accordingly, an immediate response to the call of Jesus does not necessarily imply an abrupt give up of all responsibility to be fulfilled.

Moreover, it is possible to conceive disciple Matthew's restitution in Matt 19:27; Mark 10:28; Luke 18:28 because Peter states that all the disciples gave up everything (πάντα, Matt 19:27, Mark 10:28) and followed Jesus.[18] Although this story does not tell about his restitution, Matthew must have given up his possessions and made restitution if he had defrauded anyone. Among five passages on following Jesus, only Matt 19:21; Mark 10:21; Luke 18:22 attest the condition of following Jesus. There is scholarly consensus on the authenticity of this story except for some minor additions in Matt 19:17a and v 22b par. [Best, 1986: 19]. Jesus asks this man to sell his possessions and to give them to the poor (v. 21). There is no hint of the profession of this young rich man (v. 22). If Jesus asked a rich man, who is under no suspicion regarding his way of making his fortune, to take up such a weighty moral responsibility as that of giving his possessions to the poor, it is most likely that Jesus asked the tax-collector to return his ill-gotten gains to the defrauded.

Further, according to Jewish standards offences against fellow Jews required repentance as well as restitution if necessary. Repentance is fundamental in the O.T and the presupposition of the prophetic message. There is evidence that the Jewish people at the time of Jesus continually obeyed rules stipulated in Lev 6:1-7 (Philo, *The Special Laws*, 1. 234-238 (victims); m. Yoma 8. 9, Sifra Lev 26. 27; Josephus, *Jewish Antiquities*, 3. 230-232 (sin offering) [Abrahams, 1917: 139; Buechler, 1928: 460]. Just repenting was of no use. Restitution was essential: restitution

---

[18] Best argues that "...the historical Peter had not at his call (1:16-18) left house and wife (1:29-31), and many even had continued to possess a boat (3:9; 4:1, 36) and a net (Mt 17:24-27), and so *he could not have said* 'we have left all'; if the saying of vv.29f had originally been addressed to Peter it would surely have contained a reference to 'ships' rather than 'fields'" [1988: 18]. What seems certain is that Peter and other disciples gave up their main professions to follow Jesus, cf. [Luke 12:33.] (italics mine).

precedes guilt offering (Lev 6: 1-7).

Given these general practices as reliable evidence, Sanders seems to go too far when saying that Jesus did not ask of the wicked any restitution if they heeded him [1985: 207]. Sanders argues that restitution need not be applied to those who follow him [1985: 255]. This argument is particularly striking because Sanders affirms that Jesus did not explicitly oppose those parts of the Law, nor did he abrogate the law in general [326]. Sanders even concedes that "he (Jesus) accepted obedience to the law as the norm." [336]. In regard to the Temple sacrifice Sanders particularly mentions that "Jesus did not tell sinners that, before purifying themselves, and without bringing a sacrifice and a prayer of repentance, they could enter the temple." [205]. Then Sanders needs to admit that "follow" includes restitution: "...some of the traditional practices of Judaism may be forgone by those who follow Jesus" [207] seems to be an overstatement.

Sanders argues that "Jesus put 'following him' above the law" in the case of his implied suspension of fasting (Mark 2:19 & par.), "for at least the fast of the Day of Atonement (Lev. 16.29) was emphatically observed." [207]. Sanders' argument seems to harmonize with his argument on Jesus' attitude toward the Law: "...he (Jesus) made the moral requirements more stringent, but relaxed the external ones. The relaxation of external requirements allowed him to associate with the wicked..." [263]. But the Jewish people at the time of Jesus would hardly have distinguished the moral requirements from external requirements. The Jewish people viewed the law as a unity, which Sanders also affirms [1985: 56]. Hence Jesus would hardly have relaxed either external requirements or moral requirements. Jesus was the teacher of the Law who taught his followers to keep the law [O'Neill, 1980: 27, 43].

Sanders argues that "the absence of passages which call for repentance and restitution at least shows that Jesus did not aim at restoring the wicked to the community." [1985: 203]. Sanders builds his case based on the absence of passages in which Jesus asks repentant sinners to make restitution [1985: 206-207]. However, the scarcity of the explicit command to make restitution to the repentant sinners does not indicate that Jesus had excused this obligation. There are not many passages in which Jesus commands people to fulfil this obligation, but Jesus gives no explicit positive command to dismiss or discontinue this obligation in the synoptic gospels. The absence of this command does not prove that Jesus did not expect the fulfilment of these requirements on the part of the people who had offended against their fellows. It is a case of an *argument from silence*. Sanders hinges his argument too much upon this alleged silence. Contrary to the way Sanders argues, no explicit command would have been necessary. Sanders' argument remains unconvincing because his case depends on rejecting or ignoring the authenticity of some certain sayings in which Jesus explicitly or implicitly directs the repentant sinners to go to the wronged or to the Temple when necessary [see section 3. c]. His case becomes untenable if those sayings turn out to have originated from Jesus.

Sanders even argues that Jesus would have been a national hero if he led tax collectors to repent, repay those whom they had robbed and leave off practicising their profession [203]. It remains unclear whether all the tax collectors who followed Jesus left their professions. However, Jesus could have assumed a repentant tax-collector knew how to restore what he had defrauded because most Jews knew of the Law in detail (Josephus, *Against Apion* 2. 175). Following Jesus does not allow a person to bypass the obedience of the law.[19] Jesus was a national hero not in the way Sanders conceives. The Jews would not be surprised to see the repentance and restitution of tax collectors; they had already watched tax collectors asking John the Baptist what they had to do. John and the

[19] Harvey [1982: 55]: "In no case would the following of Jesus' precepts have placed a person actually outside the law." "Further, the cares of poverty was no defence against the charge of neglecting the Torah" [Abrahams, 1917: 115] Γαζοφυλακîον, the "contribution box or receptacle" [BAGD, 149], attested in Mark 12:41, 43 and Luke 21:1 could have been used for the purpose of charity. This fund could have been allowed for very poor people who were unable to offer even small sacrifices.

Jewish people and even tax collectors themselves knew that they must "collect no more than is appointed" (Luke 3:12). This teaching suggests that when they break this rule they need to repent and make restitution. If Jesus countermanded the Law at this point, he would have had to say so. Sanders also affirms that "...they (the repentant sinners) all would have known perfectly well what to do if they wished to be considered members of the covenant in good standing." [1985: 203].

Moreover, the repentant tax collector does not need to quit his job because he could continue his profession with clean hands after finishing the due restitution [see my close examination on Luke 18:9-14: arguments 4.12 and 4.13]. John the Baptist only commands the tax collectors to collect no more than is appointed to them in their baptism (Luke 3:13). Asking the repentant sinners to quit their profession as a sign of repentance would have been too much. A tax collector could have quit his job to follow Jesus as one of his disciples. In this case it is more than to quit the job. He is giving up everything (πάντα) (Mark 19:27; Mark 10:28; cf. Luke 18:28).

However, Sanders' argument could be supported by the claim: at the time of Jesus, tax collectors' restitution could have been particularly difficult. We know that the tax collector must make restitution to all those whom he knew he had defrauded (b. B. Qam 94b-95a; t. B. Mes. 8:26; b. Ber. 23a). Another problem further compounds this difficulty. Although the tax collector had to make restitution (Lev 6:1-7) the community could have been reluctant to accept it (t. B. Qam. 94b-95a) because sometimes rabbis regard tax-collectors' money as the proceeds of robbery (m. B. Qam 10.1). Hence the possibility of tax-collector's restitution could have remained blocked.

If the people of a community accept restitutions (t. B. Qam, 10. 2), a tax-collector could return what he defrauded to the wronged. Afterward, he must offer the guilt offering to the temple. However, there could be something left even after rigorous restitution because tax-collectors tended to collect more than was required in order to avoid paying the difference when their collection does not reach to the ceiling [Schuerer, 1973, vol. 1:376]. In such case the repentant sinner could deposit the remainder to the temple.

If the people of a community did not accept a tax collector's restitution, would anybody take the risk of keeping a sinner's restitution money? Under such circumstance the repentant tax collector could deposit his restitution in the House in the Temple [Abrahams, 1917: 58], probably the Temple itself. Although Prov 21:27 attests the sacrifice of the wicked as an abomination, priests accept gift offerings of sinners in order to encourage them to repent (b. Hul. 5a): "one should accept sacrifices from the transgression in Israel, so that they may be inclined to repent." [Abrahams, 1917: 58].

If the defrauded is absent, the amount of restitution with *the additional fifth* could be deposited in the *court of the law* to facilitate repentance (Num 5:8) [Buechler, 1928: 460]. The additional fifth means the guilt offering (Lev 6:1-5). In this context it is important to make the following points. When sinners bring offerings to the Temple they are supposed to confess their sins to the priests explicitly (Lev 6:1-7; Num 5:6-8) [Maimonides, 1981: 109] and true repentance (m. Yoma 8:8). Certainly priests are supposed to question the character of the sacrifice and to remind the sinner of the preliminary and essential duty of restitution before sprinkling the blood of the atoning guilt offering [Buechler, 1928: 410]. Accordingly the repentant tax collector brings only what is left after faithfully having fulfilled restitution in order to answer this anticipated question. Consequently, whether the community accept a tax collector's restitution or not, or whether the wronged is present or not, a repentant tax collector needs to go to the Temple and to give the guilt offering.

Sanders affirms that Jesus' actions and his sayings against the Temple did not mean that Jesus objected to the sacrifices instituted by

God [1985: 269]. But Sanders argues that "Jesus himself looked to a new age, and therefore he viewed the institutions of this age as not final, and in that sense not adequate." [269]. However, to regard a system as not being adequate means objecting it. In case of the sacrifice in the Temple no position in the middle would have been allowed: people must have decided whether to obey or disobey the law about sacrifice. Furthermore, to allow the unrepentant sinners not to do what is stipulated in the law is tantamount to breaking it and reforming it. Hence there seems to be no definite reason not to make restitution.

With regards to the cultic offering Sanders asks only for evidence which can be definitely dated back before A.D. 70 [1985: 18]. This is a difficult question, but answerable. If the repentant tax collectors were not asked to follow this practice at the time of Jesus, the Jewish people at the time of the making of the Talmud would not have continued to obey this rule. They would not have discussed such difficulties unless it was strictly required at that time. If any rule was laid down in the O.T. and in the later time after Jesus, it is reasonable to think that this rule has been continually obeyed even during the intervening period.[20]

One of the reasons why Sanders argues for this unusual position can be derived from his conviction: "His (Jesus') eschatological expectation did lead him to think that the Mosaic law was neither absolute nor final. In the new age which was about to dawn, God would go beyond the Law" [1985: 336]. For Sanders, this argument meant that the wicked did not need to fulfil the Law's obligations. However, the eschatological consciousness in the first century Judaism seems to have led people to

---

[20] At this point it would be worth citing T. W. Manson's illuminating argument on Jesus' attitude to the Torah: "He (Jesus) fulfills them by understanding them in their deepest meaning, and second by going beyond them in action." [1960: 45]. "The Torah is the Law of the Kingdom of God, that is to say God's revealed will as the standard and pattern of human conduct." [52]. "...the Jewish ethic did insist on inward motive as well as on outward good." [54].

obey the Law more stringently, rather than to lapse from it. That at least was the case in the Qumran community and among the Essenes in general. Accordingly, it could be held that eschatology uplifts the authority of the Law.

According to Sanders' argument Jesus' community consisted of wicked sinners. It is hardly likely that the other Jews would recognize this lawless circle as the legitimate group to lead Israel which is founded on the Law. Further, this unscrupulous inclusion of the sinners, who indefinitely remained sinners, would be against the expectation of the Jewish people who believe that the kingdom comes when people radically repent (T. Dan 6:3-11; 4 Ezra 4:38-43; Acts 3:19-21): 4 Ezra 4:39, "...the time of threshing is delayed for the righteous on account of the sins of those who dwell on earth." [Charlesworth's edition, vol. 1: 531]; b. Sanh 97b, "If Israel does not repent she will not be delivered; but if she does she will be delivered." (cf. 2 Apoc. Bar. 78:6-7; b. Sanh, 98a).

One of the functions of making restitution is helping the repentant sinners to have confidence that they have finished what is required to repair the broken relationship between the offender and offended. It is hardly likely that the repentant sinners would have this confidence if they knew somebody still suffered greatly because of their sins. So making restitution is necessary. The cultic obligation is also compulsory. "Sin-offerings were brought not to effect a primary atonement for the sin, but only as the final step in a process of atonement." [Maccoby, 1989a: 91] However, "giving a sense of finality and peace to the repentant person" must have its own value [Maccoby, 1989a: 91].

Jesus certainly asks repentant sinners and his followers to fulfil the law of restitution. If Jesus does not ask his disciples to fulfil the requirement of making restoration according to the law, the following propositions would likely to be true. The early church, especially the Palestinian church, would not have accepted Matthew's apostleship because he did not obey the law. Also, the Pharisees would have offered at Jesus' trial this decisive evidence of Jesus' breaking the law.

Jesus could hardly have uttered important sayings such as "the Golden Rule" (Matt 7:12; Luke 6:31), "be perfect as God is perfect" (Matt 5:48) "love your neighbour as yourself" (Matt 22:39). Paul would not ask Philemon to charge to his account anything Onesimus did wrong, if believing Jesus attenuates the obligation of restitution (Philem 18). The early church must have debated restitution if they suspected that Jesus had disregarded the law at this point. But there is no account of this debate. It is hardly possible that Jesus keeps Passover [Matt 2:17-20; Mark 14:12-16; Luke 22:7-13] without expecting his followers to obey the law. The most convincing argument would be that Jesus could have assumed that the repentant sinners would make restitution according to the practice in the Judaism at his time.

c. I will rely on the following passages.

(1) Mark 1:41-44; Matt 8:2-4; Luke 5:12-16
(2) Matt 5:23-24; Matt 6:14; Mark 11:25
(3) Matt 5:25-26; Luke 12:58-59
(5) Luke 19:1-10

Sanders regards (2) (3) (4) (5) as secondary. He is not sure of the authenticity of (1).

4.

a. My counter thesis is as follows.

Jesus teaches that people destined for the kingdom should keep the highest moral standards. "To follow" includes keeping the highest moral standards.

b. My general argument against Sanders is the following.

Eschatology conditions ethics [Wilder, 1950: 164]. Sanders states that "he (Jesus) demanded that his followers observe the highest of moral standards." [1985: 263]. If that is Sanders' main position it is hard to understand his argument about the abrupt shift from ethical radicalism to a radical proclamation of the grace of God to sinners [1985: 227]. Sanders' thesis seems to be based upon this underlying argument: "It seems somewhat more likely that, in view of the eschaton, he simply did not deal in detail with their behaviour, and thus could truly be criticized for including the wicked in his 'kingdom'." [323]. But where is the evidence that this view of the eschaton leads to dealing with the behaviour of the wicked in a relaxed way? The opposite case seems to be more likely. The imminence of the 'kingdom' includes judgment. Sanders agrees that Jesus was not opposed to the idea of judgment and selection [115]. Accordingly, this urgency could impress on the Jewish people the need to keep their distinctive moral teaching. In their expectation of the imminent end the Qumran community stresses that imminence of the 'kingdom' includes judgment. Sanders agrees that Jesus was not opposed to the idea of judgment and selection [115]. Accordingly this urgency could impress on the Jewish people the need to keep their distinctive moral teaching. In their expectation of the imminent end the Qumran community stresses the perfect obedience to the Torah of all the congregation of Israel e.g., 1QS 1:15. A call to repentance and the "intensification of norms" were widespread in the Judaism of the time (m. Ber. 2:2: "A man should take upon himself first the yoke of the kingdom of heaven and thereafter the yoke of commandments.") [Theissen, 1977: 103 (ET); Hengel, 1971: 56,[21] 74 (ET)]. This was because they suffered under the rule of the Gentiles (2 Macc.). In this context it is much more

---

[21] "This ideology could be considered the final consequence of a long bitter experience with gentile hegemony. Its basic axioms were *ardent expectation of God's reign and fanatical zeal for the law*." (italics mine).

likely that Jesus stresses that people destined for the kingdom should keep the highest moral standards. Jesus could intend to build a new Israel which would awaken individuals' conscience to God by personal obedience [cf. Dodd, 1971: 62; Moule, 1981: 54].

Sanders argues that "it is possible that Jesus imposed a higher righteousness on those who accepted him without requiring them to observe the machinery of righteousness according to the law." [1985: 323]. How could it be possible to impose a higher righteousness without asking obedience to the law which best stipulates the way to become righteous? Fulfilling what the law requires could be the short-cut to achieving the higher righteousness. Further, it must be noted that the teachings which Jesus imposes upon his followers for the higher morality seem to be mostly derived from this stringent interpretation of the law (cf. the Sermon on the Mount), not from the antinomian interpretation of the Law.

Jesus works within a framework of eschatological expectation. The prophets in the O.T. call for national repentance in the face of imminent danger of attack by foreign countries. The law was known, but it was not kept with all their hearts. The result was the imminent destruction of Israel. In the face of this danger they asked the people to obey faithfully. Jesus could call for radical obedience to the Law with the same urgency. For Jesus what mattered could be to keep the law wholeheartedly, while still requiring the people destined for the kingdom to observe the normal machinery of righteousness according to the law. John the Baptist asked them to be righteous and merciful (Luke 3:10-14). Like his predecessor, Jesus could ask them to do the same thing rather than merely to "follow him."

In the face of the impending end two sharply opposite attitudes could emerge among the people. One attitude is to ignore all responsibility and to become relaxed in obeying the Law's requirement. The other attitude is to keep the law and its requirements more faithfully and to become more sensitive in keeping the higher righteousness. The Jewish people who live according to the Law would be more inclined to take the latter view. Receiving the kingdom needs a change of personality (Mark 10:15). So it could include ethical reforms. What Jesus proclaims could be to admonish the Jewish people to make morality utmost in their life along with their cultic obligations before the imminent end. The command to repentance, restitution, reconciliation and forgiveness implies a higher morality.

c. I will rely on the following passages.

(1) Matt 5:23-24; 6:16 (Mark 11:25)
(2) Matt 5:25-26; Luke 12:58-59
(3) Matt 6:12; Luke 11:4
(4) Matt 18:12-14; Luke 15:4-7
(5) Luke 18:9-14
(6) Luke 19:1-10

Sanders regards (4) as authentic. He conceives of (1) (2) (5) (6) as inauthentic. Sanders does not deal with the authenticity of (3). I do not include Matt 18:21; Luke 17:3 (The command to forgive) and Luke 15: 8-10, 11:32 (The Parables on Forgiveness) in my close examination. Sanders affirms the authenticity of these passages [1985: 112]. The obligation to forgive repentant sinners already assumes the higher morality.

a. My counter thesis is as follows.

Jesus works and speaks forgiveness in an eschatological context.

b. My general argument against Sanders is the following.

Sanders pushes his arguments as hard as he can. He argues that sayings concerning forgiveness have little eschatological thrust [1985: 111]. Then he concludes that in the message of Jesus, forgiveness does take on the tone of eschatological restoration [112]! There is no firm evidence that sayings on forgiveness have little or no eschatological thrust. Although each saying, edited by evangelists, could reflect the non-eschatological post-Easter life situation of the early church, it is still possible that Jesus could speak these sayings in the pre-Easter eschatological context. It is improbable that Jesus speaks some sayings in an eschatological context, other sayings in a non-eschatological contest. Sanders concedes that Jesus expects the eschaton in the near future [1985: 156, 267], and he argues that Jesus' temple cleansing fits into eschatological expectation [90]. Hence, Sanders should admit that the sayings on forgiveness are also spoken in the eschatological context because he also argues that Jesus' whole work is set in the frame of Jewish eschatology [1985: 8, 10, 264].

c. I will rely on the following passages.
(1) Matt 5:23-24; 6:14; Mark 11:25
(2) Matt 5:25-26; Luke 12:58-59
(3) Matt 6:12; Luke 11:4
(4) Matt 10:5-7; Luke 10.9
(5) Matt 11:16-19; Luke 10:13-15
(6) Matt 11:41-42; Luke 11:31-32
(7) Matt 23:37-39; Luke 13:34-35

(8) Luke 13:1-5
(9) Luke 13:6-9

All these passages have an eschatological tone. Sanders regards (1) (2) (4) (6) (8) as secondary. He does not deal with the authenticity of (3) (7) (9). Sanders agrees only partly with the authenticity of (5) (a ring of authenticity).

D. *Prima facie* passages which could support Sanders' position: Jesus' silence about repentance in the case of healings

It is generally assumed that at least some cases of illness, if not all, resulted from sin. Jesus' general silence about the need for repentance in his healings might lend support to Sanders' case that Jesus did not require sinners to fulfill the law's requirement before he accepted them into his company. It is particularly in the healing incidents that we find *prima facie* passages in which seemingly unconditional forgiveness is offered. Thus it would be necessary to examine closely all passages in which Jesus seems not to ask repentance of sinners or people who are healed.[22] I note the following cases of healing.

1. Jesus' healing of individuals
   a. The centurion of Capernaum (Matt 8:5-13; Luke 7:1-10; John 4:46-54): Jesus was described as being amazed at the faith of this centurion (Matt 8:10; Luke 7:9).
   b. Peter's mother-in-law (Matt 8:14-15; Mark 1:29-31; Luke 4:38-39).
   c. The healing of the man brought by others (Matt 9:1-8; Mark 2:1-12; Luke 5:17-26).
   d. Jairus' daughter (Matt 9:18-19, 23-26; Mark 5:21-24, 35-42; Luke 8:41-42, 49-56).

---

[22] I isolate stories on exorcism from healing stories. The exorcism stories seem to have no direct connection with the sins of the sick. a. In the synagogue at Capernaum (Mark 1:21-28; Luke 4:31-37) b. The Gadarene demoniac (Matt 8:28-34; Mark 5:1-20; Luke 8:26-33) c. The Syrophenician woman (Matt 15:21-28; Mark 7:24-30) d. The epileptic boy (Matt 17:14-21; Mark 9:14-29; Luke 9:37-43) e. The dumb man possessed of a devil (Matt 9:32-34; 12:22-24; Luke 11:14-23)

e. A woman with the issue of blood (Matt 9:20-22; Mark 5:25-34; Luke 8:43-48): Jesus said to her "Your *faith* has made you well" (Matt 9:22; Mark 5:34; Luke 8:48).
f. Two blind men (Matt 9:27-31).
g. A deaf and dumb man (Matt 15:29-31; Mark 7:31-37).
h. A blind man at Bethsaida (Mark 8:22-26).
i. A man with a withered hand (Matt 12:9-14; Mark 3:1-6; Luke 6:6-11).
j. A blind man (Bartimaeus) (Matt 20:29-34; cf. Matt 9:17-31; Mark 10:46-52; Luke 18:35-43). This blind man asks Jesus to have mercy on him. Was it a sign of repentance?
k. The widow's son at Nain (Luke 7:11-17).
l. The healing of a crippled woman on the Sabbath (Luke 13:10-17).
m. The healing of the man with dropsy (Luke 14:1-6).
n. The healing of the ten lepers (Luke 17:11-19).
o. The healing of a man born blind (John 9:1-4)
p. The raising of Lazarus (John 11:1-44)

2. Jesus' healing of a multitude of people.
   a. Healings by the lakeside (Matt 4:24; 12:15; Mark 3:7-12; Luke 6:17-19).
   b. Healings in the evening (Matt 8:16-17; Mark 1:32-34; Luke 4:40-41).
   c. Healing the sick in Gennesareth (Matt 14:34-36; Mark 6:53-56).
   d. The healing of many people (Matt 15:29-30).

It is noteworthy that not all healing stories fit Sanders' argument. In the story of the ten lepers (Luke 17:11-19) *fulfillment of the Law is clearly required*: "Go and show yourselves to the priests" (Luke 17:14).

This explicit command to offer a sacrifice along with the account in John 5:14 could support the argument: Jesus could have asked or assumed the repentance of sinners and their fulfilling of the Law's requirements. Sanders' position could be consolidated only if there is an account in which Jesus explicitly dismisses or commands the discontinuation or the breaking of the cultic obligation. However, there is none. On the contrary many accounts attest Jesus; conformity to the law and the Temple. To sum up, Sanders' argument from silence remains weak.

Perhaps another *prima facie* passage upon which Sanders could rest his case would be Matt 9:1-8; Mark 2:1-12; Luke 5:17-26.[23] This story has no account in which Jesus commands the healed paralytic to fulfill his cultic obligations. Jesus may be seen simply declaring that the paralytic's sin is forgiven (Matt 9:5; Mark 2:5; Luke 5:20). No sign of repentance or a resolution of making a sacrifice before or after the healing is attested in this periscope. However, a more careful reading of this passage could lead to a different result.

John 5:14 shows another possibility. Although the setting of the Matt 9 passage (Galilee, Capernaum) is not paralleled in John 5:1-15 (which happened around the porticoes in Jerusalem), Jesus' command "take up your pallet and go walk" (John 5:8) is the same as in the synoptic accounts. Hence it is possible to assume at least that Jesus healed another paralytic in Jerusalem. *What is noteworthy is that the healed paralytic was found by Jesus in the temple* (v. 14). The healed paralytic could have gone to the temple to offer the sin offering. Jesus

---

[23] It would be unnecessary to deal with the authenticity of this story because Sanders does not dispute the historicity. Sanders seems to concur with the historicity of Jesus' announcement of forgiveness [1985: 111, 273; 1990: 61-63, 96] at least for the sake of his thesis: Jesus' unconditional forgiveness was an offence to many of his contemporaries [293].

could have assumed that the healed man would go to the temple because Jewish people in Jerusalem at the time of Jesus always did so. Furthermore, Jesus commands him: "See, you have become well! Sin no more, that nothing worse befalls you" (v. 14). The underlying assumption is that Jesus understood this man's sickness as a punishment of sin.[24] This is one of the cases in which Jesus' silence about repentance does not necessarily imply his rejection of the obligation of repentance.

We can also find an implicit teaching on repentance embedded in Matt 9:1-8; Mark 2:1-12; Luke 5:17-26. πίστις is used to describe the obedient attitude of the Jews toward God in the O.T. Deut 9:23, "you rebelled against the commandment of the Lord your God, and did not believe him or obey his voice" (ἠπειθήσατε τῷ ῥήματι κυρίου τοῦ θεοῦ ὑμῶν καὶ οὐκ ἐπιστεύσατε αὐτῷ καὶ οὐκ εἰσηκούσατε); Deut 32:20, "they are a perverse generation, children in whom is no faithfulness" (γενεὰ ἐξεστραμμένη ἐστίν υἱοί, οἷς , οὐκ ἔστιν πίστις ἐν αὐτοῖς); 1 Sam 26:23, "The Lord rewards every man for his righteousness and his faithfulness" (κύριος ἐπιστρέψει ἑκάστῳ τὰς δικαιοσύνας αὐτοῦ καὶ τὴν πίστιν αὐτοῦ); Sir 1:27 "he delights in fidelity" (ἡ εὐδοκία αὐτοῦ πίστις καὶ πραότης); 15:15 "to act faithfully" (πίστιν ποιῆσαι).[25] Hence Jesus could have healed the

---

[24] This command has a fair chance of being an authentic saying. The early church would hardly have made up this saying because for them sin means unbelief in the risen Christ. Schnackenburg accepts the possibility of tracing it back to the oral tradition [1971: 96 (ET)].

[25] Pesha. 118a-118b; For R. Huna said: "The Israelites of the generation [sc. of the Egyptian Exodus] were men of little *faith*, and as Rabbah B. Mari expounded: What is taught by the *verse, But they were rebellious at the sea, even at the Red Sea*? This teaches that in that moment the Israelites were rebellious and said: Just as we ascend at one side [of the sea] so do the Egyptians ascend from another." b. Sota. 48b-49a: "What is the cause that the tables of the righteous are despoiled in the Hereafter? The smallness [of faith] which was in them, that they did not trust in the Holy One, blessed be He." b. Taan. 8a: "*But they beguiled Him with their mouth, and lied unto Him with their tongues. For their heart was not steadfast with Him,* neither were they faithful in His covenant; and yet, But *He being full of compassion,*

paralytic by forgiving his sins because Jesus saw the sinner and his friends revivifying their faith in God by repentance.

Why did Jesus say the same command to the healed paralytic, "to take the pallet and go home" in all four gospels? There could be a reason. κράβαττον (Mark 2:11) or κλίνη (Matt, Luke) indicates a bed of a sick man. But we don't need to imagine a bed made of wood. It could be a big linen mattress which people could lie. It is possible that the healed sick brought their pallets to priests as a sign of their healing. Jesus could have asked them to carry their pallets to the priests for this reason.[26]

---

forgiveth inequity etc.?" (italics mine).

[26] Jewish people were particularly careful not to take on "the uncleanness caused by an unclean person lying on an object" [Jastrow, 1926, vol. 1: 854]: on 'bed' (מִשְׁכָּב: *mishcab*). This concern raises another question. How can the already uncleaned object to be purified? The healed person would have saved his bed because even a sheet of linen was precious at the time of Jesus. So the healed paralytics needed to have brought their beds to priests to be declared clean at the same time. (italics mine)

CHAPTER II-V

The Problem of Authenticity: A Systematic Treatment of the Relevant Passages

If we accept the Synoptic Gospels as they stand as an accurate account of Jesus' teaching and ministry, there would be little doubt that Jesus expected Israel to return to God and sinners to repent according to the highest teaching of the Law. However, we cannot assume that the records of Jesus' words and deeds are entirely reliable. The later church may have distorted Jesus' teaching on just this point. Each case is dealt with under the following five headings.

1. The Greek text to be defended so authentic and accurate

2. The reasons for setting aside some parts of the usual Greek test is a later embellishment or addition.

3. The reasons given against the authenticity of the text as given in 1.

4. The reasons that can be set against the arguments in 3.

5. A conclusion pointing out the connection between the defended passage in 1 and Jesus' teaching in general.

5.1 The main thrust of this saying.
5.2 The bearing on the forgiveness of sins.

CHAPTER II

Passages In All Three Synoptic Gospels

A. Did Jesus call for national repentance in Mark 1:15; Matt 4:17?

1. The conjectured original text

ἤγγικεν ἡ βασιλεία

2. Arguments against the authenticity of the excluded parts

τοῦ θεοῦ] Scribes and their predecessors could have expanded an original short form with this word [O'Neill, 1980: 116-117].[1]

καί πιστεύετε ἐν τῷ εὐαγγελίῳ] The early church or Mark could have expanded this part. The term εὐαγγέλιον in Rev. 14:6 could hint at its Jewish origin. Nonetheless the preceding πιστεύτε ἐν seems to suggest the Christian origin of this clause.

I mainly work on the authenticity of ἤγγικεν ἡ βασιλεία although

---

[1] "Scribes and their predecessors, the oral teachers, expanded an original short form "the kingdom" in order to explain to their hearers and readers either way what would have been obvious to the first audiences." [117].

there seems to be no decisive evidence that the other parts are secondary.[2]

3. Arguments against the authenticity of 1.

3.1. Mark 1:15 could be a Marcan formulation: Mark 1:15 "is a quite secondary formulation made under the influence of a specifically Christian terminology (πιστεύετε ἐν τῷ εὐαγγελίῳ) which might very well derive from Mark himself. Reference to the Person of Jesus is involved in the fact that Jesus is himself part of the gospel" [Bultmann, 1931: 118, 127 (ET); 1948: 5 (ET)].

3.2. Jesus did not make his appearance with a call to repentance [Jeremias, 1971: 42 (ET)]. Hence Mark 1:15 is secondary [Sanders, 1985: 374, 113].

3.3. In view of the passages on the already in-breaking kingdom, the theme of nearness of the kingdom was imported from the preaching of John the Baptist [Bammel, 1964: 8-9, 18; Fiedler, 1976: 101, 324[3]]. The concept of βασιλεία is misunderstood as summarizing the content of Jesus' eschatological preaching [Bammel, 1964: 10].

3.4. This passage was ascribed to the risen Jesus [Fiedler, 1976: 101-

---

[2] The similar expression ἥκει ὁ καιρὸς appears in Ezek 7:7 ἰδου ἡ ἡμέρα. Hence Jesus could have said this phrase. Jesus could also have said which lies before ἤγγικεν ἡ βασιλεία in Matt 4:17. It is possible to argue that Jesus uttered Mark 1:15 and Matt 4:17 on different occasions.

[3] Fiedler suspects the argument that Jesus' proclamation is linked to John the Baptist' proclamation of the imminence of the kingdom [1976: 101, 324 n 340] arguing against Hiers [1973: 52] who cites Schweitzer [1901: 147, 150 (ET); 1951: 123-124 (ET)]. Schweitzer [1901: 150 (ET)]: "He feels himself obliged to lead the people up climactically from the conception that John is a prophet to the presentiment that he is the Forerunner, with whose appearing the hand of the world clock nears the fateful hour...".

102]. The coming of the kingdom refers only to present reality; Jesus did not regard this phrase as referring to the future, but to an already ongoing event [Fiedler: 1976: 101].

3.5. Once the picture of the reign of God and its imminent coming are excluded from this saying the call for repentance remains as purely a natural way of thinking in Judaism. "Believe in the Gospel" is not a Jewish idea. All these ideas lead to a conclusion that no particular Jewish idea is embedded in Mark 1:15 [Fiedler, 1976: 102].

3.6. Mark 1:14f is the summary of Jesus' preaching by the evangelist, not the received single saying of Jesus [Fiedler, 101].[4]

3.7. Some scholars regard this saying as secondary with or without putting forward any additional reasons; K. L. Schmidt, 1964: 33 (ET); Marxen, 1956: 132 (ET)[5]; Haenchen, 1968: 73-74; Gnilka, 1978, vol. 1:65[6]].

4. The counter arguments against 3.

4.1. (3.1) seems to be too sweeping an argument. Mark could have formulated v. 15 from traditions and some of those traditions could have come from Jesus. ἤγγικεν ἡ βασιλεία seems to fit into this case; it could

---

[4] Fiedler selectively cites Kuemmel[1972: 32 (ET)].

[5] However Marxen still implies that some parts of Mark 1:14f contain the tradition of the early Jesus [1956: 133 (ET)].

[6] Gnilka is sceptical about the existence of some authentic sayings in Mark 1:15 [1978, vol. 1: 65]. However he argues that ἤγγικεν ἡ βασιλεία could be traced back to the Palestinian tradition (Matt 10:7; Luke 10:9) [1978, vol. 1:65].

be a true summary of Jesus' preaching.[7]

4.2. The suspicion on the authenticity of πιστεύετε ἐν τῷ εὐαγγελίῳ need not be extended to the entire preceding clause. The early church or Mark could have expanded Jesus' sayings with post-Easter traditions.

4.3. (3.2) seems to remain not entirely convincing. What Jeremais argues is that Jesus did not make his appearance with a call to repentance; in other words μετανοεῖτε is secondary [1971: 42 (ET)]. Sanders uses this argument in defence of the secondary nature of Mark 1:15 [1985: 374]. Contrary to the way Sanders interprets him, Jeremias clearly affirms the authenticity of the saying that "Jesus himself proclaimed its nearness with the words ἤγγικεν ἡ βασιλεία, and he sent out his disciples with same message." [1971: 100 (ET)].

---

[7] Bultmann does not deal with the authenticity of each tradition in Mark 1:15. He simply states that Mark 1:15 is a Marcan formulation. He does not clearly state that he casts doubt on the authenticity of ἤγγικεν ἡ βασιλεία, a particular part of Mark 1:15. In *The History of the Synoptic Tradition* (translated by J. Marsh from the second German edition published in 1931) Bultmann argues that Mark 1:15 is secondary [1931: 118, 127 (ET)]. However, in his later work, *Theology of the New Testament* vol. 1, published in 1952 (translated by K. Groebel from one of the German editions published in 1948) he seems to accept the words I am arguing are authentic: "But it is evident that Jesus has this conviction: This age has run out. *The summary* [scilicet by Mark] *of his preaching in the saying "The time is fulfilled, and the Reign of God is at hand*" (Mark 1:15), is appropriate." [1948: 5, 21 (ET)] (italics mine). Wellhausen isolated individual traditions in Mark 1:15 and dealt with each of them separately. He does not reject that Jesus could proclaim "the kingdom of God is at hand" [1907: 7]. Bultmann's two statements "The dominant concept of Jesus' message is the Reign of God" and "Reign of God is an eschatological concept" [1948: 4 (ET) already affirms that Jesus preached a certain message; "the kingdom is at hand". Bultmann seems not categorically to reject the possibility; v. 15 includes some authentic Jesus traditions along with some post-Easter traditions. Although Mark 1:14-15 is the substance and essential meaning of the whole public ministry and could, therefore, be ascribed to the creative work of Mark [Nineham, 1963: 67-68] this passage nevertheless may have some authentic Jesus tradition too.

4. 4. Further ἤγγικεν ἡ βασιλεία alone could all for national repentance sufficiently. The call for the coming of the kingdom is tantamount to asking for the repentance of the whole Jewish nation (Luke 17:26-35): "The radical moral demands made by Jesus that form part of the most unchallengeable tradition are based primarily on eschatological motives: entry into the kingdom of God, a share in the divine banquet, reign with God etc." [Schnackenburg, 1963: 84 (ET)]. "The clamour for divine vengeance upon the godless and sinners, on persecutors and oppressors is at least as emphatic as the yearning appeal for salvation and future glory. This is only too evident even in the austere members of the Qumran community" (CD VII.9; VIII.1-3; 1QS IX.23; 1QH II.24; IV.26 (cf. IV.20); 1QH III.27-28; 1QM XI.14, 16; XII.5; XIV.5-6; XIX.2) [Schnackenburg, 1963: 87 (ET)]. CD 7.9 "And all those who despise (Ms. B the commandments and the statutes) shall be rewarded with the retribution of the wicked when God shall visit the Land" [Vermes, 1987: 88]. CD 8:1-3 "...so shall it be for all the members of His Covenant who do no hold steadfastly to these (Ms. B: to the curse of the precepts). They shall be visited for destruction by the hands of Satan. That shall be the day when God will visit." [Vermes, 1987: 89]. "God shall (will) visit the Land" probably indicates the time of the coming Kingdom. These are good evidence that the coming kingdom accompanies judgment.

4.5. In (3.3) Bammel cites Martyr's work but gives an incomplete quotation. However, this passage in full supports the claim that Jesus proclaimed ἤγγικεν ἡ βασιλεία. Justin Mart., Dial. 51:2 Εἰ δὲ Ἰωάννης μὲν προελήλυθε βοῶν τοῖς ἀνθρώποις μετανοεῖν, καὶ χριστὸς ἔτι αὐτοῦ καθεζομένου ἐπὶ τοῦ Ἰορδάνου ποταμοῦ ἐπελθὼν ἔπαυσέ τε αὐτον προφητεύειν καὶ βαπτίζειν, καὶ εὐηγγελίζετο, καὶ αὐτὸς λέγων ὅτι ἐγγύς ἐστιν ἡ βασιλεία τῶν οὐρανῶν [Goodspeed, 1914: 150]: "But if John came as forerunner, exhorting men to repent and then Christ came and brought to a close his prophesying and baptizing at the River Jordan, and preached the Gospel in person, *affirming that the Kingdom of Heaven is imminent...*". [Justin

Martyr, 1977: 225].

4.6. Despite his stringent argument based on an exhaustive study, Bammel' s case seems not to be entirely convincing. Although Bammel argues that the early church had Jesus import what John the Baptist preached [1964: 8-9], in his recent article "the Feeding the Multitude," he confirms that "...he (Jesus) proclaimed a message that could be summarized in the same words as are found in tradition as characterizing John's preaching (cp. Matt 3:2 with 4:17)." [1984: 226].

4.7. Sanders also in his conclusion does not concur with Bammel's argument: "Bammel's analysis of the sayings about the kingdom deserves careful consideration, but the facts keep us from accepting his far-reaching conclusion" [1985: 117]. However in the previous paragraph Sanders already accepts Bammel's argument as his own: "We must doubt the authenticity of most of the passages that depict him as doing so, either because they conform his Jesus message to that of John the Baptist (e.g. Mark 1:15 and par.)..." [Sanders, 1985: 117]. Even if μετανοεῖτε is secondary ἤγγικεν ή βασιλεία τοῦ θεοῦ could be authentic. As a result of this hesitant acceptance of other scholar's argument on repentance (Mark 1:15; Matt 4:17), Sanders comes to rest his case mainly upon the argument of Bultmann [Sanders, 1985: 374] and Bammel [Sanders, 1985: 117], which seems to remain not entirely convincing. Sanders does not put forward his own argument. He merely cites arguments of other scholars [Bultmann, Bammel, Fiedler]. Consequently he ends up resting his argument only upon names.

4.8. (3.4) seems to be hardly convincing. Some accounts illustrate how the early church thought of Jesus as the king (Christ) who reigned in the kingdom (Eph 5:5; Col 1:13; cf. 2 Tim 4:1, 18; 2 Pet 1:11; 1 Cor 15:24). Hence the early church would have been reluctant to have Jesus call for the imminence of what might be understood to be another kingdom.

4.9. Along with Bammel [1964: 6-10, 28-32] Fiedler seems to interpret Jesus' proclamation in terms of the present reality of the kingdom of God as Bultmann does think [1948: 51-54 (ET)]. But Bultmann clearly argues that the kingdom is entirely future: "Rather, the Kingdom of God is a power which, *although it is entirely future, wholly determines the present* " [1926: 51 (ET)]. Further Fiedler does not seem to pay due attention to the authentic sayings of Jesus, which indicate the future aspects of the kingdom. Jesus seems to distinguish the future and present aspects of the kingdom; his instruction to pray "thy kingdom come (ἐλθέτω ἡ βασιλεία σου)" (Matt 6:10; cf. Mark 14:25; Luke 22:16; Matt 8:11; Luke 13:29) and Mark 9:1 (if authentic) also indicates the kingdom's coming in the future as does the remark that the kingdom is already breaking in (Luke 11:20; Matt 12:28). Further, what Jesus means in Luke 11:20; Matt 12:28 does not indicate that the kingdom is already fully realized, but that the sign of the imminent kingdom already begins to appear.

4.10. Fiedler's point in (3.5) could rather confirm the distinctiveness of Jesus' preaching. Jesus is unique in proclaiming the kingdom in the context where the Jewish people were anticipating the imminent kingdom accompanying judgment.

4.11. Fiedler's presupposition, that the proclamation of the post-Easter salvation message is not distinguished from the message of the earthly Jesus [1976: 102], is convincing to a certain degree. However, it is hardly possible to imagine a post-Easter Christian proclamation that has nothing to do with Jesus' preaching. It would be more convincing that the early church could have reshaped the pre-Easter traditions into kerygma. Jesus who preaches and Jesus who is preached could have had a close relation. In the course of pressing his argument Fiedler seems to make an error by saying that the kingdom already was present in Jesus [1976:101, 323 n 338]. However, Fiedler seems not to recognize that this interpretation runs counter to his main argument. If the early church understood Jesus' reigning in the kingdom only as a historical progress of the future coming of Christ's revelation as Fiedler speculates, it is much more unlikely that they would have made Jesus say "the kingdom is at hand".

4.12. Further it must be noted that even in Luke 11:20; Matt 12:28 Jesus still distinguishes himself and the kingdom.

4.13. It is much more likely that the Christian prophets or missionaries would have preached the death and resurrection of Christ [Jeremias, 1971: 108 (ET)] than the imminent kingdom.

4.14. In Judaism the disciples are expected to repeat what their master commands. "A man's agent is like to himself" (m. Ber. 5.5). Rengstorf translates this verse "he who is sent by a man is as he who sent him" [1933: 415 (ET)]. Accordingly Jesus' disciples would only have repeated what their master proclaimed rather than proclaiming something different. They could only add something more if Jesus endorsed it: "...the transaction could not be properly conducted without a resolute subordination of the will of representative to that of the one who commissioned him " [Rengstorf, 1933: 415 (ET)]. This consistency and continuity is essential in confirming the authority of a messenger [Flew, 1938: 110] (Matt 10:40; Luke 10:16). Accordingly it is hardly likely that Jesus' disciples proclaimed ἤγγικεν ἡ βασιλεία (Matt 10:7; Luke 10:9, 11) while their master did not.

4.15. By the same toke it is unlikely that Jesus commanded his messengers to preach this message, ἤγγικεν ἡ βασιλεία (Matt 10:7; Luke 10:9, 11), unless he proclaimed the same message. It is difficult to imagine a charismatic figure who restrained himself from proclaiming something before the public when his disciples already proclaimed something to the public.

4.16. What Kuemmel means in (3.6) is that Mark 1:14f was a summary of preaching by Mark; "not a specific saying of Jesus, in the present wording in Mark 1:15, has been handed down" [Kuemmel, 1972: 32 (ET)]. Kuemmel clearly argues that "The evangelist correspondingly did not place the announcement of the imminent judgment at the beginning of their account of Jesus' proclamation, but the message; "the kingdom is at hand" (Mark 1:15 par)" [1972: 33 (ET)]. The same conviction appears in another place too, "...by adding Jesus' announcement that "the kingdom of God is at hand"" [1972: 36, 43, 65, 325 (ET)].

4.17. One of the most detailed studies on the kingdom of God in Mark's Gospel was done recently by Ambrozic. Ambrozic argues that Mark himself is responsible for the formulation f Mark 1:14-15 [1972: 4-6]. However, Ambrozic still leaves 1:15a intact [1972: 5-6]. Further, he admits that some of the terms, kingdom and conversion should be traced back to the preaching practice of Jesus himself. Cabraja in his work on the repentance in the synoptic gospels clearly confirms that Jesus spoke ἤγγικεν ἡ βαοιλεία [1985: 86].

4.18. It is very likely that tradition could come from Jesus because this phrase is multiply attested in three gospels in different literary settings: proclamation, mission, and parables.

4.19. The continuity with the O.T. needs to be considered here. Pesch rightly cites passages (Isa 56:1; Ezek 7:3, 12; 9:1; Lam 4:18) as evidence for the authenticity of Mark 1:15 [1976, vol. 1: 102]. Jesus stands in the prophetic tradition and draws his proclamation for these passages calling for the national repentance of Israel.

4.20. Contrary to (3.7) many scholars regard ἤγγικεν ἡ βασιλεία as an authentic saying of Jesus with or without additional reasons: Bousset, 1906: 71-73 (ET); Montefiore, 1927, vol. 1: 23-27; Dodd, 1930: 62; T. W. Manson, 1948: 180; W. Manson, 1943: 97; Kuemmel, 1956: 24-25 (ET); Cranfield, 1959: 63; Gaechter, 1963: 123; Perrin, 1963: 200; 1967:

201; Hahn, 1963: 44 (ET); Schmid, 1958: 29-30 (ET); Conzelmann, 1968: 110 (ET); Braun, 1969: 40-41 (ET)[8]; H. Anderson, 1976: 83-85; Schweizer, 1967: 45 (ET); Chilton, 1979: 27, 56-59, 65, 86-88; Mussner, 1979: 156 (ET); Charlesworth, 1982: 467-468; Best, 1983: 39, 139; Uro, 1987: 150-156: Schrage, 1982: 28 (ET); Davies, 1988: 389]. Ambrozic puts Trilling's argument on the side of inauthenticity [Ambrozic, 1972: 4 n]. However, Trilling in his commentary on Matthew argues that in Matt 10:7 "The apostles are to make the same proclamation that Jesus made: "The Kingdom of heaven is at hand."" [1965: vol. 1: 178 (ET); pace Ambrozic, 1972: 4].

5.

5.1. The main thrust of this saying

When a saying was uttered with the desire to reach out to the nation it could be classified as "proclamation" although it was delivered to a relatively small group of people even in a quiet voice. It is not necessary to assume that every proclamation for the nation should have had the form of strong rhetoric before a large crowd as some contemporary politicians do. When Jesus' sayings include words like "kingdom" or "generation" "the house of Israel" it would be reasonable to assume that these sayings were aimed at the whole Jewish nation. The whole nation could be his audience because this type of saying could spread to the whole nation. In this respect Jesus' kingdom saying should be defined as "proclamation" because it could have a far-reaching impact on the nation which could have heard about the message from Jesus' audience. Further, when John the Baptist draws a multitude of people although he seems to have proclaimed in the wilderness of Judah (Matt 3:2-5) how much more effective could Jesus' proclamation to the Jewish people be when he

---

[8] Braun thinks that the community correctly caught the meaning of Jesus' message: "Repent, the kingdom of God is at hand" (Matt 4:17).

made trips to several places! ἤγγικεν ἡ βασιλεία could be part of the firm evidence of Jesus' calling for national repentance to all Israel. Jesus could call for national repentance with the appropriate means of communication ideal to the context: proclamation, parables, teachings. Jesus could call for repentance with this message immediately after John the Baptist was put into prison. "In a sense, the whole of Jesus' ministry was a call to change" [Borg, 1987: 163]. "Though Jesus used the word "repent" itself relatively infrequently, the notion is everywhere in his teaching" [Borg, 1987: 164]. These are counter arguments against Sanders. "Indeed, the call to change was at the heart of his various roles "[Borg, 1987: 164]. Like the Baptist, Jesus did indeed direct his proclamation and summons to all Israel [O'Neill, 1980: 44-58; Borg, 1987: 164; B. Meyer, 1990: 89-97]. "Like the Baptist (Luke 3.8=Matt 3.9), he consistently affirmed that the maintenance of election in the sight of God hinged on response to the final call of God." [B. Meyer, 97]. "Response to Jesus' eschatological and election-historical mission was not optional, but absolutely requisite." [Borg, 1990:97].

5.2. The bearing on the forgiveness of sins.

Contrary to what Sanders argues [1985: 110] the authenticity of Mark 1:15 seems to be sturdy. Standing in the prophetic tradition Jesus could call for national repentance with the proclamation, ἤγγικεν ἡ βασιλεία.

B. Did Jesus ask the leper to offer a sacrifice in the Temple as Moses commanded (Matt 8:2-4; Mark 1:40-45; Luke 5:12-16)?

1. The conjectured original text

Matt 8:2 καὶ ἰδοὺ λεπρὸς προσελθὼν προσεκύνει αὐτῷ λέγων, κύριε ἐὰν θέλῃς δύνασαί με καθαρίσαι. 3 καὶ ἐκτείνας τὴν χεῖρα ἥψατο αὐτοῦ λέγων, θέλω, καθαρίσθητι καὶ εὐθέως ἐκαθαρίσθη αὐτοῦ ἡ λέπρα. 4. καὶ λέγει αὐτῷ ὁ Ἰησοῦς ὅρα μηδενὶ εἴπῃς ἀλλὰ ὕπαγε σεαυτὸν δεῖξον τῷ ἱερεῖ καὶ προσένεγκον τὸ δῶρον ὃ προσέταξεν Μωϋσῆς, εἰς μαρτύριον αὐτοῖς.

Mark 1:40 καὶ ἔρχεται πρὸς αὐτὸν λεπρὸς παρακαλῶν αὐτὸν καὶ γονυπετῶν καὶ λέγων αὐτῷ ὅτι ἐὰν θέλῃς δύνασαί με καθαρίσαι. 41 καὶ σπλαγχνισθεὶς ἐκτείνας τὴν χεῖρα αὐτοῦ ἥψατο καὶ λέγει αὐτῷ, θέλω, καθαρίσθητι. 42 καὶ εὐθὺς ἀπῆλθεν ἀπ᾽ αὐτοῦ ἡ λέπρα, καὶ ἐκαθαρίσθη· 43καὶ ἐμβριμησάμενος αὐτῷ εὐθὺς ἐξέβαλεν αὐτὸν 44 καὶ λέγει αὐτῷ, ὅρα μηδενὶ μηδὲν εἴπῃς ἀλλὰ ὕπαγε σεαυτὸν δεῖξον τῷ ἱερεῖ καὶ προσένεγκε περὶ τοῦ καθαρισμοῦ σου ἃ προσέταξεν Μωϋσῆς, εἰς μαρτύριον αὐτοῖς.

Luke 5:12 καὶ ἐγένετο ἐν τῷ εἶναι αὐτὸν ἐν μιᾷ τῶν πόλεων καὶ ἰδοὺ ἀνὴρ πλήρης λέπρας· ἰδὼν δὲ τὸν Ἰησοῦν, πεσὼν ἐπὶ πρόσωπον ἐδεήθη αὐτοῦ λέγων, κύριε, ἐὰν θέλῃς δύνασαί με καθαρίσαι 13 καὶ ἐκτείνας τὴν χεῖρα ἥψατο αὐτοῦ λέγων, θέλω, καθαρίσθητι· καὶ εὐθέως ἡ λέπρα ἀπῆλθεν ἀπ᾽ αὐτοῦ. 14 καὶ αὐτὸς παρήγγειλεν αὐτῷ μηδενὶ εἰπεῖν, ἀλλὰ ἀπελθὼν δεῖξον σεαυτὸν τῷ ἱερεῖ καὶ προσένεγκε περὶ τοῦ καθαρισμοῦ σου καθὼς προσέταξεν Μωϋσῆς, εἰς μαρτύριον αὐτοῖς.

2. Arguments concerning the excluded part

This identical account appears in all three gospels in different wording. Many of the differences could have arisen during the translation from an Aramaic original text.

Mark 1:41 καὶ σπλαγχνισθεὶς] D a ff^1 r^2 have οργισθεὶς. It is more likely that οργισθεὶς was changed to σπλαγνισθεὶς than vice versa.[9] Dalman assumes that this textual variation could have arisen from a misreading of the Aramaic origins of two words σπλαγνισθεὶς and οργισθεὶϛ [1898: 65 (ET)]. This seems to be evidence of the Aramaic origin of this text.

Mark 1:43 καὶ ἐμβριμησάμενος αὐτῷ εὐθὺς ἐξέβαλεν αὐτὸν] Matt and Luke do not have this part. W b c (e) omit it. It is perhaps unlikely that this important segment was omitted by Matthew and Luke. This Marcan segment could have come, as an isolated tradition, from a healing story like Matt 9:30 (καὶ ἠνεῴχθησαν αὐτῶν οἱ ὀφθαλμοί, καὶ ἐνεβριμήθη αὐτοῖς. ὁ 'Ιησοῦς λέγων ὁρᾶτε μηδεὶς γινωσκέτω).[10]

Mark 1:45 ὁ δὲ ἐξελθὼν ἤρξατο κηρύσσειν πολλὰ καὶ διαφημίζειν τὸν λόγον, ὥστε μηκέτι αὐτὸν δύνασθαι φανερῶς εἰς πόλιν εἰσελθεῖν, ἀλλ' ἔξω ἐπ' ἐρήμοις τόποις ἦν· καὶ ἤρχοντο πρὸς αὐτὸν πάντοθεν] This part, paralleled in Luke 5:15-16 in different wording, could be a pre-Marcan or a Marcan end formulation [Bultmann, 1931: 341 (ET); Branscomb, 1937: 39]. However it would have been natural that a person freed from the deadly disease could not have kept silent along the path to a priest: especially if the leper interprets this

---

9 Cranfield [1959: 92].

10 Bultmann argues for the Marcan addition [1933: 212 (ET)].

command for silence as having arisen from the modesty of the healer.[11]

3. Arguments against 1.

3.1. Mark 1:40-44 comes from the Palestinian church [Bultmann, 1931: 240[12] (ET)].

a. Some scholars argue that Mark 1:43-44 was another tradition that emerged in the early church, which was later merged with the core healing tradition vv. 40-42 [Bultmann, 1931: 212[13] (ET); Lohmeyer, 1937: 47; Grundmann, 1968: 50].

b. The early church made up this saying to exalt Jesus as an eschatological prophet; this fitted the mission setting of the church [Pesch, 1976, vol. 1: 147-148]. Jesus is portrayed as a Hellenistic healer superior to Moses (Lev 13-14) or Elisha (2 Kings 5:1-14) [Pesch, 1976, vol. 1: 141, 143, 147].

3.2. The command to offer a sacrifice to the Temple ἀλλὰ ὕπαγε σεαυτὸν δεῖξον τῷ ἱερεῖ καὶ προσένεγκε περὶ τοῦ καθαρισμοῦ σου ἃ προσέταξεν Μωϋσῆς, εἰς μαρτύριον αὐτοῖς is a later

---

[11] K. L. Schmidt also takes v. 45, except from ὥστε to ἦν, as of belonging to the original story [1919: 66-67]. J. K. Elliott puts forward a similar argument: Jesus, not the leper, was the subject of ἤρξατο κηρύσσειν πολλὰ καὶ διαφημίζειν τὸν λόγον [1971: 153-157; 1978: 175-176].

[12] "The healing of the leper (Mk. 1:40-45) will also have come from the Palestinian Church; σεαυτὸν δεῖξον τῷ ἱερεῖ κτλ. Could hardly be formulated in an Hellenistic environment. The same does not hold of Lk. 17.14, for it is fashioned on the pattern of Mk. 1.44." [Bultmann, 1931: 240 (ET)].

[13] "Additions by Mark are to be found in the words ἐμβριμησάμενος αὐτῷ εὐθὺς ἐξέβαλεν αὐτὸν in v. 43, and ὅρα μηδενὶ μηδέν εἴπῃς ἀλλὰ in v.44 and in v. 45."

expansion, made to demonstrate Jesus' superiority over, even opposition to, the temple or priestly class[14] εἰς μαρτύριον αὐτοῖς could confirm this hypothesis.

4. Arguments against 3.

4.1. In (3.1) Bultmann advances no reasons for his argument; it is unclear whether the entire section or a segment was made up by the early church. One thing seems to be certain: many accounts support the conclusion that Jesus did miraculous work, including healing the sick. Jesus was accused of having been a magician [Origen, *Contra Celsum* 1. 28; Josephus, *Jewish Antiquities* 18. 63 (ἦν γὰρ παραδόξων ἔργων ποιητής: "wrought surprising feats"].[15] Otherwise healing with the name of Jesus would not have been prohibited (t. Hul. 2.22-23). Papyrus Egerton 2 (Fragment 1 r.) also supports Jesus' healing of the leper. Accounts on the healing of the leper, Luke 7:22 ("lepers are cleansed") and Luke 17:14 (healing of ten lepers) (cf. Luke 24:19) could support the historicity and authenticity of this passage.

4.2. Pesch also regards this passage as secondary[16] because the time and

---

[14] Lohmeyer regards this passage as a saying of Jesus: "The conflict, not apparent until that incident, appears again in another story of healing (Mk. 1.40-45) in Jesus' own words." [1942: 25 (ET)]. However I deduce a possible argument against the authenticity of the passage from Lohmeyer's interpretation of this passage. "The conflict between Jesus' healing power and priestly sacrifice is thus made abundantly clear; the sacrifice is to point to the means "which Moses commanded", but at the same time to the end of sacrifice and priesthood, and Jesus' work has the as yet veiled object of "destroying sacrifice," to quote from an apocryphal saying." [26 (ET)]:ἦλθον καταλῦσαι τὰς θυσίας...[Aland, 1985: 78].

[15] If we are able to rely on this as Josephus' report.

[16] Gnilka still admits the possibility that Jesus healed a leper [1978: 94].

place of healing and the name of the healer and healed[17] are not specified [1976: 142, 147]. Certainly there is no guarantee that only stories having such details could claim historicity. There are other healing stories where some of these details do not appear: Mark 1:30-31 (place), 5:21-24, 35-43; 5:25-34 (place and time), 7:31-37, 8:22-26 (Jesus).

4.3. Contrary to (3.1.a) this whole story seem to form a single unitary passage. It is not impossible that vv. 40-42, 44b form a single healing story. However vv. 41-42 squares so well with 43-44 that it would be reasonable to read this passage as a single unit.[18] The command to go to priests (vv. 43-44) would hardly have been associated with other stories than the healing of a leper (vv. 41-42).

4.4. Against Bultmann's argument [1931: 212 (ET)] the healing action ἐκτείνας τὴν χεῖρα αὐτοῦ ἥψατο and the command on sacrifice δεῖξον τῷ ἱερεῖ play pivotal roles in this healing incident. These descriptions are more than healing gestures or a demonstration of the consequent action. The early Palestinian church would have been reluctant to describe Jesus as healing the leper by touching, especially in their Jewish mission context.[19] They need not have irritated the Jews with this way of healing when they could have portrayed Jesus as healing leprosy by a word (2 Kings 5:11; Luke 17:14).[20] The healing section (vv.

---

[17] Pesch [1976, vol. 1: 142] counts the absence of the name of the healer, Jesus, as one indication of a secondary Healing setting. But the name Jesus appears in Matt 8: 14; Luke 5:12. Further, the leper's name could have been disclosed later in the phrase "Bethany in the house of Simon." (Mark 14:3; Matt 26:6).

[18] Schuermann also dismisses this two segment hypothesis [1969: 279].

[19] Matt 8:4; 1:43-44; Luke 5:14 indicates the Palestinian context.

[20] His touching the leper does not imply disrespect for the Law, but rather reflects his consciousness of being the Son [Cranfield, 1959: 93]. However Jesus still does not intend to reveal his Messiahship. What needs to draw our attention is that the leper, not Jesus, breaks the segregation law initially. Further a rabbinic evidence

41-42) would hardly have been made to reflect the polemic situation. Rather this description seems to suit the way Jesus heals the leper. One reason remains. The early church would have avoided Jesus' physical touch of the sinner as much as possible, to discourage the early Christian from resting their faith upon the earthly physical Jesus.[21] The early church seems to have already begun to encourage their members to be faithful to the spiritual risen Jesus (cf. Rom 8:9-16).

4.5. (3.1.a) remains unconvincing. The early Palestinian church would hardly have composed a saying consisting of two sharply contradicting segments, against and for the Law: the leper's abrupt approach (v. 41), which is against the rule of segregation (Lev 13:45-46; Num 5:2), and the command to offer sacrifice (v. 44), stipulated by Moses (Lev 14:1-32).

4.6. Pesch's argument (3.1.b) seems only partly convincing. Jesus' prophetic role would have made some positive contribution to the Jewish mission. However, this motive seems not to have been so strong as to lead them to make up this account. The point that the early church would have made in order to convince the Jewish people would have been that the risen Jesus is the Messiah (Acts 2:36; 3:15-20), not the prophetic authority of Jesus. Contrary to Pesch's argument Acts 3:15, 19 (cf. 26:22-23) focuses on the fulfilment of the prophecy, not on a superiority or rivalry, between Moses and Jesus. Likewise the difference of healing

---

shows that helping the leper at the emergency situation takes precedence over the observance of the purity law (Midrash Rabbah on Ecclesiasticus 9.7.)[Abrahams, 1917: 109-110].

[21] Vermes correctly points out that the twelve apostles also received the gift of healing. He rightly reminds us that disciple's method of treatment was, however, the more conventional one of anointing the sick with oil (Mark 6:13; Jas 5:14) [1973: 25]. However the following statement "...although in the Acts of the Apostles reference is nevertheless made to healing by command and touch" seems to be wrong. He cites Acts 3:6-7; 9:34; cf. 5:15-16. These texts do not say anything about disciples' touching of the sick.

between Elisha (by word) and Jesus (by touching) shows that Jesus did not follow quite the model of Elisha, as Pesch argues [1976: 143, 147].

4.7. Against what Pesch argues the setting of this passage is clearly a Jewish cultic setting. The argument that it is framed as a typical Hellenistic healing story [Pesch, 1976: 147] does not indicate its Hellenistic Jewish setting. Further the term "Hellenistic Jewish church" seems to be too arbitrary. If the early church maintained such an attitude of conformity, many conflicts caused because of the sharp difference between the Jewish church and the Hellenistic church would not have arisen, e.g., circumcision, food law. If we assume that this saying was made up in the Hellenistic Jewish church, the person who was asked to make up stories as reflections of their life setting could not easily have ignored the anticipated irritation and opposition from the Hellenistic Christians.

4.8. (3.2) is too tendentious an and hardly a convincing interpretation. Jesus "announces", not "declares", the leper "to be clean". καθαρίζειν could have both meanings, announce "to be clean" and declare "to be clean" as Taylor points out [1952: 187]. However in this passage it must mean "make clean" (heal) [Cranfield, 1959: 91]. The leaving of the leprosy (ἀπῆλθεν ἀπ᾽ αὐτοῦ ή λέπρα) confirms this interpretation. Although men of God could appeal to (Num 12:13) or announce the healing from leprosy (2 Kings 5:10-14) only priests can "declare" clean (Lev 14).

4.9. If the command to go to the Temple and to show the healed body to the priests (σεαυτὸν δεῖξον τῷ ἱερεῖ) for the proof of the healing (εἰς μαρτύριον αὐτοῖς) was made up as an evidence of Jesus' challenge to the Temple or priests, the command to offer a sacrifice (καὶ προσένεγκε περὶ τοῦ καθαρισμοῦ σου ἅ προσέταξεν Μωϋσῆς) would hardly have been necessary.[22] The simple and most powerful way of describing Jesus' challenge to the temple would have been "declare clean" and not to direct the healed to the Temple.[23]

4.10. Contrary to Lohmeyer [1942: 25-26[24] (ET); and Grundmann [1968: 52] εἰς μαρτύριον αὐτοῖς[25] does not have an "adversative sense" as Cave names it [1979- 249]. It rather has an "advocating sense". εἰς μαρτύριον αὐτοῖς hardly means to show the healed body to priests as a sign of the protest against the Temple. Schuermann adds another reason: εἰς μαρτύριον αὐτοῖς is not used with such a negative connotation in

---

[22] Hence Lohmeyer's argument "The conflict between Jesus' healing, power and priestly sacrifice is thus made abundantly clear" [1942: 25-26 (ET)] seems too remote from the original meaning of this saying.

[23] Theissen argues that Jesus "declared" clean, not "made clean" [1974: 146 (ET)]. "A sending to the priest would be meaningless if the cured man appeared claiming that he had already been pronounced clean. He has to keep this fact a secret and outwardly conform to the Jewish custom which is really *superfluous* for him. That is why in the story he is referred not to God, but to Moses, as the authority." [ibid] (italics mine). So he argues that the leper is directed to offer sacrifice as Moses, not the Law, stipulated. However what *Moses* commands is the Law (Lev 13, 14). The two words are equivalent.

[24] "But the more correct exegesis is rather different, for whenever the formula "for a proof unto them" occurs the reference is to the proof over against an unbelieving, God forsaking world. Therefore here it is the priests who are the unbelieving enemies of Him who performed this miracle; they are enemies even before they see it; and the sacrifice offered by the healed leper is to serve not merely to prove the "cleanness" of the man but by means of this proof to bear witness to the power of the agent of eschatological fulfilment, to whom in reality the commandment of Moses refers."

[25] Opinions differ to whom αὐτοῖς refers to, priests, the people having watched Jesus' healing, or people in general. The most likely reference would have been both "the priest" who was supposed to examine the healed leper and the people having watched Jesus' healing.

Luke 21:13 [1969: 277 n 29].[26]

4.11. Other accounts attests Jesus' respect for the Temple system and offering, They occur in multiple forms: narrative (Matt 5:23-24; 23:23; cf. 17:24-27; the exemplary temple offering (γαζοφυλάκιον Luke 21:1), parable (Luke 18:9-14), poetic forms (Matt 9:13; cf. Hos 6:6)), and in two different gospels. This could support the authenticity of Matt 8:2-4; Mark 1:41-44; Luke 5:12-14. Papyrus Egerton 2 (Fragment 1 r.) also contains the command to go to a priest[27] Jesus' positive command to offer (Mark 1:41-44; Matt 5:23-24) is clear. The passages in which Jesus is supposed to betray a negative attitude to the Temple or suspicion of the place of the Temple are obscure. They do not state at all clearly what the scholars think they imply (e.g. the cleansing of the Temple; the citation of Hos 6:6 (Matt 9:13; 12:7)), the statement about destroying the Temple that was cited by opponents at his "trial" (Matt 26:61, Mark 14:58; Mark 15:29, Matt 27:40, Acts 6-.14; cf. Mark 13:2). It seems wiser to accept clear statements than to prefer what are at best obscure statements. Jesus is not likely to have expressed his intentions in obscure words or deeds.

4.12, The frequent καὶ (v. 40, 41, 42, 43, 44) strongly hints its Aramaic

---

[26] εἰς μαρτύριον αὐτοῖς in Matt 10:18; 24:14 (εἰς μαρτύριον); Mark 6:1l; Mark 13:9 (par. Matt 24:14) may fit to the case of the negative use. But in these two cases the phrase is used in the context of being persecuted due to the preaching, of the gospel, not due to the temple offering (Mark 1:44 par.). Pesch also rejects the adversative meaning of this phrase [1976: 146 n 34].

[27] There is a sharply opposed argument on this issue: one guild of scholars argues against Jesus' respect to the Temple. These scholars draw their argument from the episode in the Temple (Mark 11:15-18; Matt 21:12-16; Luke 19:45-47). However "cleansing" seems to be still the main motive of Jesus' action. Jesus' reverence for the Temple could have driven him to show anger and anxiety over the abuse of the merchant activity which was originally adopted for the assistance of the sacrificial service. It would have been most likely that merchants would have tended to advance to the inside of the Temple in the more aggressive pursuit of business: as a result they could have been crossing, the limit of access.

origin.

4.13. Some scholars regard this incident as authentic saying of Jesus with some additional reasons: Jeremias, 1971: 207-208[28] (ET); Hengel, 1983: 43[29] (ET)].

5.

5.1. The main thrust of this passage

This passage illuminates two main points on Jesus' teaching in respect to the relationship between sickness, repentance, forgiveness and offering sacrifice. Firstly, the relationship between sickness and repentance. In Judaism diseases are sometimes regarded as a consequence of sin (Mark 2:9; cf. John 9:2; b. Arak. 6a; b. Ned. 4la[30]; 4QprNab) [Abrahams, 1917: 108-111]. Leprosy was believed to occur to Jews as a result of sin. This idea of retribution seems to have prevailed in the time of Jesus because this idea was stressed in the O.T. and rabbinic Judaism

---

[28] "Jesus demands with some vigour a reverential attitude towards temple and altar. This positive attitude also extends to sacrificial worship, the practice of which is presupposed in Matt 5:23f." "In Mark 1.44f par. he requires the leper to fulfil the ritual precepts for cleansing. Thus we cannot say with E. Lohmeyer that Jesus fought against the sacrificial cult. Had he done this, the earliest tradition would hardly have kept silence about it and the early church would hardly have taken part in sacrificial worship (Acts 21.26)."

[29] Hengel takes Jesus' warding of "the press of the masses, in contrast to the popular miracle workers and magicians of the Hellenistic and the Roman period, who could often be encountered in die Jewish sphere as well" as the evidence of authenticity.

[30] R. Alexander said in the name of R. Hiyya b. Abba. "A sick min does not recover from his sickness until all his are forgiven him; as it is written, who forgiveth all thine inequities; who health all thy diseases."

(b. Sabb. 55a).[31] The slander of Miriam on Moses' marriage causes leprosy (Num 12:1-10).[32] Leprosy struck Gehazi because of his ill-gotten gains and deception (2 Kings 5:27). The leper was a sinner and regarded as dead (Num 12:12) and could be healed only by God (Exod 4:6; Num 12:10-14; 2 Kings 5:10-14). However that was not the dead end. When lepers repented, God healed them through the men of God. Repentance, uttered by Aaron and appealed to by Moses to God, heals Miriam (Num 12:11): "We have done foolishly and have sinned." Further, although the breakout of this disease caused enormous pain, it was understood as a chance of reaching to repentance through self examination (t. Neg. 6.7[33]; Tractate Ber. (5a).[34] Jesus worked and spoke in a world where this idea of retribution prevailed. Then did this leper show any sign of repentance? This leper's desperate approach to a prophet stressing repentance in his proclamation could already imply repentance. Further this leper's word

---

[31] "There is not death without sin, and there is no suffering without iniquity."

[32] b. Arak. 16a: "Because of seven things the plague of leprosy is incurred. These are *slander*, the shedding of blood, vain oaths, incest, arrogance, robbery, and envy." (italics mine). Similar idea, Midrash Leviticus Rabba, 18.4.

[33] Neusner [1977: 1591: "He would come to priest, and the priest says to him, "My son, Go and examine yourself and return [from your evil ways]." "For Plague comes only because of *gossip,* and leprosy comes only to those who are *arrogant.*" (italics mine) [ibid].

[34] See Babylonian Talmud: Tractate Beracoth in Bibliography. From Cohen's translation [1921: 21]: "Raba (another version: Rab Hisda) said: Should a man see sufferings come upon him, let him scrutinise his actions; as it is said, "let us search and try our ways, and return unto the Lord," (Lam iii. 40). If he has scrutinized his actions without discovering, the cause, let him attribute them to neglect of Torah; as it is said, "Happy is the man whom Thou chastenest, and teachest out of Thy law (Ps xciv. 12)." If he attributed them to neglect of Torah without finding any justification, it is certain that his sufferings are chastenings of love, as it is said, "For whom the Lord loveth He correcteth" (Prov. iii.12)." Midrash Rabbah Leviticus 18:4 also teaches the idea of retribution. Midrash Rabbah Leviticus 17: God give punishment for chastisement.

καθαρίσαι could imply the liberation from sin: e.g. Ps 50:4 LXX, ἐπὶ πλεῖον πλῦνον με ἀπὸ τῆς ἀνομίας μου καὶ ἀπὸ τῆς ἁμαρτίας μου καθάρισόν με [Wojciechowski, 1989: 118]. Accordingly the leper's appeal ἐὰν θέλης δύνασαί με καθάρίσοι could imply his repentance.[35]

Secondly, Jesus directs this leper to the priests for restitution as the Law stipulates. If Jesus was so keen that a sick person should make restitution, how much more would he have been eager to see restitution made by sinners who clearly violated the, Law (e.g, robbery, fraud). Along with this significance, Jesus' directing this leper to the priests aims at the full restoration of the social position of a person who was once segregated from society.[36] In this case the command to go to the priests benefits the leper. That is one of important functions of the Law: Law is not for law itself but for human beings. How consistent was the work of priests, who were responsible for the whole process, from the diagnosis, through the treatment, to the declaration of cleanness. When this system collapses, the rehabilitation of the leper becomes virtually impossible, and no effective means could have deterred the spread of this infectious disease. This social function of the law and of the priestly system needs to be granted its positive value. In this sense, Law was not a burden but a blessing for the Jewish people.

---

[35] "The same word καθαρίζειν is used of removal of sin (Acts xv.9; II Cor. 7.1; Eph. v. 26; 1 John i. 7, 9, etc.) and of cleansing from leprosy (i. 40, 41, 42)." [Best, 1965: 106]. Best concedes that leprosy is then a type of sin: more generally sin and sickness are related [ibid] He derives a similar idea from the comparison of ἁμα ρτία (Matt 8:17) and LXX translation of Isa 53:3, 4. "In the LXX rendering of Isa Iiii. 3, 4 the servant is said to bear both μαλακία and ἁμαρτία implying their equivalence; μαλακία may mean "moral wickedness", but in Hellenistic Greek certainly means "sickness" (cf. Matt iv. 23; ix. 35; x. 1)."

[36] The special provision, a simple offering designed for the poor persons recovered from the deadly leprosy, is unique (Lev 14:21-32) and indicates that this purity rule did not aim at imposing the law irrespective of the situation of the people.

5.2. The bearing on the forgiveness of sins

The causality between sickness and repentance and the authenticity of this passage dismisses one of Sanders' main arguments on Jesus' attitude toward sinners: "...the absence of passages which call for repentance and restitution shows at least that he did not aim at restoring the wicked to the community." [1985: 203]. Sanders does not state his position on the authenticity of this passage clearly. He neither rejects nor affirm the authenticity [1985: 207].[37] He merely argues that Mark 1:40-45 and par. in any case does not deal with transgression [1985: 207]. Sanders seems to consider restitution only in terms of the civil law, etc., that is, in terms of offender's retribution of damage to the harmed. Certainly the leper is not a transgressor of a civil law. However in the Mosaic law and

---

[37] It is important to remember the fact that Sanders does not support the authenticity of this passage clearly, as I have pointed out in the section on Matt 5:23-24. One may perhaps believe that Sanders affirms the authenticity of this passage, because of his clear position in his later work *Jewish Law, from Jesus to the Mishnah* published in 1990: "A major biblical purity law which figures in the synoptics is that governing leprosy, and here Jesus acts in general conformity with the law (Mark 1:40-44)," [1900: 21]. "The synoptic Jesus lived as a law-abiding Jew." "He accepted the sacrificial system both as atoning (Matt. 5.23f.) and purifying (Mark 1:40-44). In common with other teachers, he cautioned his followers not to sacrifice until wrongdoing had been rectified and grievance assuaged." [1990; 90]. Here it is unclear what Sanders means by the words *Jesus figured in the synoptics or the synoptic Jesus.* If it equals the historical Jesus, Sanders affirms Jesus' full confirmation to the teaching of the Judaism of his time on repentance and restitution, if not, Sanders hints that Jesus takes a different position from the Judaism of his time. In the end we may have to conclude that Sanders rejects the authenticity of this saying, because in the heading of this book he states that "For the purpose of this study I shall for the most part work on the basis of two assumptions which I do not actually hold: that all the materials which is attributed to Jesus in fact goes back to Jesus..." [1990: 1].

in the world of Judaism at the time of Jesus there seemed to be no clear distinction between the purity and ceremonial and civil law. Any breach of these laws was regarded equally as a transgression of the law. Sometimes an offence against ceremonial law, like the blasphemy of the Temple or God, was regarded as more serious than a breach of a civil law. Further, if Jesus said that the offering of sacrifice for a transgression of the purity law should be strictly obeyed, he is unlikely to have condoned any excuse or evasion of the obligation to make restitution for a transgression of the civil law. Accordingly, the distinction of two types of transgression seems to give hardly any support to Sanders' argument. Josephus also wrote an account on the sin-offering of a person in sickness: "There are also sacrifices offered for escape from sickness or for other reasons" (*Jewish Antiquities* 3. 236). This account supports the continuation of sin-offerings at the time of Jesus. A similar account on the leper's offering appears in m. Neg. 14:1-13. If a certain cultic regulation was observed in the O.T. and at the time of the rabbinic Judaism, it would be reasonable to assume that the same rule was practiced at the time of Jesus. Hence it would be more convincing to argue that Jesus would have directed the healed leper to offer what Moses commanded (Lev 14; cf. Mark 7:11).

C. Did Jesus call for national repentance in Mark 8:12?

Matt 12:38-41; Mark 8:11-13; Luke 11:29-32 consist of independent traditions. In order to examine more closely I divided this passage into three pericopes, Mark 8:12; Man 12:39, Luke 11:29; Matt 12:41-42, Luke 11:31-32.

1. The conjectured original text

Mark 8:12 καὶ ἀναστενάξας τῷ πνεύματι αὐτοῦ λέγει, Τί ἡ γενεὰ αὕτη ζητεῖ σημεῖον; ἀμήν λέγω ὑμῖν, εἰ δοθήσεται τῇ γενεᾷ ταύτῃ σημεῖον.

2. Arguments concerning the authenticity of 1.

I accept the entire text as a genuine saying of Jesus.

3. Arguments against the authenticity of 1.

3.1. Mark 8:11-12 is designed to serve as another saying to emphasize the Messianic secret: Mark 8:12 rejects the idea of using miracles as the evidence of the legitimizing the Messiah [Luehrmann, 1969: 35].[38] The setting of Mark 8:11-13 is secondary: the Pharisee's asking a question immediately after Jesus puts his feet on earth after crossing the lake is clumsy [Wellhausen, 1909: 60].

4. Arguments against 3.

4.1. The rhetorical feature of Τί ἡ γενεὰ αὕτη ζητεῖ σημεῖον [Black, 1967: 123] does not appear in γενεὰ πονηρὰ καὶ μοιχαλὶς σημεῖον

---

[38] However Luehrmann still affirms that this saying could have come from Jesus [1969: 35, 42].

αὕτῇ ἐπιζητεῖ. This feature is likely to be original; it is a Semitic idiom (cf. Matt 16:4).[39]

4.2. The early church would have been reluctant to describe Jesus as refusing to give a sign because they portrayed Jesus as having already given many signs (Acts 2:22; cf. Acts 4:30). For them Jesus' flat rejection of rendering a sign could be unusual because the early church responded many signs performed even by apostles (σημεῖον Acts 4:16, 22; 8:6, 13; 2 Cor 12:12) (τέρας Acts 4:30; 6:8; 15:12; Rom 15:19; 2 Cor 12:12)).

4.3. The rhetorical feature of Τί ἡ γενεὰ αὕτη ζητεῖ σημεῖον (e.g. Τί στενὴ ἡ πύλη Matt 7:14) could echo Jesus' distressed response to the testing attitude of the unrepentant Jews who seek signs constantly while repudiating even the obvious signs. This distress seems to be coherent with that of Jesus in Luke 12:54-57. Luke 17:21 could also echo the same distress of Jesus; why do you ask the sign of the coming Kingdom when the kingdom is in your grip? [O'Neill, 1980: 24].

4.4. The Semitism εἰ in Mark 8:12 [Wellhausen, 1909: 61; Swete, 1913: 168] also supports the authenticity of this saying. ἀμὴν λέγω ὑμῖν in the beginning part of the speech and the passive form δοθήσετι could also support its authenticity. These linguistic, along with rhetorical, features could be reckoned as significant pieces of evidence of the authenticity.

4.5. One piece of evidence for the authenticity is that this type of teaching is coherent with the saying in which Jesus refuses to answer the question on his authority (Mark 11:27-33; Matt 21:23-27; Luke 20:1-8).

4.6. The word ἀναστενάξας which appeared only here in the N.T.

---

[39] Marshall already hints this possibility [1978: 483]. Along with the argument of Marcan omission [1978: 492-3, 495] Marshall argues for another possibility: a different strand of tradition could have reached Mark [483].

could indicate that Mark 8:12 is an old tradition [Edwards, 1971: 76].

4.7. The argument (2.1) on the Messianic secret seems unconvincing because Jesus' feeding of the five thousand (Mark 8:1-10) is a sign of his Messiahship. Moreover "The sign from heaven" asked from Jesus need not be a sign for testing Jesus' authority necessarily [Luehrmann, 1969: 35]. It could mean a sign of the coming Kingdom or the End.

4.8. Sanders does not write on the authenticity of this saying in detail. He states that Jesus' refusal to give a sign is a "tradition" [1985: 172]. However he seems to endorse the authenticity of Mark 8:12: "We can now see the situation in the Gospels clearly. Jesus, we read, was asked for a sign, and we may be reasonably sure that the report is accurate. According to Matt 12.38-42 and par.; Mark 8.11f and par., he refused." [1985: 172].[40]

4.9. The following scholars regard this saying as an authentic saying of Jesus with or without giving any significant reasons: Rawlinson, 1925: 105; Montefiore, 1927, vol. 1: 174-175; Dibelius,[41] 1933; 159 (ET); Lohmeyer, 1937: 154; Hengel, 1968: 59 (ET); Nineham, 1963: 212; Edwards, 1971: 75[42]; H. Anderson, 1976: 198-199; Pesch, 1976, vol. 1: 409; Gnilka, 1978, vol. 1: 307; 1986: 468-469[43]; Trautmann, 1980: 163; Merklein, 1981: 126; Bayer, 1986: 131.

---

[40] What Sanders means by "the situation in Gospels" is that some people considered Jesus as the special figure in God's plan when convinced by his miracles and signs; but some people probably called him a magician when not persuaded by these miracles [1985: 172].

[41] Debelius suspects Mark 8:11f as a form of "Chriae".

[42] Edwards argues that Mark's version is close to an early account of Jesus' refusal to give a sign to the Pharisees.

[43] Gnilka claims that the mysteriousness of this answer to the request of signs could be traced back to Jesus.

5.

5. 1. The main thrust of the saying

ἡ γενεὰ meaning "contemporaries" [BAGD, 154][44] could point to the whole nation of Israel at the time of Jesus. Thus Jesus' flat rejection in Mark 8:12 could indicate his assumption that Israel as a whole needed to repent. What could Jesus mean by rejecting the request that he gives a sign? A pejorative connotation used when accusing somebody is embedded in this flat refusal [Pesch, 1976, vol. 1: 408] and in the use of "this generation". In this solemn refusal Jesus could stress what the nation of Israel fails to catch: the need for the repentance of Israel before the kingdom which was on the threshold. In 2 Esdras (4 Ezra) 5:13 Ezra says he has given signs but will give no more signs until Israel repents by praying, weeping and fasting. The prophet and his proclamation could function as a sign; Ezek 4:3, 12:6 "I have made you a *sign* for the house of Israel." Therefore Jesus could refuse to give signs by reminding them of a sign which suggested that if his questioners could not see it for themselves it was useless to do anything further.

If σημεῖον ἀπὸ οὐρανοῦ was meant to be the sign of the end or the kingdom[45] Jesus' rejection could indicate the impending end or the destruction of Jerusalem. If σημεῖον ἀπὸ οὐρανοῦ was put to Jesus to check whether he is the Messiah[46] he could avoid justifying himself and revealing his authority.

5.2. The bearing on the teaching on the forgiveness

---

44 Kuemmel, 1956: 61 (ET); Cranfield, 1959: 258-259; Nineham, 1963: 212; Luehrmann, 1969: 35; Jeremias, 1971: 72 (ET).

45 Linton; 1965: 128.

46 Schniewind; 1952: 110; 1954: 162; Linton, 1965: 128.

In short, Jesus could be calling for the national repentance of Israel in his flat rejection of giving signs. Their groundless confidence prevents them from perceiving the explicit signs revealed in the words and actions of Jesus. Further Jesus could intend to lead the Jewish people into repentance as they asked themselves about the reason for Jesus' flat rejection; how perverted they were!

D. Did Jesus call for national repentance in Matt 12:39; Matt 16:4; Luke 11:29?

1. A conjectured original text

Matt 12:39, Matt 16:4, Luke 11:29,

Γενεὰ πονηρὰ καὶ μοιχαλὶς σημεῖον ἐπιζητεῖ, καὶ σημεῖον οὐ δοθήσεται αὐτῇ εἰ μὴ τὸ σημεῖον Ἰωνᾶ.

2. Arguments against the authenticity of the excluded parts.

2.1. τοῦ προφήτου seems to be a Matthean addition [Harnack, 1907: 23 (ET)].

2.2. ἡ γενεὰ αὕτη γενεὰ πονηρά ἐστιν σημεῖον ζητεῖ] This Lucan text could be a translation variant of the Matthean text. p^{75} does not have second γενεὰ. The original text seems to have the distinctive words μοιχαλὶς and ἐπιζητεῖ [Hawkins, 1899; 71; Harnack, 1907: 23 (ET)]. There is no difference between Luke and Matthew in the second half. Other half is paralleled in Matthew 16;4 καὶ σημεῖον οὐ δοθήσεται αὐτῇ εἰ μὴ τὸ σημεῖον Ἰωνᾶ.

3. Arguments against the authenticity of 1.

3.1. εἰ μὴ τὸ σημεῖον Ἰωνᾶ was inserted as an addition to the original text in Mark 8:12 by Matthew and Luke [Bousset, 1913: 38-39 (ET); Branscomb, 1937: 139] or this phrase was already inserted in Q [Wellhausen, 1914: 36, 62; Dobschuetz, 1927: 39; Luehrmann, 1969: 37, 40-42; Edwards, 1971: 80-87, 106; G. Schmitt, 1978: 128]. Some scholars argue that εἰ μὴ τὸ σημεῖον Ἰωνᾶ was brought in as an addition to the original text. Mark 8:12 at the time of making the link with the following pericopes, Matt 12:41-42; Luke 11:31-32 [Bousset, 1913: 38-39 (ET); Luehrmann, 1969; 35, 42; 1988; 137; Edwards, 1971: 56]. Some scholars put forward this argument without giving any particular reasons [Branscomb, 1937: 139].

3.2. Jesus contradicted himself by saying that a sign would be given on one occasion and no sign on another occasion. He is unlikely to contradict himself. Therefore one of the sayings is inauthentic and the longer of the two is likely to be the inauthentic one.

3.3. The early church made up this saying for polemic reason [Luehrmann,1969: 42; Schulz, 1972; 253 n 534, 255-257]. They could criticize unbelieving Jews with this saying.

3.4. It is unlikely that some Jews asked Jesus to perform a sign because an appeal for a sign was discouraged in some part of Judaism (b. Mes. 59b): The school of Shammai is particularly reluctant to allow this appeal [Gerhardsson, 1961: 213 (ET)].

3.5. Sanders casts doubt an the authenticity of Matt 12:39; Luke 11:29 indirectly [1985:143]. According to Sanders "the Marcan accusation of "this generation" in Mark 8:38 is similar to the criticism of "this generation" of Matt 12:39-41; Luke 11:29f., a criticism which Matthew repeats in 12:45." [143]. Thereafter he argues that (ὃς γὰρ ἐὰν ἐπαισχυνθῇ με καὶ τοὺς ἐμοὺς λόγους) ἐν τῇ γενεᾷ ταύτῃ τῇ μοιχαλίδι καὶ ἁμαρτωλῷ in Mark 8:38 shows the influence of Christian redactional activity [Sanders, 1985: 144]. Consequently the authenticity of "in this adulterous and evil generation" in Matt 12:39; Luke 11:29 is called into question.

4. Arguments against 3.

4.1. Contrary to (3.1) Matt 12:39; Matt 16:4; Luke 11:29 seem to have come to our present text as independent traditions.

4.2. Both Matt 12:39; Luke 11:29 and Matt 12:41-42; Luke 11:31-32 could have had "the reference to Jonah", εἰ μὴ τὸ σημεῖον Ἰωνᾶ and τὸ κήρυγμα Ἰωνᾶ before they were put together in Q [Bultmann, 1931: 118 (ET)]. It is much more likely that the common reference to Jonah led to the combination of these two sayings.

4.3. It is unlikely that εἰ μὴ τὸ σημεῖον Ἰωνᾶ was added because of its enigmatic features [Kuemmel, 1956: 68 (ET)] or because of its essential role in an idiom: a denial is made only to be followed by an exception (e.g. Matt 15:24; Gal 2:16) [Colpe, 1972: 449[47] (ET); Perrin, 1967: 193; Schweizer, 1976: 292; Marshall, 1978: 485; Bayer, 1986: 126[48]]. The early church or Matthew or Luke would not easily have made up such an enigmatic or idiomatic saying. The longer text is claimed as the original saying for similar reasons [Schweizer, 1973: 292 (ET); Marshall, 1978; 485; Bayer, 1986: 126]. Some scholars regard this text as original without providing any particular reason [Mussner, 1979: 167 (ET); Cabraja, 1985: 63; Schnackenburg, 1985: 113; Gnilka, 1986: 468; Beasley-Murray, 1986: 254].

4.4. If a phrase was added to make a link between Matt 12:39; Luke 11:29 and Matt 12:41; Luke 11:32, it is more likely that they would put εἰ μὴ τὸ κήρυγμα Ἰωνᾶ than εἰ μὴ τὸ σημεῖον Ἰωνᾶ. εἰ μὴ τὸ κήρυγμα Ἰωνᾶ would have settled the question as to whether originally

---

[47] Colpe cites some passages from Kuschke's list [1950-51: 263], But Colpe seems to confuse the case of the real relative negative (Mark 2:17; 9:37; John 1: 13; John 7:16; Matt 25:29b) with the case of the idiomatic exception (Matt 15:24; 25:29b; Gal 2:16).

[48] Following Marshall [1978: 484] Bayer interprets this phrase to mean "only the sign of Jonah will be given" [1986: 125 n 111].

Matt 12:39; Luke 11:29 had any direct connection with Matt 12:41; Luke 11:32.[49] The κήρυγμα of Jonah in Matt 12:41; Luke 11:32 would have pointed directly to the sign which Jonah gave, the message of Jonah on repentance. The early church would hardly cause confusion by bringing in εἰ μὴ τὸ σημεῖον which could yield three different meanings: the sign which was the prophet Jonah (appositive genitive), the sign which Jonah gave (subjective genitive), the sign which Jonah experienced (objective genitive).[50] This confusion is puzzling εἰ μὴ τὸ σημεῖον if was the intended meaning.

4.5. Was the phrase εἰ μὴ τὸ σημεῖον added to Mark 8:12 by Matthew and Luke in light of the passage in The Lives of the Prophets 10:10, Jonah's giving a portent concerning the destruction of Jerusalem [G. Schmitt, 1978:126-1281? The evidence remains flimsy. The word τέρας, not, σημεῖον is used in the Lives of prophets 10:10. Moreover, the date of this text is not settled. This text is usually dated from the first quarter of the first century to the end of the first century [Hare, 1985: 392-293, 486]. Even if this text is dated around A.D. 66-70 [G. Schmitt, 1978: 128] it could have been written after the destruction of Jerusalem in A.D. 70.

4.6. Contrary to (3.2) many scholars regard this saying as authentic [Kuemmel, 1956: 68, 113 (ET); Grundmann, 1981: 242; Jeremias, 1938: 409 (ET); 1971: 135 (ET); Perrin, 1967: 193; Mussner, 1979: 167 (ET); B. Meyer, 1979: 158; 0. Betz, 1965: 35 (ET); Hengel, 1969: 59 (ET); Marshall, 1978: 485; Merklein, 1981: 126; Trautmann, 1980: 163; Cabraja, 1985: 63; Bayer, 1986; 131; Schnackenburg, 1985: 113; Uro,

---

[49] Wellhausen argues that originally this following part has nothing to do with the preceding rejection saying [1914: 62-63].

[50] Jeremias [1938: 408 (ET)].

1985:171-172; Beasley-Murray, 1986: 254; Gnilka, 1986: 468[51]; Fitzmyer, 1986: 930-932; Stanton, 1989: 219; Evans, 1990: 497-498].

4.7. Is the hypothesis (3.3) compelling? Does Matt 12:39; Luke 11:29 contradict Mark 8:12? Jesus could be seen as being inconsistent in saying "no sign is given" on one occasion and "a sign is given" on another occasion. However, Jesus' progressive answer could clarify this seeming contradiction. Jesus' initial refusal to heal the daughter of the Syrophenician woman (Mark 7:27) ends with his healing her when her mother appeals for help persistently (Mark 7:28). The absolute negative answer in Matt 19:24 is followed by the positive answer in Matt 19:26. These two sets of seemingly contradictory sayings do not illustrate Jesus' inconsistency: they rather elucidate how realistic these sayings were.

4.9. The point of two sayings is the same; to give the sign of Jonah means to give no sign. This sign puzzles the people who ask it. I know that this is a different argument from (4.7); if (4.7) fails, (4.8) may hold.

4.9. In answer to the hypothesis (3.4) the early church would hardly make up this saying to portray their polemic situation.[52] This hypothesis fails to

---

[51] Gnilka claims that Mark 8:12 is the secondary against Matt 12:39; Luke 11:29. The enigmatic feature of "the sign of Jonah" could possibly be traced back Jesus.

[52] Contrary to Luehmann [1969: 42: Schulz, 1972; 253 n 535] Uro argue that the polemic against "this generation" in Luke 11:29-32 does not stem from the latest stage of the composition of Q [1985: 171-172]. Along with other traditional sayings Luke 10:12-15//Matt 11:20-24 Luke 11:29-32//Matt 12:39-42 could be spoken against unrepentant Israel in the pre Q stage [Uro, 172]. Bayer correctly points out why Schulz' argument on the late composition of this saying in Q is not convincing [1985: 127 n 126]; γενεὰ could be used as the term portraying Jesus' criticism) of the unrepentant Israel. The early church could keep this collection of sayings and could use it in their mission along with reference to the death and resurrection of Jesus and the judgment at the future coming of the Son of Man [Cabraja, 1985: 63; Uro, 1985: 171-172].

take into account the possibility that Jesus could criticize his contemporaries with the term "this generation". Must the term; ἡ γενεὰ Luke 11:30, 31f reflect a sharp contrast only between the Q community and Israel? [Luehrmam, 1969: 35, 42-43; Schulz, 1972: 253 n 534, 255-257]. Had this phrase really become a stereotype used in polemical contexts mostly against unbelieving Jews? Standing in the prophetic tradition Jesus could criticize his unrepentant contemporaries with the term ἡ γενεὰ[53]

4.10. The early church could repeat the collected traditions of Jesus' saying in the polemic setting of the early church [Mussner, 1979: 181; Uro, 1985: 171-172].[54]

4.11. The presupposition of hypothesis (3.4) could work the other way. The Palestinian church was keen to get more Jewish members. Therefore they were unlikely to irritate Jews deliberately by making up a story of a request for a sign which went against a trend of some parts of Judaism (The school of Shammai).

4.12. The hypothesis (3.5) does hold true only for one stream of Judaism. Unlike the school of Shammai, the school of Hillel was less sceptical about the appeal to signs [Gerhardsson, 1961: 213 (ET)]. Further a sign could be asked of a man who seems to be given a prophecy to confirm his divine commission [Rengstoff, 1964: 235; Schlatter, 1948: 414]. The

---

53 Jeremias confines the use of the term γενεὰ to "Jesus' contemporaries" be-cause of the eschatological and linguistic features [1971: 135 (ET)]. He points out that the Greek γενεὰ can have the meaning of "race", but not the Hebrew *dor* or *dar*. If this text was originally written in Aramaic his argument would be convincing. However if it was originally written in Greek this argument could not stand firm. However the Semitic features of this text seem to support its Aramaic origin.

54 Recent works on Q affirm that the collection of traditions in Q could pre-serve the sayings of the historical Jesus [Aune, 1983: 245; Piper, 1989: 195-196].

stricter attitude to miracles and signs was developed only after A,D 70 [Montefiore, 1930: 249; Gerhardsson, 1963: 213].[55] Accordingly it is historically possible that some Jews asked a sign from Jesus and that their request was turned down by him.

4.13. In his hypothesis (3.6) Sanders does not give any firm evidence of the Christian editorial activity. "In this adulterous and sinful generation" could have come to Mark 8:38 from an isolated floating saying. Or Luke could have omitted this phrase in Luke 4:26. Luke seems to have omitted μοιχαλὶς in Luke 11:29. Further the spuriousness of "in this adulterous and sinful generation" of Mark 8:38 does not need to dictate that all the passages which have this phrase in the synoptic gospels are inauthentic. The same phrase in a similar wording is attested in three gospels in the passages: the asking of a sign from Jesus (Matt 12:39, 45; Matt 16:4; Luke 11:29), the description of Jesus' distressed response to the absence of the faith which is required for the healing (Mark 9:19; Matt 17:17; Luke 9:41), the rejecting of Jesus (Luke 16:8; Luke 17:25). Hence, the frequently attested phrase in slightly different wording γενεὰ πονηρὰ καὶ μοιχαλὶς in Matt 12:39 (Luke 11:29) could have come from Jesus.

4.14. The early church would be reluctant to have Jesus refusing to offer a sign because they portrayed Jesus as having given many signs (Acts 2:22; cf. Acts 4:30). For them Jesus' flat rejection of giving a sign could be unusual because the early church reported many signs performed even by apostles.

---

[55] This reluctant attitude toward signs seems to have spread as time went on. Gehardsson argues that by the third Tannaitic generation matters had gone so far that a rule was formulated to the effect that "one should not (when deciding halakic questions) mention miracles" (b. Hul. 43a; b. Ber. 60a; b. Yeb. 121b) [1961: 213 (ET)]. But until the destruction of the Temple the Jews could ask signs for a special purpose [Montefiore, 1930: 248]. cf. Acts 9:9-16 [Gerhardsson, 1961: 213 (ET)].

4.15. Justin Martyr., *Dial.* 107.1 parallels Matt 12:39 (except τοῦ προφήτου); Luke 11:29. If Justin Martyr is independent of Matt and Luke [O'Neill, 1961; 35, 41, 42; 1970: 29-44] his testimony lends added support to the authenticity of this text.

4.16. The first half of Matt 12:39; Luke 11:29 γενεὰ πονηρὰ καὶ μοιχαλὶς σημεῖον ἐπιζητεῖ is markedly different from Mark 8:12 in wording. This feature seems to support the view that it is a distinct saying from Mark 8:12 [Cabraja, 1985: 531].

4.17. The text in Matt and Luke retains no rhetorical feature from Mark 9:12.

4.18. A Semitism in the passive form οὐ δοθήσεται could also support the authenticity.

4.19. The strong derogatory connotation in πονηρὰ, μοιχαλὶς, ἐπιζητεῖ is absent in Mark 8:12. If the early church made up this saying they were likely to have used the word σκολιᾶς (crooked) (Acts 2:40; Phil 2:15) or διεστραμμένης (perverse) (Phil 2:15). The early church would need to condemn Jewish lack of faith not Jewish lack of morality. Hence they would not need to use πονηρὰ or μοιχαλὶς as a description of the Jewish morality. Further if the early church made up the saying, they would have been unlikely to confine Jesus' strictures to this one generation.

4.20. Jesus could have been responding to questioning people with a good example of a σημεῖον ἀπὸ τοῦ οὐρανοῦ which they needed to think out. He could have taken the approach, a good teacher answers one question by raising another, especially when faced by an embarrassing question he does not wish to answer (Mark 12:27; Matt 21:24; Luke 20:3-4).

5.

5.1. The main thrust of the saying

The proclamation of Jonah has many features that recur in the proclamation of Jesus: the preaching of the imminent end (Jonah 3:4), the clear sign of repentance (3:5,6,7), national repentance (3:5,8), renouncing of the evil and violent behaviour (3:8), the expectation finding mercy of God in repentance (3:9), God's decision not to bring in the disaster before their resolute renunciation of evil ways (3:10). εἰ μὴ τὸ σημεῖον Ἰωνᾶ could emphasize the notion that God saved even wicked Gentiles destined for judgment when they responded with repentance, the message of judgment.[56] Sanders argues that "...and the saying about Jonah has produced a good deal of debate; but the uncertainty that hangs over the saying is well expressed by Perrin: What did this [the sign of Jonah] mean in the teaching of Jesus? The answer to this question is simply that we do not know, because we do not know what Jesus and his contemporaries would have understood by the phrase..." [1985: 110, 374 n 631. That is

---

[56] This interpretation comprises two possible interpretations of the sign of Jonah, taking the genitive as either appositive or subjective. It is not necessary to interpret the sign of Jonah only as an objective genitive which refers to the miracle of the deliverance of Jonah from the belly of the great fish [Jeremias, 1938: 409 (ET)]. Rengstorf clearly points out that Jeremias' interpretation does not answer the question of in what sense Jonah is taken to be a sign. Rengstorf attempts to answer this puzzling, question by integrating all three possible interpretations into one which Jeremias detests: "According to the context and also the meaning of a tip σημεῖον it seems very probable that the saying characterises Jonah as the one in whom God Himself shows Himself to be present with the prophet and work through him and his call for repentance." [1964; 233 (ET)]. Bayer complements this integrated interpretation by the argument "The giving of a sign is not separate from the person through whom the sign occurs." [1986: 131]. Although each of the three different interpretations is relevant for this passage the subjective genitive interpretation of this sign of Jonah seems to be the most important. δοθησέται in Luke 11:29 may hint at this interpretation [Bayer, 131].

hardly likely. "The sign of Jonah" could mean God's end time forgiveness of repentant sinners. This interpretation seems to make excellent sense in the whole context of this passage. Jesus could intend to lead Jews into repentance by directing their attention to a story with which they were familiar. Jesus could call for the repentance of all Israel with this saying.[57]

5.2. The bearing of the saying on the forgiveness of sins.

By using the term γενεὰ, Jesus seemed to show his far-reaching concern at the wickedness of the people of Israel who vainly and anxiously seek for a sign of the end only to delay their radical change. Jesus' use of this collective term has a significant meaning. γενεὰ has a national scope.[58] The whole of Israel needs to repent! This strong remark with its derogatory tone could have had a resounding impact on the whole of Israel.

---

[57] Bultmann [1951: 20-21 (ET)]: "...Jesus' knowledge of the absolute validity of the divine demand is the basis of his radical verdict over "this evil and adulterous generation" ripe for divine judgment (Matt 12:39 par., Mark 8:39)." But the original German text does not have the word Jesus [1948: 20].

[58] Against Sanders who argues that the sayings about judgment do not have a national scope [1985: 117].

E. Did Jesus ask national repentance in Matt 12:41-42; Luke 11:31-32?

1. The conjectured original text

Matt 12:41 ἄνδρες Νινευῖται ἀναστήσονται ἐν τῇ κρίσει μετὰ τῆς γενεᾶς ταύτης καὶ κατακρινοῦσιν αὐτήν, ὅτι μετενόησαν εἰς τὸ κήρυγμα Ἰωνᾶ, καὶ ἰδοὺ πλεῖον Ἰωνᾶ ὧδε. 42 βασίλισσα νότου ἐγερθήσεται ἐν τῇ κρίσει μετὰ τῆς γενεᾶς ταύτης καὶ κατακρινεῖ αὐτήν, ὅτι ἦλθεν ἐκ τῶν περάτων τῆς γῆς ἀκοῦσαι τὴν σοφίαν Σολομῶνος καὶ ἰδοὺ πλεῖον Σολομῶνος ὧδε.

Luke 11:31 βασίλισσα νότου ἐγερθήσεται ἐν τῇ κρίσει μετὰ τῶν ἀνδρῶν τῆς γενεᾶς ταύτης καὶ κατακρινεῖ αὐτούς, ὅτι ἦλθεν ἐκ τῶν περάτων τῆς γῆς ἀκοῦσαι τὴν σοφίαν Σολομῶνος καὶ ἰδοὺ πλεῖον Σολομῶνος ὧδε. 32 ἄνδρες Νινευῖται ἀναστήσονται ἐν τῇ κρίσει μετὰ τῆς γενεᾶς ταύτης καὶ κατακρινοῦσιν αὐτήν. ὅτι μετενόησαν εἰς τὸ κήρυγμα Ἰωνᾶ, καὶ ἰδοὺ πλεῖον Ἰωνᾶ ὧδε.

2. Argument concerning the authenticity of 1

The two accounts are almost the same, except that the two verses are in different positions. There are no inauthentic features in these two sayings.

3. Arguments against the authenticity of 1.

3.1. Some scholars regard this passage as inauthentic on the basis of its polemical features [Fridrichsen, 1925: 75[59] (ET); Kaesemann, 1965: 95[60]

---

[59] Fridrichsen argues for the origin of this saying from the early church: "The two groups of speeches exhibit a strictly uniform structure, and the final phrase is

(ET); Luehrmann, 1969: 38-40; Schulz, 1972: 253-257; Sanders, 1985: 110, 114]. Some scholars propose this argument without giving any significant reason [Hengel, 1969: 70 (ET); Schnackenburg, 1985: 114].

3.2. The saying presupposes a Gentile mission which did not exist during Jesus' ministry.

3.3. These scholars cast doubts on the authenticity of Matt 12:41-42; Luke 11:31-32 on the basis of their suspicion of Matt 11:21-24; Luke 10:13-15 and related sayings on judgment.

4. The counter arguments against 3.

4.1. (3.1) needs a careful examination. Fridrichsen seems to go too far. Matt 12:41-42 and Luke 11:31-32 do not exhibit a "strictly uniform structure." The tense of the two sayings are different (κατακρινοῦσιν future Matt 12:41; κατακρινεῖ present; Matt 12:42). Further ἦλθεν ἐκ τῶν περάτων τῆς γῆς ἀκοῦσαι seems to go against what he calls the "strictly uniform structure". Sanders also remains unpersuaded at the argument on the structure [1985: 374 n 60].

4.2. The hypothesis (3.1) does not take into account the possibility that this saying could have come from the pre-Easter tradition. καὶ ἰδοὺ πλεῖον Ἰωνᾶ ὧδε could point to the coming kingdom [Dodd, 1936-. 46-47; T. W. Manson, 1948: 92; Fenton, 1963: 202-203; Mueller, 1977: 434] or the proclamation of Jesus [Fuller, 1954: 34-35]. This saying does

---

repeated as a refrain". "Here we undoubtedly have an outline of primitive Christian polemic in a gnomic and stylized form" [1925: 71 (ET)]. For him this passage is seen to reflect the polemical context between the Palestinian church and the unbelieving Jews [ibid].

[60] Kaesemann adds one more reason, the rejection of the poetical parallelism of this saying.

not necessarily reflect the polemical situation of the early church. Rather, Jesus could have called for the urgent repentance of the whole of Israel which was in danger of becoming more hopeless than the Gentiles whom Israelites assumed to be the most hopeless of people.

4.3. If the early church made up καὶ ἰδοὺ πλεῖον Ἰωνᾶ ὧδε for polemic reasons they would have used the explicitly clear masculine form of πλεῖων to highlight Jesus' Messiahship rather than the ambiguous neutral form of πλεῖον.[61]

4.4. By the same token, the early church would not have made up enigmatic words like ὧδε if the intention was polemical [Mussner, 1968: 171-171]. If they did they would have exposed Jesus more explicitly with a phrase like "behold more than Jonah (Solomon) am "I""[62]

4.5. Against (3.2) the positive presentation of the Gentiles does not necessarily imply the existence of a Gentile mission.[63]

4.6. The Palestinian church would hardly have, made up Matt 12:41-42; Luke 11:31-32. They would have refrained from describing contemporary Jewish people as being condemned by the Gentiles even in an imaginary setting. Their aspiration and endeavour could have been nothing but to call their fellow Jews into faith in the risen Christ. Hence, they would

---

61 Later I found that Mussner count this enigmatic reference to Jesus as one piece of the evidence of the pre-Easter christology [1968: 171].

62 Mussner argues that the early church could expose Jesus more clearly with the phrase like "behold more that Jonah (Solomon) is "Jesus"" [1968: 170]. However, I am not convinced at this argument because in this saying Jesus is portrayed as the speaker. Thus it could be more convincing that if the early church made up this saying they would have described Jesus as "I" or "me".

63 Against Sanders [1985: 114; Luehrmann, 1969: 87]. Luehrmann cites Steck [1967: 287].

hardly need to describe detested Gentiles as judging their fellow Jews. When Peter, who could be regarded as the forerunner of the Palestinian mission, described the unbelieving Jews with the phrase "the crooked generation", he did not use a phrase which has a stronger derogatory tone. Hence his followers in the Palestinian church would hardly have made up the comparison which shows the fundamental reversal of Israel's position. Further the judgment of the Jews by the Gentile was unusual in Judaism at the time of Jesus; the Jews believed that some of the foreign kings and wicked sinners could not stand in judgment (m.Sanh 10.3). They generally believed that angels (Matt 13:41, 49) and only the righteous Jews (Isa 3:14; Dan 7:10, 22) could judge them. It is much more unlikely that the Hellenistic church made up this passage. This story has too many Jewish features, the story in the O.T., the resurrection and the judgment of the dead. If they made up the saying in the Hellenistic church they would have described the people as asking Jesus for "wisdom" rather than "a sign" (1 Cor 1:22-23).

4.7. Contrary to (2.3) this saying coheres with Jesus' contrast between Israel's sinfulness and the likely repentance of Gentiles (e.g. Matt 11:20-22; Luke 10:13-15).

4.8. The tone of the some of the arguments which support the hypothesis (3.3) seems to be too strong: "We must doubt the authenticity most of the passages that depict him as doing so [calling for national repentance]... because *the condemnation of Israel and praise of Gentiles* makes one suspect the activity of the later church (Matt 12:41f)" [Sanders, 1985: 117] (italics mine). The urgent appeal for the repentance of Israel seems to be the intention, not the condemnation of Israel and the praise of Gentiles. The contrast of the Jews with the Gentiles coheres with Jesus' praise of the Gentiles for their love, faith or trust in his power and teaching which excels over that of the Jews e.g. the Good Samaritan (Luke 10:33-37) [Perrin, 1976: 194-195], the Roman Centurion (Matt 8: 10; Luke 7:9).

4.9. The eschatological feature of this saying could support its authenticity.

4.10. The Aramaism in Matt 12:41-42; Luke 11:31-32 ἀναστήσονται ἐν τῇ κρίσει μετὰ τῆς γενεᾶς ταύτης could be one piece of evidence in favour of authenticity [Dalman, 1902: 64 (ET); Wellhausen, 1914-63; Black, 1967: 93, 134].

4.11. Contrary to hypothesis (3.2) some scholars regard this saying as authentic for particular reasons [Bultmann, 1931: 112-113[64] (ET); Rengstorf, 1964: 234[65] (ET); Mussner, 1968: 170-171; 1979: 217-218 (ET); Jeremias, 1971: 82[66] (ET); Perrin, 1976: 194-195[67]; Fitzmyer, 1986:

---

[64] It is difficult to know the clear position of Bultmann on the authenticity of this saying. Bultmann clearly states that in its original context this saying could have pointed to the coming of the kingdom [Bultmann, 1931:112-113 (ET); 118 (German)]. He categorically denies that this saying originated in the early church: "...originally it was a minatory saying directed against this generation (i.e., the Jews), which failed to recognize the decisive hour. If one regards the saying for itself, there is no need to take it as a community formulation." (italics mine). Nevertheless Bultmann gives an impression of harbouring some slight suspicion of the authenticity of this passage in the light of Fridrichsen's argument [1925: 75 (ET)]: "Yet it has a striking parallelism with the passage just considered, Matt 11:21-24//Luke 10: 13-15." [1931: 112-113 (ET)]. However the authenticity of Matt 11:21-24//Luke 10: 13-15 seems to stand firm. Many scholars assume that Bultmann actually regards Matt 12:41-42; Luke 11:31-32 as secondary. Sanders understands that Bultmann's conclusion is in agreement with that of Fridrichsen who argues for the Christian construction [1985: 110]. Luehrmann also assumes that Bultmann [1969: 38]. Mueller also thinks the same way [1977: 434].

[65] On the basis of Bultmann's argument on Jesus' prophetic self consciousness Rengstorf argues that it is possible to regard the saying as a genuine testimony which uses prophetic categories in self-portrayal.

[66] πλεῖον has an eschatological ring.

[67] Perrin argues that "... the point at issue is the question of repentance in face of a challenges certainly a major concern of the message of the historical Jesus."

931[68]; Gnilka, 1986: 469[69]]. Some scholars put forward this argument without giving any particular reasons.[70]

5.

5. 1. The main thrust of this saying

Hardly any nation would be comfortable when their morality is compared with that of other nation's. This unwanted comparison could show the need for their fundamental change and for learning a significant lesson from other nations. The proclaimer of this kind of an unpleasant message could risk the loss of his life particularly when the concerned nation glories in its superiority to other nations. Jews could hardly bear this message because they usually thought of the Gentile nations as wicked. Hence Jesus' unfavourable contrast of Israel to the Gentile nation could sharply expose Israel's wickedness and their need of repentance. Jesus could stress the need for national repentance of Israel in this saying: If you do not repent, even the Gentiles, whom you think of as most wicked, will judge you because they repented when they heard the message of repentance or they cherished the wisdom at least. Now you are in danger. The kingdom which brings in judgment is already at hand.

---

[68] Fitzmyer accepts the authenticity of Matt 12:41-42; Luke 11:31-32. However he points out that Matt 12:42; Luke 11:31 is intrusive in the story of the sign of Jonah. Nonetheless he affirms that Jesus could have said this saying on another occasion.

[69] Gnilka argues that vv. 41f could be the authentic saying of Jesus (jesu-anische) because "more than Jonah" undoubtedly points to Jesus' kingdom. Gnilka relies upon the argument of Mueller [1977: 434] who cites Mussner [1968: 170-171 (ET)].

[70] Dodd, 1936: 82; T. W. Manson, 1949: 91; Kuemmel, 1956: 113 (ET); Grundmann, 1981: 242; Hahn, 1963: 36 (ET); 0. Betz, 1965: 35 (ET); Schweizer, 1973: 291 (ET); Goppelt, 1981: 166-167 (ET); Uro, 1985: 168-172; Marshall, 1978: 486-487; Cabraja, 1985: 62.

5.2. The bearing of the saying on the forgiveness of sins.

Is it really true that the authenticity of every saying on national repentance is not sturdy [Sanders, 1985: 110]? Matt 12:41-42; Luke 11.31-32 would support the opposite case, γενεᾶς ταύτης, the whole of Israel, could face the danger of being condemned by the Gentiles unless they repented. This urgent call implies the national repentance of the whole of Israel.

CHAPTER III

Passages which appear in Matthew and Luke but not in Mark.

A. Did Jesus call for an eschatological forgiveness and reconciliation in Matt 5:25-26; Luke 12:57-59?

1. The conjectured original text

Matt 5:25 ἴσθι εὐνοῶν τῷ ἀντιδίκῳ σου ταχύ, ἕως ὅτου εἶ μετ᾽ αὐτοῦ, ἐν τῇ ὁδῷ, μήποτέ σε παραδῷ ὁ ἀντίδικος τῷ κριτῇ καὶ ὁ κριτὴς τῷ ὑηρέτῇ καὶ εἰς φυλακὴν βληθήσῃ. 26 ἀμὴν λέγω σοι, οὐ μὴ ἐξέλθῃς ἐκεῖθεν, ἕως ἂν ἀποδῷς τὸν ἔσχατον κοδράντην.

Luke 12:58 ὡς γὰρ ὑπάγεις μετὰ τοῦ ἀντιδίκου σου ἐπ᾽ ἄρχον τα, ἐν τῇ ὁδῷ δὸς ἐργασίαν ἀπηλλάχθαι ἀπ᾽αὐτοῦ, μήποτε κατασύρῃ σε πρὸς τὸν κριτήν, καὶ ὁ κριτής σε παραδώσει τῷ πράκτορι, καὶ ὁ πράκτωρ σε βαλεῖ εἰς φυλακήν. 59 λέγω σοι, οὐ μὴ ἐξέλθῃς ἐκεῖθεν, ἕως καὶ τὸ ἔσχατον λεπτὸν ἀποδῷς.

2. Arguments concerning the excluded parts

Luke 12:57 Τί δὲ καὶ ἀφ᾽ ἑαυτῶν οὐ κρίνετε τὸ δίκαιον] Some scholars argue that Luke or pre-Lucan scribe could have added this part as the introduction [Bultmann, 1931: 91, 172 (ET); Klostermann, 1929:

141; Schulz, 1972: 421]. However Schuermann and Marshall are less certain [1968: 116; 1978: 550-551].

The texts in Matt and Luke are not so markedly different as to lead us to assume two independent sources. The essential contents of two synoptic accounts are almost identical except for some differences in wording. Because opposite arguments on the originality of wording of texts between Matt and Luke sharply contend against each other it would be wise, to leave the texts as they stand, unless a very compelling reason emerges. It would be perhaps reasonable to assume the same Aramaic origin of these two texts.

3. Arguments against the authenticity of 1.

3.1. Matt 5:25-26; Luke 11:58-59 is secondary [Braun, 1957, vol. 2: 85 n 2; Klein, 1969: 383; Schulz, 1972: 424; Strecker, 1985: 68-69[1] (ET)].

3.2. Matt 5:25-26 is an allegory: v. 25 is combined with an Amen-saying v. 26 [Gnilka, 1986: 151[2]]. Matt 5:25; Luke 12:58 was made up from a passage like Proverb 6:1-5 [Gnilka, 1986: 151[3]].

3.3. The non-Jewish setting could hint at its secondary nature.[4]

---

[1] Strecker seems to regard this saying as secondary: "In accord with the present composition, this means with fellow Christians, even if in the wider context it is clear that the Sermon on the Mount reaches beyond the level of disciples and includes the people. Here a rule of life is established which...". [1985: 69 (ET)] (italics mine).

[2] Juelicher notes the uncertainty on the relationship between these two accounts [1999: vol. 2:240].

[3] However Gnilka regards Matt 5:25-26 as the pre-Matthean material.

[4] A Hellenistic court setting and terms like πράκτορι, λεπτὸν could be put forward as a sign of the Hellenistic origin. "καὶ εἰς φυλακὴ βληθήσῃ: imprisonment for debts, and imprisonment as punishment in general, are unknown to Jewish law. Hence we must conclude that Jesus is deliberately referring to non-Jewish legal practice which his audience considered inhuman (the same is true of the,

4. Arguments against 3.

Bultmann neither affirms nor rejects the authenticity of this passage. What Bultmann means by "he (Luke) seems to have retained the eschatological thrust in better state than Matthew" is that the Lucan text seems to preserve the eschatological thrust of the passage [1931: 96 (ET)] better than Matthew, not that the Lucan text is more primitive than the Matthean text. The summary of Bultmann's argument is as follows: a parable of the Parousia, of which the original setting is impossible to recover, turned into a rule of piety [1931: 149 (ET)]. The original meaning of this parable of timely agreement, as claimed by Bultmann [1931: 172 (ET)], does not exclude its origin from Jesus. "We must do penance at the right time" [1931: 96 (ET)] could indicate repentance in conjunction with fulfilling the obligation of making restitution. It is noteworthy that Bultmann does not put forward any argument doubting the authenticity of this saying. Bultmann's statement "This is a typical example of a similitude made out of a "figure""[5] [1931: 172 (ET)] does not reject that Jesus could have made up this parable.

4.1. (3.1) is hardly convincing. The early church would have been reluctant to make up Matt 5:25-26 par. which would not have happened in their life setting. They would not have left their colleague in the prison because he was in financial straits. Rather they would have bailed out the person imprisoned quickly by paying the debt with the money drawn from the community common fund made from voluntary contribution. "They had everything in common" (Acts 4:32). In particular, the apostles distributed to each as any had need (Acts 4:35). Accordingly, a substantial period of imprisonment of Palestinian Christians for the

---

καταποντισμός Mark 9.42, selling one's wife, Matt 18.25, torture, Matt. 18.34)." [Jeremias, 1962: 180 (ET); cf. Deissmann, 1923: 279 (ET)].

[5] Strecker calls it "a parable developed from an *image* saying." [1995: 68 (ET)] (italics mine).

payment of the financial damage would hardly have happened.[6]

4.2. If the early (Palestinian) church made up this saying they would have made it up to reflect perhaps the most important problem in their life setting, the conflict between the Palestinian church and the Jews over faith e.g., the imprisonment of some of the apostles and the Jewish Christians (Acts 8:3; 22:19). Hence the early church would have been reluctant to put this sort of saying in the setting of a dispute over an unfulfilled financial obligation. Some accounts describe how some unbelieving Jews were persecuting Christians (Acts 7:57-58; 9:1-2; 9:23, 29; cf. 5:40). However hardly any accounts describe imprisonment because of an unfulfilled financial obligation. By the same token the early church would have been reluctant to use the term ἀντίδικος (adversary)[7] in connection with describing the legal adversary in financial matters.[8] If κριτής refers to the Sanhedrin, the early church would have been reluctant to appeal to this authority which indirectly led to the stoning of Stephen (Acts 6:9).

4.3. Marshall correctly rejects Klein's argument: "For Klein, the parable exhorts men to throw in their lot with the church and make a clean break with its opponents"; "the point of the parable lies in the danger of falling under judgment rather than in getting rid of the adversary" [Marshall, 1978: 551].

---

[6] This story could refer to a criminal law e.g., robbery, fraud. However the early Christians would hardly have committed such kind of sins because they are strongly commanded to keep a distinctive morality.

[7] ἀντίδικος has the meaning of "adversary" which could refer to a legal adversary (Luke 18:3) (the widow asks a vindication (ἐκδίκησον)) or an enemy (1 Pet 5:8) (like a roaring lion).

[8] Further I also assume that early Christians would have finished making restitution before joining the Christian community.

4.4. Contrary to his usual practice, Schulz does not put forward any significant reason supporting his case. Schulz merely speculates that this eschatological narrative, "a rule of community", incorporates the prophetic enthusiastic imperative of the oldest Q tradition [1972: 424]. He is simply summarizing Braun [1957, vol. 2: 85 n 2]. However "the prophetic enthusiastic imperative of the oldest Q tradition" could have come from Jesus as an isolated saying tradition. Further, as (4.1) and (4.2) illustrate, the early church seems to have no particular reason to make up this saying.[9] The alleged main reason of the conflict between the Q community and their contemporary Judaism, belief in Jesus as Messiah, claimed by Schulz, hardly suits the emergence of this saying framed in the setting of fulfilling financial obligation. The argument is rather convincing that this passage came from the pre-Matthean oral tradition.

4.5. If the early church's motive of making up this saying was the threat of the last judgment[10] they would hardly have needed to add ἕως ἂν ἀποδῷς τὸν ἔσχατον κοδράντην. They would have believed that the punishment, once made, lasts eternally (Heb 6:2): there is no chance of coming out from judgment (cf. Jas 2:13).[11] Further, the early church would not have reconciled with their adversary for reasons of faith.

---

[9] In another work, Braun gives the impression that he is affirming the authenticity of this saying: "In the Lukan text it is likely *the historical Jesus* himself who warns that just as someone accused in earthly matters does everything he can to settle accounts with his accuser..." [1969: 67 (ET)] (italics mine). Braun notes Matt 5:25f was used in "Jesus' words" and calls this passage as a "Jesus tradition" [1969: 91 (ET)].

[10] Although not following this line of argument Bultmann argues that the original requiring of this parable was the threat of the last judgment.

[11] If Matt 5:25 originally indicated that the Jews put some of the early Christians to prison for their belief in Jesus, they would not have added v. 26, which does not share their belief, eternal judgment.

4.6. Strecker's argument, the later addition of v. 26 to v. 25, seems not to rest upon hard evidence. Contrary to Zeller's argument "the unique feature" of this parable, the form of admonition, supports its authenticity [1977: 65]. Zeller argues that a common Jewish saying v. 25 acquires eschatological meaning only at the stage of merger to v. 26 [1977: 66]. However v. 25, as well as v. 26, already has an eschatological meaning. No intrinsic difference can be discerned in their view of judgment between these two verses. A quick (ταχύ) reconciliation with the accuser while going to court indicates the same urgency. Further the threat of judgment, "being put to prison" in v. 25, hardly needs to be taken differently from the theme of imprisonment in v. 26.

4.7. Gnilka's argument on the two segments hypothesis (3.2) is hardly convincing. Once detached from v. 25 v. 26 ceases to have any single unitary meaning: circumstances surrounding this imprisonment remain enigmatic unless explained in the preceding verse. What does ἐκεῖθεν refer? Why must ἔσχατον κοδράντην (λεπτὸν) be given back? From which place does the accused come out (ἐξέλθῃς)? On the contrary βληθήσῃ (v. 25) squares with (v. 26). V. 26 would have been too puzzling to be regarded as a single unitary saying. Hence it would be reasonable to assume that Matt 5:25-26; Luke 12:59-59 was handed down as a unitary passage from the beginning.[12] The similar phrase in Matt 18:30 ὁ δὲ οὐκ ἤθελεν ἀλλὰ ἀπελθὼν ἔβαλεν αὐτὸν εἰς φυλακὴν ἕως ἀποδῷ τὸ ὀφειλόμενον could support its authenticity.

4.8. Gnilka's argument on the wisdom source of this saying (3.2) remains

---

[12] If v. 25 was made up by the early church to reflect the persecution of Christians by Jews it could lead to a misunderstanding that even faith can be sacrificed to be reconciled with an adversary. Concession or compromise to the adversary for reconciliation would have taken place only in the matter of financial obligation, not at all in the matter of faith.

unconvincing. A fundamental difference emerges when these two texts are compared.

Firstly, Prov 6:1-5 has no eschatological tone (no pressing imminence of the judgment).[13] Moreover Prov 6:1-5 is not framed in the legal setting unlike Matt 5:25-6; Luke 12:58-59.

Secondly, unlike Prov 6:1-5, Matt 5:25-26; Luke 12:58-59 assumes that the legal proceeding is ongoing. Prov 6:1-5 does not stress the harassment and danger of wasting time when going through this tedious process. The reason of the imprisonment is the surety for other people, not the unfulfilled financial responsibility.

Prov 25:8-9 stresses the need to be prudent and not to put neighbours to shame in the course of justice. Further, this account deals with a case of a plaintiff, not a case of a defendant. Prov 25:8-9 and a proverbial exhortation Sir 18:19 seem too remote to serve as an archetype of Matt 5:25-26, in particular in the absence in them of eschatological overtones.

4.9. (3.3) raises a significant question. Could Jesus not have said something not practised at his time in his country? Jeremias' inference seems to rest upon the assumption that this passage describes a case of unpaid debt. Certainly the imprisonment of a debtor is not directly attested in any accounts.[14] However the imprisonment of a person for robbery is attested in *Jewish War* 2.273: καὶ τοὺς ἐπὶ λῃστείᾳ δεδε-μένους ὑπὸ τῆς παρ᾽ ἑκάστοις βουλῆς ἢ τῶν προτέρων ἐπιτρόπων ἀπελύτρου τοῖς συγγενέσι"... but he [Albinus] accepted

[13] ἐκλυόμεονς (Prov 6:3) is translated as "hasten" in RSV or "humble yourself" in some manuscripts. But REB translates as "bestir".

[14] B. T. D. Smith points out the obscurity over the arrangements for the administration of justice in Palestine at the time of Jesus [1937: 149].

ransoms from their relatives on behalf of those who had been imprisoned for robbery by the local councils or by former procurators; and the only persons left is goal as malefactors were those who failed to pay the price."[15] Josephus uses ληστής to refer to a "robber" *(Jewish War* 2. 125; 228) and a "revolutionary" *(Jewish War* 2.253; 4. 504; *Jewish Antiquities* 14. 159-160; 20. 160-161, 167) [BAGD, 473]. However the jurisdiction of the local councils seems to support that Josephus referred to a "robber" in this text.

Further Jas 2:6 also attests that the rich drag the poor to the law court (εἶς κριτήρια). It could mean that when the poor could not pay back a financial obligation the creditor could drag the debtor to a law court (cf. 1 Cor 4:3). The early church would have made up our present saying by using κριτήρια instead of κριτής. The point of the matter is that κοδράντην or λεπτὸν do not exclude the possibility that this saying refers to the case of robbery. Further the verb ἀποδῷς (Matt 5:26; Luke 12:59) does not dismiss this case.[16] The speaker could have meant various cases of financial wrongdoings, robbery, fraud: If it was a minor financial affair, the Jews need not have brought this case to a legal court: Rabbis

---

[15] "For the Roman period, there is evidence of the existence of local councils, for example in the statement of Josephus that Albinus, out of greed, *set free* for a monetary reward certain persons who had been imprisoned *for robbery* by their local council (βουλή). This shows that it was the βουλή itself which exercised the functions of both police and judiciary." [Schuerer, 1979, vol. 2: 185 (ET)] (italics mine). Deissmann found papyri and inscription which attest such imprisonment in Graeco-Roman Egypt [1923: 270 (ET)]. But Deissmann does not state that the imprisonment of a debtor was absent in Judaism:"...this was in Graeco-Roman Egypt, and elsewhere a widespread legal custom."

[16] In many instances ἀποδίδωμι implies "that the person to whom payment or repayment is made is the rightful owner or recipient of whatever is paid or repaid; the action amounts to giving back to someone property to which he is entitled." [Bruce, 1984: 258]. Bruce refers to Luke 4:20; Lev 6:4 LXX; Luke 10:35; Luke 19:8; Matt 18:34; Luke 7:42; Matt 5:26; Luke 12:59; cf. Rom 13:7.

could have mediated such a problem. It means that the affair referred here is a serious case. This passage consists of affairs what could have happened in the daily life of Israel at the time of Jesus. Jesus seems to have spoken mainly Jewish ideas.[17] However Jesus need not have been constrained to be ignorant of affairs and cultures around Israel. He was described as having been outside of Israel.

4.10. The strong eschatological tone of this saying, attested in many other Jesus' authentic sayings, could support its authenticity.

4.11. Some scholars regard this saying as authentic with additional reasons; Dodd, 1936: 137[18]; 1971: 41[19]; Jeremias, 1962: 43-44[20], 180

---

[17] Further Jeremias' argument on the un-Jewish features is not compelling be-cause Matt 5:25-26 and Luke 12:57-59 have un-Greek un-Roman words like κριτής [Sherwin-White, 1963: 133-134]. Thus this saying's Jewish origin seems fairly strong. Further the Hellenistic church would hardly have made up a saying with a un-Roman phrase like κριτής. "The profession of Christianity was not a religious offence punishable by imprisonment." [Hare, 1967: 47]. A similar idea was reiterated by Marshall:"...the language may suggest that a Hellenistic court is meant, since a Jewish dispute would have been settled by a scribe (12:13f.) acting as a judge." [1978: 551].

[18] The sermon on the Mount is in fact a compilation of religious and moral maxims, drawn from the teaching of *Jesus,* for the guidance of Christians. (italics mine).

[19] Dodd assumes that Jesus addresses this parable "in a situation in which a decision was urgent and delay dangerous."

[20] Although arguing for the deliberate referring to non-Jewish legal setting Jeremias firmly believes that "Jesus rebukes the populace for the failure to grasp the gravity of the present moment" in this saying. Jeremias counts the eschatological tone, in contrast to the much watereddown eschatological tone of the early church, as signs of an authentic saying of Jesus.

(ET); Marshall, 1978: 551-552[21]; Luz, 1985: 281[22] (ET); Davies, 1988: 519.[23] Bornkamm [1959: 118-119 (ET)] and Fitzmyer [1986: 1002] concede the authenticity of this saying without giving any particular reason.

4.12. At a later stage the early church could have put this isolated authentic saying of Jesus into an appropriate place in order to teach, along with the need for repentance and making restitution, the need to fulfil financial obligations in society.

5.

5.1. The main thrust of this saying

Jesus' strong urging of the need to come to terms with an adversary could have been made in order to avert two dangers. Mainly, the imprisonment of a person at the time of the imminent end would make manifest his violation of the Law and his restitution along with repentance. As a result the people who failed to come to terms with their adversaries would have been doomed to punishment. The scholarly consensus on the meaning of reconciliation before the imminent eschaton seems to overshadow an equally significant meaning, the emphasis on the urgent need of making restitution. The final warning, "You will never get

---

21 Marshall takes ἀμήν at the outset (Matt) and the emphatic future negative (οὐ μή) as good reasons for accepting the authenticity of the sayings.

22 The striking double reference to "judgment" fits into the proclamation of Jesus.

23 The role of the κριτής which is exclusively Jewish, the eschatological tone and the solid unity of this saying were put forward as reasons in favour of authenticity. "Nothing stands in the way tracing, 5:25-6=Luke 12:58-9 to Jesus."

out till you have paid the last penny" (Matt 5:26; Luke 12:59) clearly attests that repentance and restitution along with reconciliation is a condition for averting judgment at the end. Making restitution is just as important as reconciliation before the eschaton.

5.2. The bearing on the forgiveness of sins

We have seen reason to question to Sanders' argument in favour of the Christian origin of this passage [1985: 263].[24] The strong eschatological tone of this passage undermines one of Sanders' main arguments:"Sayings concerning forgiveness have, as might be expected, little eschatological thrust" [1985: 111]. Jesus stresses repentance, restitution and reconciliation in the prospect of the coming end. "the eschatological perspective defines ethical behaviour!" [Strecker, 1985: 69 (ET)].

---

[24] "Since negatives are so difficult to prove, I do not wish to argue that we can know that Jesus said none of these things attributed to him in the sections under consideration. I am inclined to reject the entire section, Matt. 5.17-6.18, except for the prayer (6.9-13)."

B. Did Jesus teach that it was necessary to forgive others before praying for God's forgiveness in Matt 6:12; Luke 11:4a?

1. The conjectured original text

Matt 6:10a ἐλθέτω ἡ βασιλεία σου

Matt 6:12 καὶ ἄφες ἡμῖν τὰ ὀφειλήματα ἡμῶν, ὡς καὶ ἡμεῖς ἀφήκαμεν τοῖς ὀφειλέταις ἡμῶν.

Luke 11:2b ἐλθέτω ἡ βασιλεία σου

Luke 11:4 καὶ ἄφες ἡμῖν τὰς ἁμαρτίας ἡμῶν, καὶ γὰρ αὐτοὶ ἀφίομεν παντὶ ὀφείλοντι ἡμῖν.

2. Arguments concerning the original text.

It is almost impossible to recover the original text.[25] But at least in Matt 6:12; Luke 11:4 there is scholarly consensus that the Matthean text of whole prayer is closer to the original text with regard to wording than the Lucan text [T. W. Manson, 1948: 265; Jeremias, 1962a: 92-93 (ET)]. The different wording between the two texts seems to be caused by translation variants.

3. Arguments against 1.

3.1. The entire petition Man 6:12 (Luke 11;4) was made up by the early Jewish (or Hellenistic) Christian church [Schulz, 1972: 86[26], 931.

---

[25] Streeter assumes two different sources [1927: 277].

[26] Schulz argues that the Lord's prayer takes a "prayer-form" of an old Jewish-Christian Q community (or of the Hellenistic church) in Palestine [1972: 87].

3.2. A particular form of (3.1). The entire verse Matt 6:12 (Luke 11:4) was the Matthean expansion of Mark 11:25 and 14:36, 38 [Goulder, 1963: 34-38, 45; 1974: 298[27]]. Luke pruned the Matthean version [Goulder, 1974: 298; 1963: 35, 37-38].

3.3. This section only affects Matt 6:12b; Luke 11: 4b.

a. Some scholars argue that Matt 6:12b; Luke 11:4b is a later addition [Harnack, 1907: 64-65 (ET); Strecker, 1985: 119-121 (ET)].[28] Matt 6:12b was made up by the early church [G. Schwarz, 1968-69: 239[29]; Ford, 1968:[30] 130 (ET)]. The early church could have put in this

---

This prayer follows the prayers of late Judaism in respect to its form [93]. However Schulz still admits that clearly the Lord's Prayer used old traditions [86].

[27] "Matthew has thus composed a prayer that may properly be called the Lord's Prayer, since the greater part of it is his own prayer, and teaching on prayer. [Goulder, 1974: 300]. So Goulder argues that the substance of the prayer goes back to Jesus, the form to Matt.

[28] Strecker [1985: 107 (ET)]: "Perhaps during this period of tradition the *substantiation* for the petition for forgiveness (v. 12b) was also added." "Thus, the petition for forgiveness of debt is expanded through a substantiation (Luke) and a comparison (Matthew)." (108 (ET)]. "The second clause (Matt 6:12b; Luke 11:4b) may not have belonged to the original version of the Lord's Prayer, since it goes beyond the.series of individual petitions." (120 (ET)] (italics mine). Strecker thinks that ὡς καὶ has "substantiating significance" [120-121 (ET)].

[29] Matt 6:12b is a *commentary* on Matt 6:12a. Schwarz argues that the original prayer for forgiveness was expanded: only followed by a commentary when the early church felt something deficient. This passage must be a later addition which was put in to fill this deficient part, with an assumption that it corresponds to Jesus' intention. Schwarz argues that once the additional parts are taken off, a concise form of original text showing a perfect poetic form appears. (italics mine).

[30] Ford assumes that Matt 6:12b may represent an ancient form of the Lord's Prayer for use in the Jewish-Christian community on the liturgical occasion of Yom Kippur [1968: 127-131]. Ford proposes that St. Matthew's Sermon on the Mount may have been composed for use in the Syrian Church on the occasion of Yom

conditional clause to stress the need for forgiveness within the community [Strecker, 1985: 121[31]].

b. A group of scholars reject the authenticity of Matt 6:12b (Luke 11: 4b) in terms of the idea that Jesus held that God's forgiveness is hardly conditional [Fiedler, 1976: 204-211; Strecker, 1985: 121[32]].

4. Arguments against 3.

In the reformed tradition the relationship between repentance and grace has come down to us as an intriguing question. Some argue that repentance is necessary along with grace. Others argue that grace entirely rejects the need of repentance. How can we arrive at the truth? The ideal solution would be to read the natural meaning which springs from the text itself, rather than to impose a certain theological presupposition upon the text.

4.1. Schulz's argument is hardly convincing. The clear eschatological

---

Kippur and one clue to this embolism [addition] is to be found in the Pater Noster in St Matthew, namely vv. 6.14-15 [1968: 128].

[31] "In the Matthean understanding, the fifth petition is not only the expression of the Christian certainty of forgiveness but also the demand of Jesus that the Christian community must be ready to forgive."

[32] The idea that human forgiveness is made the very condition for God's forgiveness differentiates Matthew's theology from Paul's message of justification, according to which the deeds of the believer are understood as the *consequence,* not as the precondition, of God's redeeming, and forgiving activity (Gal 5:25; Rom 6:1ff). Here Matthew—as also the pre-Matthaean version of the Lord's Prayer that was expanded in this way—*stands in the tradition of Jewish thinking,* according to which human readiness to forgive is demanded as the prerequisite of divine forgiveness of sins." (italics mine).

character of the Lord's prayer could support its authenticity[33] even in terms of the criteria of the dissimilarity test set up by Bultmann. However Schulz argues that the eschatological character of the Lord's Prayer reflects that of the early church, not the time of Jesus [1972: 87, 89-90]. Two "you" petitions are eschatological but the following three "we" petitions are not eschatological: it merely reflects the early church's waiting for the parousia [Schulz, 1972: 89 90]. This argument is hardly convincing. The three "we" petitions could also have taught Jesus' disciples and followers how to prepare themselves before the imminent end (Matt 6:10; Luke 11:2). In view of the imminent judgment, Jesus' disciples and his followers could have been commanded to live free of sin. At the same time they could have been commanded to help others avoid judgment, possibly inflicted upon sinners due to their failure to seek forgiveness. Jesus could have commanded his disciples to pray for daily bread and for the avoidance of temptation in the context of a proclamation of the imminent kingdom (Matt 6:33-34).

4.2. With few exceptions, there is a scholarly consensus on the authenticity of the first part of the petition for forgiveness, καὶ ἄφες ἡμῖν, which already assumes the repentance of the petitioners; even scholars who reject the authenticity of the following part affirm the authenticity of this preceding part [G. Schwarz, 1968-69: 233, 239; Strecker, 1985: 107-108[34]].

4.3. The early church would have been reluctant to put "their forgiving

---

[33] W. D. Davies, 1987: 593.

[34] Although he rejects the authenticity of the later part, Strecker is firm on the authenticity of Matt 6:12; Luke 11:4 [1985:107-108 (ET)]: "The earliest version—derivable through synoptic comparison belongs to the proclamation of the historical Jesus." "The conception and practice of the "forgiveness of sins" have an original place in the oldest Jesus tradition." [Strecker, 1985: 108 (ET)]. Strecker states that Schulz' position is untenable [1985; 107 (ET)].

others" as a reason for their claim to receive God's forgiveness. They would have been mainly interested in the forgiveness of the Lord, made at the crucifixion, which impinged upon themselves.

4.4. Despite his contribution, Goulder's argument (3.2) seems to remain not convincing.[35] Contrary to Goulder, Mark does not have to contain all the important teachings of Jesus. The common source or sources in Matthew and Luke, not in Mark, could also have contained important sayings of Jesus.

4.5. If Matthew made up the Lord's Prayer from Mark, and Luke copied Matthew why then are there two versions rather than one unitary version?[36] There seems to be no inevitable reason why Luke should alter the Matthean version which was given to him. Further the assumption that Luke copied Matthew is still disputed. Goulder seems to have arrived at his conclusion because he does not consider the possibility that variants could have emerged in the course of translation from the original Aramaic to the present Greek text. By doing that Goulder allows no possibility of the emergence of variants although that process seems to result in a minor discrepancy between two versions.[37]

---

[35] Marshall correctly asseses Goulder's argument [1978: 455]: "M. D. Goulder assigns its composition to Matthew (from whose Gospel it was copied by Luke); his article has the merit of showing the links between the prayer and other aspects of the teaching of Jesus, but it fails to prove that Matthew composed the prayer on the basis of these parallels."

[36] Goulder asks the same question for a different reason. He argues that it is hardly likely that a Prayer composed by Jesus was corrupted into two variant versions, Matt and Luke, by the early church [1963: 33].

[37] Two slightly different versions seem to have emerged in the course of translation from Aramaic to Greek. Nonetheless Goulder rejects this hypothesis which Manson concedes [Goulder, 1963: 33].

4.6. Although Goulder argues that this part of the Lord's Prayer is based on Mark 11:25 and 14:36, 38, these alleged verses lack the explicit eschatological character that is manifested in the context of Matt 6:12; Luke 11:4 (cf. 6:10; 11:2).

4.7. Is (3.3.a) cogent? Schwarz's argument remains unconvincing. It is not absolutely necessary to accept the shorter poetic form which Schwarz puts forward [1968-1969: 235-239].[38] Further, the longer text which includes Matt 6:12b; Luke 11:4b forms a perfect poetic parallelism [Burney, 1925: 112-113].

4.8. Ford's contribution lies in her argument that if the Lord's Prayer was recited after the Days of Repentance, when reconciliation between men was made, it is understandable to pray 6:12b with 6:12a [Ford, 1968: 130]. In a sense Ford assumes that the Lucan text is original and the Matthean text could have arisen in the liturgical context of the Matthean church. However that hypothesis is hardly cogent. The liturgical context of the early church would hardly have led to the emergence of a text of conditional character.[39]

4.9. (3.3.a) is hardly likely. If the early church intended to add something to stress the mutual forgiveness between their members they would have put an account like Matt 6:14-15, outside, not inside, the prayer form not

---

[38] Marshall correctly points out the fallacy of Schwarz's assumption [1978: 415]:"Attempts to emend the text of the prayer, based on the assumption that Jesus followed OT poetic rules without deviation (G. Schwarz), are unconvincing."

[39] "Liturgically, however, the Synagogue (the name of a Jewish prayer) did not make man's repentance a precise condition of God's pardon" [Abrahams, 1924: 97]. One other reason is that the Matthean text (ὀφειλήματα, Matt 6:12b) could be more primitive than the Lucan text (ἁμαρίας Luke 11:4b) in terms of the primitiveness of its wording and the Semitism.

to destroy the unity of this prayer.[40] Further, the early church would have been reluctant to alter a prayer which their revered Lord taught them.

4.10. Would the Matthean church alone have been experiencing the absence of mutual forgiveness? The Marcan and Lucan church could have had the same kind of problem. Repentance as a condition of forgiveness occurs also in other passages where no such words μετανοέω or μετάνοια appear (e.g. Luke 13:6-9; 18:9-14; 19:1-10). Further Luke 11:4b is not much different from Matt 6:12b in its conditional character. Hence the argument that ὡς clause emerges only in Matthew is not convincing.

4.11. If Luke 11:4b (par. Matt 6:12b) was made up by the Lucan church, why would they not have used a word which has less Semitic colour than ὀφείλοντι? In Matthew ὀφειλήματα matches with the following ὀφειλέταις.

4.12. The strong Aramaism in Matt 6:12b; Luke 11:4b could support the authenticity (ὀφειλήματα, ὀφειλέταις (Matt); ὀφείλοντι (Luke) [Burney, 1925: 112-113; Torrey, 1933: 309[41]]. Others follow Burney's work [Black, 1967: 129, 140, 194; Lohmeyer 1946: 28-29 (ET); Kuhn, 1950: 32-33; Jeremias, 1962a: 93-94 (ET)].[42]

---

[40] Nevertheless Matt 6:14-15 is not secondary.

[41] "The καὶ γὰρ is Luke's own interpretation of the Aramaic particle (probably the simple "and"). Luke's Aramaic verb could be taken equally well as present or future, "will forgive", as I have rendered."

[42] The argument of Strecker that "Recourse to a hypothetical Aramaic model contributes nothing to the understanding of the Matthean version, since Matthew's community prayed the Lord's prayer in the Greek language" [1985: 121 (ET)] seems to be too sweeping a statement which unduly rejects the examination of the significant question, what Jesus, not Matthew, could have meant with this saying. Schulz also notes the strong Semitism particularly in this verse [1972: 87].

4.13. (3.3.b) seems to derive from a dogmatic presupposition. Fiedler puts forward three reasons why Matt 6:12b; Luke 11:4b are secondary.

Firstly, Matt 6:12b; Luke 11:4b looks "alien" to the preceding 6:12a; Luke 11:4a [1976: 204-205]. Fiedler's claim of on "alien" character seems to be due to his theological presupposition. This protruding character could turn the other way: it could indicate significance and authenticity.[43]

Secondly, Fiedler argues that the Lord's Prayer indicates the element of the present and future at the same time. But he focuses on the fact that forgiveness in 6:12b refers more to the present. He counts the "present" character of the "forgiving" as evidence of its origin in the early church. Fiedler counts the petition for the "daily" bread and the present perfect tense of ἀφήκαμεν as evidence of the "present" character of this prayer which the early church prayed [1976: 206-207]. Contrary to Fiedler's argument, the petition for daily bread, the way of sustenance of Jesus' disciples, still retains its eschatological character. Further Matt 6:12b; Luke 11:4b hardly refer to the experience of forgiveness between disciples in the church, as Fiedler draws out in the course of painting out the contradictory elements in the arguments of Perrin and Schuermann [Fiedler, 1976: 206-207]. If members of the early church forgave each other they hardly needed to have made up this clause.

Thirdly, Fiedler also argues that Jesus need not have taught Matt 6:12b; Luke 11:4a because the Day of Atonement could have forgiven all the sins of the Israelites that had accumulated for a year [1976: 208]. Even Sanders puts forward a similar argument [1985: 200, cf. 397 n 23].

---

[43] "All these consideration suggest the conclusion that this particular petition in the Lord's prayer emanates, not from Jewish models, but from the peculiar thought of Jesus himself." [Abrahams, 1927: 98]. "It looks almost like an alien body; that makes clear that a very heavy emphasis is placed on it" [Jeremias, 1971: 201 (ET)].

This is seemingly significant but hardly a convincing argument. in Yoma 8:9 dismisses Fiedler's case. Further Sanders is fully aware of a Rabbinic teaching on repentance: "Transgression of commandments governing relations among humans requires compensation as well as repentance to God.'"[44] What Fiedler fails to consider is another point: Jesus works in the consciousness of an imminent end. Accordingly, Jesus could hardly have put off the call for repentance and reconciliation until the Day of Atonement of the coming year.

4.14. Contrary to what Fiedler argues [1976: 208], the conditional element in the later part of Matt 6:12b; Luke 11:4b does not infringe God's absolute free will in forgiving man's sins. God's forgiveness is not conditioned by human beings' forgiving of others. However, men's attitude of not forgiving others could hamper genuine forgiveness. Fiedler's argument that our forgiveness of our neighbour is also God's forgiveness [1976: 207[45], 210] is hardly convincing. The pattern of forgiveness could be the same, but the source of forgiveness is different.

4.15. In what sense is Matt 6:12b conditional? What Jesus meant in Matt 6:12b seems to be the following: you should not be so shameless or impudent as to ask God to forgive your sins while you grudge forgiving other people's sin. You are not supposed to ask God's forgiveness if you store up every bit of other people's sins within your mind. Rather be more sensible! Clear away every obstacle, which might hinder your full comprehension of God's forgiveness. Give up all such grudging attitudes

---

[44] Sanders cites Sifra Ahare Mot Pereq 8.1: "For transgressions which are between man and God the Day of Atonement atones, but those between man and man the Day of Atonement does not atone until he compensates his fellow." (cf. Sifre Zuta to Num. 6.26) [1985: 397 n 23].

[45] To Fiedler the second clause is to be seen as unnecessary. Fiedler argues that a God who is ready to forgive in action and word and a God who requires the response of men contradict each other [1976: 207].

by forgiving others if they repent. Then you can pray God to forgive your sins with a free conscience. You cannot ask God to forgive you when you refused to forgive others. That seems to be what Jesus meant to teach in Matt 6:12b, a *preparatory condition* before invoking God's forgiveness. "In this petition we have *the characteristic doctrine of Jesus that God's forgiveness can only come to those who themselves show a forgiving spirit,"* [T. W. Manson, 1948: 170][46] (italics mine).

---

[46] It is noteworthy that many scholars who have made an exhaustive study on the Lord's Prayer concede the conditional meaning. "Jesus could be very exacting *in the light of his reaching on forgiveness of man by man*" [Abrahams: 1927: 98]. "...in a sense God himself forgives through man (cf. Eph iv:32)." [Abrahams, 1927: 96]. Bultmann [1949: 78 (ET)]: "Only those who themselves forgive can ask God for forgiveness (Matt 6.12; Luke 11.4)." The reason why Manson's interpretation is most illuminating and convincing is because of his clear understanding of the relationship between the parties involved: forgiveness is not a linear relation between God and man, but a triangular relation, God, my neighbour, and I [T. W. Manson, 1956: 443]. "In the matter of sin and forgiveness, man never appears before God as an isolated individual, but always as man in society. His sins have repercussions on other people and other people's sins have repercussions on him. He appears before God but linked with his neighbour in countless ways. Any effective forgiveness must penetrate this barbed-wire entanglement of human estrangements and wrongs. And if it is to do so there must be *wirecutting on man's side as well as God's.*" [T. W. Manson, 1936: 443]. "If you refuse to forgive, it is an indication that you are unfit to receive forgiveness yourself—unable to accept it. If you cannot give forgiveness you cannot begin to receive it." [T. W. Manson, 1955: 109-110]. Jeremias also reads this verse as conditional: "As Jesus continually stresses, this *readiness* is the *indispensable prior condition for God's forgiveness.*" [1971: 201 (ET) cf. 192]. God's forgiveness is conditional because reconciliation is not established without the response of sinner [Moule, 1978: 751]. "However eager the forgiver may be to offer forgiveness, *it cannot be received, and reconciliation cannot achieved without repentance.*" [Moule, 1978: 72]. "The point has to do not with deserts but with desire; God's forgiveness, although it cannot be merited, must be received, and it cannot be received by those without the will to forgive others." [Davies, 1988: 610-611]. To support the conditional connotation Davies cites some texts in which the activity of man is followed by the act of God. "For other synoptic words with the form of a two-part pronouncement, and in which the first clause states an activity of man and the other

4.16. The Lord's prayer closely coheres with Jesus' proclamation on the kingdom, forgiveness, eschatological repentance. ἐλθέτω ἡ βασιλεία σου (Matt 6:10; Luke 11:2), whose authenticity is hardly challenged[47], already indicates the need of national and individual repentance. When the kingdom comes the judgment of God happens too. Accordingly, all Israelites need to clear themselves from any obstacle between themselves

---

an eschatological act of God, and in which the same verb is used in each clause, see Mt 5:7; Lk 6:37-38; Lk 14:11=18:14=Mt 23:12; Mt 10:31-33=Lk 12:8-9. There is no compelling reason to brand Mt 6:12b=Lk 11:4b a secondary accretion." [Davies, 1988: 611]. Lohmeyer [1946: 184 (ET)]: "We *could not venture to pray for forgiveness if we refused this assurance, just as we could not give the assurance itself if we might not and could not ask the Father for forgiveness.* " Luz integrates two points into one [1995: 384 (ET)]: "...prayer and human acting do not exclude each other. On the contrary, prayer is the speaking of the *active* human being with God". Marshall [1978: 461]: "The petition has a "condition" attached. God can be asked to forgive us because we too forgive everyone who is indebted to us. "While affirming the conditional connotation of Matt 6:12b; Luke 11:4a scholars persistently warn that the meaning is not that forgiveness can be earned [Plummer, 1909: 102]. "Man ought not to expect to receive what he is not ready to give—it is good discipline to lay this truth to heart. But, none the less, God's forgiveness is absolute." [Abrahams, 1927: 96]. "God's forgiveness is not a matter of a bargain or contract or transaction" [T. W. Manson, 1955: 109]. "To make forgiveness conditional on repentance is by no means the same as saying that forgiveness has to be (or, indeed, can be) earned by the recipient." [Moule, 1978: 72]. "In neither case, however, is there the thought of laying a good work before God. Rather it is emphasised that no obstacle must stand in the way of God's forgiveness." [Marshall, 1978: 461]. "The paradoxical unity of prevenient grace and a condition to be fulfilled by human beings is destroyed only if people by their forgiving raise a claim that they could hope that God will imitate their example." [Luz, 1985: 384] (italics mine).

[47] Harnack [1907:63-65 (ET)] replaces our present Luke 11:2 with ἐλθέτω τὸ ἅγιον πνεῦμά σου ἐφ' ἡμᾶς καὶ καθαρισάτω ἡμᾶς in terms of manuscripts (162), 700, Marcion Greg. Nyssa. Harnack's argument deserves attention. However the unanimous witness of the Greek Manuscripts and the attestation of only two late Greek Manuscripts are not strong enough to overturn the authenticity of our present Lucan text [Marshall, 1978: 458].

if they are to avoid God's judgment. In view of this imminent judgment the conditional clause would have been quite natural and necessary.

4.17. Although not in a liturgical context, *the idea of conditional forgiveness was prevalent in the Judaism at the time of Jesus*. Forgiving others as the condition for God's forgiveness is apparent in some Jewish texts (Sir 29:2-4; m. Yoma 8:9; t. B. Qam. 9:29; b. Ros. Has. 17a; b. Meg. 28a; b. Sabb.151b[48]). Showing mercy toward the offender is stressed (T. Zebulon 5:3; 8:1-2; T. Joseph 18:2) (cf. 2 Sam 22:26=Ps 18:25). In this literary milieu Jesus would naturally have put Matt 6:12b; Luke 11:4a into his prayer.

4.18. What needs to be drawn to our attention is that a strenuous observance of the law or rule gives joy, instead of being a burden or constraint.[49] Thus Jesus could deliberately have inserted this part in order to teach his contemporaries the joy of restoring the relationship in repentance and forgiveness. Jesus could have put in this part to teach that "reconciliation" expedites the coming of the kingdom (Matt 5:24-25).

4.19. Even if the wording in Luke 11:4b (καὶ γὰρ) is close to the original text the conditional connotation remains. The fact that our forgiveness of others (καὶ ἄφες) and God's forgiveness of our sins (ἀφίομεν) occur at the same time indicates that two identical forgivenesses are related to

---

48 "He who is merciful to others, mercy is shown to him by heaven, while he who is not merciful to others, mercy is not shown to him by Heaven."

49 Sometimes a natural and ideal interpretation of a text seems to be hampered by the theological presupposition that Christianity does not ask of human beings any action for their salvation. Hence any idea in which Jesus stresses conditions or responsibility tends to be interpreted as not authentic. The presupposition which detests any theological ideas on law, or an conditional acceptance seems to have been deeply embedded in the Reformed tradition. This presupposition seems to have led to a fallacious interpretation.

each other. Further, the conditional meaning is obvious in the Lucan text. The Aramaic equivalent of καὶ γὰρ αὐτοὶ ἀφίομεν ("because we also forgive") could imply that we have done so, or habitually do so, or intend to do so [McNeile, 1915: 81].

4.20. Whether the petitioners forgive other sinners after or before they implore God to forgive them, their "recognition of this contemporaneity of action in the petition" [Perrin, 1967: 210] "ability and obligation and assurance" [Lohmeyer, 1946: 184 (ET)] "willingness" [Jeremias, 1966: 103 (ET)] or "readiness to forgive" [Hauck, 1954: 563 (ET)] implies a preparatory condition.

4.21. Jesus' emphasis on the distinctive morality and fulfilment of obligation to the offended are bountifully reflected in many parts of his sayings and parables. In light of his emphasis on the radical fulfilment of the Law a command for the restoration of the relationship between men would have been natural and almost necessary to Jesus.[50] For example Jesus could have taught this prayer in the spirit of "love your neighbour as yourself" (Mark 12:31; 33; Matt 19:19; 22:39; Luke 10:27; Rom 13:9; Gal 5:14; Jas 2:8).

4.22. Some scholars regards this clause as authentic and having some sort of conditional connotation with or without additional reasons: Abrahams, 1924: 98, 103; Montefiore, 1927, vol. 2: 103[51]; Stauffer, 1941: 178[52]

---

[50] Repentance, contrition, reconciliation, restitution, penance, praise and prayer are so closely connected in Jesus' teaching that it seems almost impossible to think of one without another [O'Neill, 1980: 58].

[51] "Only if we forgive others, have we a right to ask God forgiveness."

[52] "The act of reconciliation with one brother, which *needs to precede God's act of forgiveness,* is not a piece of magic of the *do ut des* kind, but rather the natural and indispensable expression of a thoroughgoing repentance which has once for all abandoned resentment and calculation of injury." (italics mine). "If our confession is

(ET); Bultmann, 1948: 24-25 (ET)[53]; Jeremias, 1962a: 103[54] (ET); Perrin, 1967: 151-153[55]; Grundmann, 1968: 202-203; Schweizer, 1973: 155[56]

---

half-hearted, then we are no longer willing to forgive our brother who has wronged us (Matt 6:15; 18:21 ff.)! But if our confession is genuine then we pray: "Forgive us our trespasses, as we forgive them that trespass us"" (Matt 6.12 cf. 6.14; 5.23; Mark 11.25) [178].

[53] Bultmann [1931: 133 (ET)] seems to argue that the introductory part Matt 6:7f is secondary: Bultmann simply states that "it is not more likely that Matt 6:7f is a formulation (by Matthew?) analogous to the other sections fashioned specially to bring the Lord's Prayer into this particular context." Schulz seems to misread that Matt 6:7f includes the Lord's Prayer too [1972: 86 n 204]. Bultmann's position on the authenticity of the Lord's Prayer is unclear. Sometimes he seems to affirm the authenticity of some parts of this prayer. However in other places he shows a sign that he regards it as secondary: " ...the early Christian community had its prayer, the Lord's prayer, which was *attributed to Jesus*, as the sect of John *ascribed their prayer to their master* (Matt 6:9-13; Luke 11:1-4)." [1926: 180 (ET)]. However Bultmann admits the possibility that Jesus' prayer could have been transmitted to the early church. "How *far* the Lord's prayer was really formulated by Jesus cannot be determined; at least it must be characteristic of him." [1926: 180 (ET)]. Bultmann's comment that "the last petition (Matt 6:13b; "lead us not into temptation") could have scarcely have come from Jesus but had its origin in the church." [1926: 181 (ET)] perhaps indicates that he does think of others parts as authentic sayings of Jesus. At this point the most reasonable conclusion on his position would be that the basic form of this prayer came from Jesus, but later it was expanded by the early church with older Jewish traditions on prayer.

[54] "With these words he who prays reminds himself of his own need to forgive. Jesus again and again declared this very point, that you cannot ask God for forgiveness if you are not prepared to forgive. God can forgive only if we are ready to forgive."

[55] Matt 6:12; Luke 11:4 satisfies the criterion of dissimilarity absolutely.

[56] Schweizer leaves the possibility open that this petition in the other half could go back to Jesus or to the post-Easter tradition [1973: 155 (ET)]: "Whether the petition here goes back to Jesus or only to the post-Easter tradition, the interruption of the rhythm shows *the importance of the supplementary clause.*" Further it is noteworthy that Schweizer balances between the rejection of earning of God's forgiveness (Matt 20:1-16) and necessity of some conditional connotation in Matt

(ET); Voegtle, 1974: 95-96[57]; Moule, 1978: 72, 76[58]; Marshall, 1978: 455[59]; Luz, 1985: 372 (ET); Fitzmyer, 1986: 899.[60]

5.

5.1. The main thrust of this saying

Jesus could have taught a prayer which is very similar to Matt 6:12 and Luke 11:4a in its form. In this prayer he clearly stipulates a condition, to be ready to forgive other sinners, before asking God's forgiveness, because a forgiving spirit in a man is an essential condition of his receiving God's forgiveness.

5.2. The bearing on the forgiveness of sins

The political context of Israel at Jesus' time could have urged him to stress the need of mutual forgiveness to expedite national

---

5:23-24 [1973: 155 (ET)] (italics mine).

[57] At the outset Voegtle argues for the inauthenticity of this clause: "Moreover, it is not only possible but even probable that the promise of one's own forgiveness which is common to both versions of the Lord's Prayer (Matthew 6:12b; Luke 11:4a), was added in the Judaeo-Christian community only after Easter, probably at a relatively early date." However Voegtle's wavering comes in the immediately following paragraph: "We could possibly consider as yet another original element, the second part of the second We-petition "as we forgive our debtors." [1974: 95]. As a whole it would be fair to say that Voegtle leaves the authenticity as an open question.

[58] "Jesus himself, from time to time, uttered both kinds [conditional and unconditional] of saying."

[59] "There are no grounds for reasonable doubt that the prayer goes back to Jesus himself."

[60] "God's forgiveness cannot he expected if human forgiveness is withheld."

reconciliation. Under the circumstance of foreign dominion the confrontation and distrust between people could have been easily exploited and manipulated only to contribute to the furthering of Israel's enslavement by the Gentiles. In view of the eschatological context this collective entreaty for forgiveness, "forgive our sins", could indicate the national repentance of the whole Israel.

Sanders does not deny that Jesus spoke the Lord's Prayer [1985: 111].[61] However Sanders argues that "Sayings concerning forgiveness have, as might be expected, little eschatological thrust. The disciples are to pray for forgiveness (Matt. 6.12, 14//Mark 11.25//Luke 11.4)" [Sanders, 1985: 111] (italics mine). But this argument remains unconvincing. How can we distinguish in Jesus' sayings little eschatological thrust from a strong or relatively strong eschatological thrust? Further, Sanders assumes Jewish eschatology as the principal context of Jesus' work.[62] Sanders clearly interpret Matt 6:10, thy kingdom come, as referring to the time yet to come [1995: 142]. By this argument he admits that Matt 6:10 was directed toward the eschatological context. Hence his argument on the little eschatological meaning of Matt 6:12 becomes unconvincing when admitting that Matt 6:9-14 was transmitted as a single form of prayer (as Sanders assumes). Accordingly Sanders' argument on the less eschatological feature of the sayings on forgiveness becomes untenable [1995: 111-112].[63]

---

[61] "Since negatives are so difficult to prove, I do not wish to argue that we can know Jesus said none of the things attributed to him in the sections under consideration. I am inclined to reject the entire section, Matt 5.17-6.18, except for the prayer (6.9-13)." [1985:263].

[62] "But we know the principal context of Jesus' work: Jewish eschatology. As I shall argue later, the line from John the Baptist to Paul and the other early apostles is the line of Jewish eschatology, and it would be misleading to move the centre of our investigation off that line." [1985: 8].

[63] Luz raises a puzzling question that Matt 6:12b; Luke 11:4b excludes the eschatological interpretation of the petition for forgiveness: "If one looks back to the

Finally, if Jesus assumed his followers would ask God for forgiveness, and if he emphasized their need to forgive others, surely he would have also assumed that no one became his followers without repenting of his sins. The emphasis of Jesus on a further condition— the need to forgive others— seems to imply that any Jew understood as comprising repentance (contrition, restitution, sacrifice) was already taken for granted.

---

human forgiveness which has already happened (aorist), then the petition for God's forgiveness cannot refer only to the eschaton" [1985: 383 n 95 (ET)]. But the aorist could be used only to describe the time sequence between two events. The point is not the time of the forgiveness, but the sincerity of reconciliation under the imminent end. Further the characteristic eschatological tension between present and future which are not found in the Jewish prayers [Perrin, 1963: 195 (ET)] could support its authenticity. Strecker also thinks of an eschatological context as the context of Jesus' activity [1985: 175-176, 181 (ET)].

C. Did Jesus send out his disciples to proclaim the coming of the kingdom in Matt 10:5-15; Mark 6:7-13; Luke 10:2-12; 9:1-6?

1. The conjectured original text: Matt 10:5-15 (cf. Mark 6:7-13; Luke 1 0:2-12; 9:1-6)

2. The Matthean text is considered authentic. This paper is focused on Matt 10:5-7; distinctive to Matt, except for verse 7.

καὶ λέγετε αὐτοῖς ἤγγικεν ἐφ᾽ ῦμας ἡ βασιλεία τοῦ θεοῦ] the Lucan text (10:9).

καὶ ἐξελθόντες ἐκήρυξαν ἵνα μετανοῶσιν] the Marcan text (6:12).

In general the Matthean text of the whole passage seems to keep the original order and wording.[64]

3. Arguments against 1.

---

64 In Luke the command on the things to be allowed to carry (Luke 10:4) precedes the instruction on mission. Preaching the kingdom and rendering healing after entering the city (Luke 10:9-10) looks natural. However the mission in the family (Luke 10:5-7) preceding the mission in the city (Luke 10:8-12) seems awkward and could hint at the artificial reversal of the order of these verses. In Matthew the instruction what to carry (Matt 10:9-10) would be more natural if it is put before 10:7. Strictly speaking v. 11 contradicts v. 12-13. V. 11, 12, 13 could have been put together later. That is the only awkward part. Otherwise the Matthean text seems to keep the order of various sayings better than the Lucan text. Matthew gives a consistent picture. The Lucan account gives an impression that disciples proclaim the coming kingdom only after people are fully ready to listen (Luke 10:9). Preaching the coming kingdom while they move on from city to city (Matt 10:6) could be more effective irrespective of the readiness of the people to listen in cities or families.

3.1. Mark 6:8-11; Matt 10:5-15; Luke 10:2-12 is a church product [Bultmann, 1931:145 (ET)]. Originally it was the risen Lord who spoke this passage (cf Matt 28:19f; Luke 24:47f) [Bultmann, 1931: 145 (ET)].

3.2. Some of the wording of this passage may have been influenced by the later missionary experience [Hahn, 1963: 40 (ET)] "...the variety of the texts shows the development of the primitive Christian idea of Mission." [Bultmann, 1931: 145 n 1 (ET)]. The early church could make up Mark 6:7, 12; Matt 10:5-6b; Luke 10:9 to establish the authority of their mission [Hahn, 1963: 40 (ET)].

3.3. Matt 10:5-7 was made up by the early church: "What we are really hearing in this saying, too, is the voice of the strictest form of Jewish Christianity", "The injunction only acquires its full weight when it is understood that the object of the polemic here is a mission among the Samaritans and Gentiles — a mission not merely planned and debated, but already begun, as the context requires." [Kaesemann, 1965: 87 (ET)].[65]

3.4. "... There is a good reason to doubt the authenticity of Matt 10:6. 1 shall argue, below that the basic theme of Jesus' mission to the "sinners" ("the lost sheep") is authentic, but that not all passages which repeat that theme, go back to Jesus." [Sanders, 1985: 104].

3.5. One of the reasons why scholars hesitate to accept this passage as a genuine saying of Jesus arises from their presupposition that Jesus hardly limits his disciples' mission to Israel [Schnackenburg: 1988: 91]. There is a conflicting account about the mission to the Gentiles (ἀπέστειλεν ἀγγέλους πρὸ προσώπου αὐτοῦ) (Luke 9:52-56).

3.6 . Some other scholars too claim that Matt 10:5-7; Luke 9:2 is made up

---

[65] Koester reads Matt 10:5-7 as a Matthean addition [1990: 162].

by the early church [Wellhausen, 1909: 44; Strecker, 1962: 107, 195-196; Hoffmann, 1972: 262; Schulz, 1972: 406; Gnilka, 1986: 361-2] or by Matthew [Schnackenburg, 1988: 91] in order to ascribe the authority of the Palestine mission of the early church to the historical Jesus [Wellhausen, 1909: 44].

4. Arguments against 3.

4.1. (3.1) seems hardly convincing. The pre-Easter saying Matt 10:5-15; Luke 10:2-12 is fundamentally different from the post-Faster saying in Matt 28:19-20; Luke 24:47-48 as follows:

a. Firstly Matt 10:5-15; Luke 10:2-12 limits mission to Israelites[66] while Matt 28:19 (πάντα τὰ ἔθνη); Luke 24:47 (πάντα τὰ ἔθνη) commands disciples to reach out even to the Gentiles.

b. Secondly the pre-Easter saying is given to the δώδεκα (Mark 6:7; Matt 10:5) while the post-Easter saying is given to the ἕνδεκα (Matt 28:16), probably a sign of the church addition.

c. Thirdly "proclaiming the coming of the kingdom" is the main task in the pre-Easter saying while "making the Gentiles disciples and giving them baptism" (Matt 28:19; Luke 24:47) is that in the post-Easter saying.

d. Fourthly Bultmann also admits that in any case the evangelist had no intention of depicting a development (from Matt 10:5 to 28:19). [1931: 145 (ET)].[67] The fact that the evangelists had no intention to depict

---

[66] Luke 10:12 seems to refer only to Israel.

[67] Bultmann argues that "But the variety of the texts shows the development of the primitive Christian idea of Mission". Certainly the evangelist seems not to have

a development implies the intrinsic difference between these sayings, the pre-Faster and post-Easter saying. Hence, unlike Matt 28:19, the command in Matt 10:5 could imply the historicity of Jesus' sending disciples only to Israel.

4.2. (3.2) does not seem to be entirely convincing. Bultmann argues that "the missionary charges were very early or originally in a connected group from which Mark has made excerpts, while Lk.10:2-12 accurately reproduces Q and Matt. 10:9-16 joins Q and Mark, and in the course of doing so Luke like Matthew adds all kinds of similar material." [1931: 325 (ET)] (italics mine). What Bultmann calls "similar material" could have come from the isolated sayings of Jesus. Synoptic evangelists could have composed the passage on a mission with received traditions comprising various isolated sayings of Jesus (e.g. Matt 10:15; Luke 10:12). This argument could be supported by that the fact Matthew and Luke seem to have added almost identical materials, except for some minor differences or translation variants in wording. Matt 10:9-15 and Luke 10:2-12 are almost identical in content although the verses are put in different positions. Many of these isolated sayings seem to fit the pre-Easter mission context. Thus it would be more reasonable to argue that Matt 10:5-15; Luke 11:1-12 comprise a collection of sayings added to the main body of Jesus' saying on a mission. The possibility that this passage comes from the historical Jesus is fairly strong.

4.3. The missionaries from the early church would have wished to preach the kerygma "Jesus was crucified and risen" rather than "the coming of

put these two different sayings in different places only to depict a development. However what Bultmann does not take into account seems to be the point that the evangelist treated the pre-Easter and the post-Easter sayings differently. They could distinguish genuine sayings of Jesus on mission preserved in the church from the sayings on the mission made up by the early church.

the kingdom".

4.4. There is a clear difference in the life style of the missionaries before and after Easter. Jesus' disciples were commanded to go out even without the bare necessities for the journey (Matt 10:9-10; Luke 10:4). Hence accompanying any members of their families would hardly have been imaginable to the twelve disciples. However the mission of the early church seems to take a much more flexible approach. Peter's being accompanied by his wife in a mission (1 Cor 9:5) could hardly have been permissable in the pre-Easter mission situation.

4.5. It is hardly likely that Peter and John suddenly begin to heal the sick and to proclaim the kerygma after Easter (Acts 3:2-8; 5:15-16) when Jesus did not endow them with the authority to heal the sick and to proclaim the message, the coming kingdom, before Easter.

4.6. Is (3.3) entirely convincing? The similar account οὐκ ἀπεστάλην εἰ μὴ εἰς τὰ πρόβατα τὰ ἀπολωλότα οἴκου ᾿Ισραήλ in Matt 15:24 in the middle of a healing story widely accepted as authentic could support its authenticity.

4.7. Jesus could have used the term τὰ πρόβατα τὰ ἀπολωλότα οἴκου ᾿Ισραήλ.[68] Trautmann argues that ᾿Ισραήλ is a unique expression which could not come from the early Jewish text [1980: 221-223, 225]. According to Trautmann from early Judaism to the time of Jesus no group describes themselves as οἴκου ᾿Ισραήλ, hence v. 6 is ascribed to Jesus [1980: 221-225].[69] Trautmann cites terms from Qumran

---

[68] Although Hahn agrees with the historicity of Jesus' sending out the disciples, he argues that Matt 10:5b, 6 hardly go back to Jesus [1963: 40 (ET)].

[69] There are derivatives of οἶκος in the New Testament such as οἴκῳ ᾿Ισραὴλ (Heb 8: 10), πᾶς οἶκος ᾿Ισραήλ (Acts 2:36). (cf. Exod 16:31; 2 Sam

texts, "the house of Holiness" (1QS IX.16), "the True house of Israel" (1QS V.6), "the Assembly of Supreme Holiness" (1QS VIII.5), "the House of Perfection and Truth in Israel" (1QS IX.6), "a sure house of Israel" (CD III.19), "Judge of the Congregation" (CD X.4-8) [222]. Contrary to Trautmann, these terms could have been used as equivalents of "all Israel" at the time of Jesus. The term occurs in a number of Jewish writings in Greek: Jdt 4:15; 6:17; 14:10 (οἶκον Ισραηλ) 8:6; 13:14 (οἴκου Ισραηλ); 14:5 (οἶκον τοῦ Ισραηλ), Bar 2:26 (οἴκου Ισραηλ), 3:24 (Ισραηλ ὡς μέγας ὁ οἶκος τοῦ θεοῦ), 3 Macc 2:10 (οἶκον τοῦ Ισραηλ), Pss. Sol. 17:21-26. Hence Jesus could have spoken of Israel using this term.

4.8. τὰ πρόβατα τὰ ἀπολωλότα οἴκου 'Ισραήλ could point to "the lost ones of Israel" (partitive genitive) and "the whole of Israel in its lost condition" (explanatory genitive) [Jeremias, 1956: 26 (ET)].[70] This non-exclusive interpretation correctly captures the scope of Jesus' mission. Certainly Jesus intends to bring back "the lost ones of Israel" rigorously (Mark 2:14-17 etc.). No Jewish groups Sadducees, Pharisees, Zealots, Essenes, or even John the Baptist, went to "the lost sheep of Israel" to include them as οἴκου 'Ισραήλ [Trautmann, 1990: 221-224]. Hence Jesus could be unique in this initiative. At the same time Jesus' concern for the lost ones of Israel does not contradict his overall concern for

---

1:12; Jer 31:31; Rev 2:36; Heb, 8:8, 10) [Schnackenburg, 1988: 92]. The underlying idea of Trautmann is to distinguish this term from Judaism. However that distinction is hardly necessary.

[70] Trautmann argues that the mission "to the lost sheep" could symbolize the mission for all Israel [1980: 220]. Weaver argues that the first two negative commands ("Go nowhere among the Gentiles, and enter no town of the Samaritans") serve as a foil for the third ("to go to the lost sheep of the house of Israel") [1990: 192]. Whether these preceding clauses are a literary foil or not the command to go to Israel seems to emerge from the urgent need of calling for the repentance of Israel before the imminent end.

Israel. The account of this mission elucidates the scope of Jesus' intention, calling for the repentance of the whole of Israel.

4.9. The church influenced mainly by Hellenistic ideas would not have made up Matt 10:5-6 because it excludes the Gentiles from the object of the mission.

4.10. Matt 10:5b-6 originally could belong to the primitive tradition transferred to Matthew and Luke. Luke could have omitted this verse because of his universal tendency [McNeile, 1915: 133]. Accordingly, Koester's argument is hardly convincing. Matthew must have noticed the contradiction between Matt 10:5-7 and Matt 28:19f.

4.11. The combination of the preaching of the coming kingdom of God and the casting out of demons seems to be unusual in Judaism. The charismatic healers mentioned by Vermes do not seem to have announced a coming kingdom: Honi the rain maker [Vermes, 1973: 69-72] and Hanina ben Dosa the healer [72-77]. There is no account that the self-proclaimed prophet Theudas *(Jewish Antiquities* 20.97*)* or the Essenes *(Jewish War* 2.159) proclaimed the kingdom and healed the sick.[71] The Jewish exorcist attested in 4QprNab asks king Nabonidus only to glorify God. Hence it would be convincing that this unique combination of preaching and healing in Matt 10:5-6b comes from Jesus.

4.12. The Semitism, ἀποστέλλειν εἰς [Jeremias, 1956: 26 (ET)], could also support the authenticity.

4.13. John the Baptist, Jesus and his disciples are in accord in proclaiming the same message ἤγγικεν ἡ βασιλεία (Matt 3:2; Mark 1:15; Matt 4:17;

[71] Sanders [1985: 171-172]. Some Essenes foretold the future (Josephus, *Jewish War* 2. 159).

Matt 10:7; Luke 9:2, 10:9). The fact that Jesus is baptized by John suggests the continuity and consistency of the work of John and Jesus who preach the same message "the kingdom has come". This unity of purpose between John and Jesus could convince the Jews of the authority and significance of this message. Mark 1:16-20, Mark 3:13-19, 9:38-40, 10:29-30 could also corroborate the continuity and consistency of the theme of sending disciples. Continuity is an important feature of the Jewish concept of agency.

4.14. In Judaism the disciples are expected to repeat what their master commands. "A man's agent is like to himself" (m. Ber. 5.5). Rengstorf translates this verse "he who is sent by a man is *as* he who sent him" [1933: 415 (ET)] (italics mine). The transaction could not be properly conducted without a resolute subordination of the will of the representative to that of the one who commissioned him" [415]. This consistency and continuity is essential in confirming the authority of a messenger (cf. Matt 10:40 ; Luke 10:16). Accordingly Jesus' disciples would only repeat what this master proclaims rather than proclaiming something different. They could only add something more if Jesus endorsed it. The disciples could not alter the message unless otherwise instructed because they could not be above their teacher (Matt 10:24-25).

4.15. (3.4) does not seem to take into account the difference between the material put before a saying as an editorial addition and the material put in the middle of a saying as a part of the essential body, Sanders' argument hinges on his understanding of Luke 15:1 where the disciples are merely supplementary figures [1985:104). This argument is not convincing. "Tax-collectors" and "sinners" are clearly additions and provide the setting for the three contained parables. But Matt 10:5-15 is a single story and there the disciples are the central figures.

4.16. Sanders regards τὰ πρόβατα τὰ ἀπολωλότα οἴκου ᾿Ισραήλ

as something of an equivalent of "the tax collectors and sinners" in Luke 15:1, an editorial addition [1985: 104]. That is hardly convincing. It may be true that Trautmann's argument points only to the authenticity of the theme of the inclusion of "the lost sheep", not to the historicity of the mission of the twelve to them. Sanders argues that we do not know what Jesus' disciples performed or with what purpose Jesus called them [1985: 103]. It is hardly likely that Jesus chose them only "to be with him" [103]. On the contrary, two facts, Jesus chose the twelve disciples (Mark 1:16-20; Matt 4:18-22; Luke 5:1-11; John 1:35-51) and Jesus had a genuine concern for the lost sheep (the whole of Israel), naturally lead to a third thesis, Jesus' disciples would play a significant role, in fulfilling Jesus' aspirations. The account of the disciples' success in their mission could support this argument (Luke 10:17-20; cf. John 12:31).

4.17. It is hardly likely that the whole passage (Matt 10:5-16; Mark 6:7-11; Luke 10:1-12; 9:1-6) came from the Palestinian Church. Even the early church influenced strongly by Jewish ideas would have been reluctant to use the expression "cast off the dust from their feet" (Matt 10:14; Luke 10:11), a prophetic action almost equivalent to reckoning as Gentiles [T. W. Manson, 1948: 76], in describing the unrepentant attitude of their fellow Jews.

4.18. The disciples' mission without carrying proper provision is unusual in Judaism (Matt 10:9-10; Luke 10:4). Even Essenes would get their food from their fellow members when they traveled (Josephus, *Jewish War* 2.125-127). This strict prohibition stands out from Hellenism where the cynic philosophers could carry staves, satchel and a single philosophers' cloak [Hengel, 1981: 28-29][72] or could make a good thing out of

[72] Diog. Laert. 6.13: "Antisthenes himself too was nicknamed a hound pure and simple. And he was the first, Diocles told us, to double his cloak and be content with that one garment and to take up a staff and a wallet." Hick's translation [1925:

preaching [Marshall, 1978: 350].

4.19. The eschatological character of some of these passages e.g. the coming kingdom etc., [Theissen, 1973: 255, 257] could support its authenticity.

4.20. It could be convincing that the unusually radical demand in this passage goes back to Jesus [Hahn, 1963: 46 (ET)]. No greetings on the road (Luke 10:4) is unusual in Judaism. It could mean an aloofness to non-community members (IQS 5:10-11:15; cf. Ps 129:8). However Elisha's command to Gehazi "If you meet anyone, do not salute him; and if any one salutes you, do not reply" (2 Kings 4:29) could arise only at the moment of life or death. Likewise the urgent need to deliver the message, the coming kingdom, could allow the disciples to bypass the ordinary etiquette.

4.21. Carrying no stick (Matt 10:10; Luke 9:3) is unusual in Judaism. Even Essenes carry at least arms as a protection against brigands (Josephus, *Jewish War* 2. 125-127).

4.22. Jesus' instruction to his disciples to copy his message and life, style is unusual in Judaism. Jesus' disciples could follow his life style τρόπους κυρίου (Did. 11:8) as his messenger [Theissen, 1973: 257].[73] In Judaism a Rabbi was more conscious of his difference from his students than of their resemblance to him [Flew, 1938: 110]. Did. 11:3-6, 8, the Gospel of Thomas 1:14, 1:40, 1:73, Oxyrhyncus Papyrus 655 have a similar text. From the point of view of allowing disciples to have the

13-14].

[73] Some of the later church seem not to have followed the lifestyle of Jesus. Did 11:8 could be an instruction to follow Jesus' lifestyle.

authority to preach his central message and his power to heal the sick there is almost no difference between the master, Jesus, and his disciples. This kind of benevolent transfer of authority is distinguished from some other Rabbis (Pharisees) who love money (Luke 16:14; cf. Mark 12:40). Thus it could be reasonable to argue that sayings that maintain an extremely simple life style could go back only to a wandering charismatic leader like Jesus.

4.23. It is noteworthy that this account is multiply attested in all three synoptic gospels (Mark 6:8, 12; Matt 10:7; Luke 9:2; 10:9, 11b). Further the content and order are too different to come from the same copies of one text. In addition, this variance of the text could hardly have arisen from the result of assimilating of the same text.

4.24. Mark 3:14-15 also witnesses that Jesus sends disciples to preach and gives the authority to cast out demons. The motif of the mission is supported in more than one source.

4.25. (3.5) is not convincing. Luke 10:9 ἀγγέλους is used with the meaning of "angels" in Mark 13:27. This word has the meaning of "apostles" or "messengers" in Luke 9:52-53. However Luke 9:52-53 does not portray the mission to Samaritans. Jesus and disciples merely intend to stay in Samaria on the way to Jerusalem. Thus it is not an account of a mission.

4.26. Against (3.6) some scholars regard Matt 10:5-7 as authentic with or without additional reasons. This passage describes Jesus' historical sending of his disciples; Harnack, 1907: 80-81 (ET), 1908, 87 (ET); Montefiore, 1927, vol. 2: 146-147; 1930: 218; McNeile, 1915: 133-134; T. W. Manson, 1948: 73, 179-180; Jeremias, 1956; 26, 72 (ET); 1971-100, 130-134 (ET); Bornkamm, 1959: 149-150 (ET); Hahn, 1963: 40

(ET); Hengel, 1968: 60, 73 (ET); Schweizer, 1973: 235[74] (ET); Kuemmel, 1956: 84-85 (ET); 1971: 33 (ET); Theissen, 1973: 253, 257; 1977: 23 (ET); Pesch, 1976, vol. 1: 330-331; Marshall, 1978: 352, 413; Trautmann, 1980: 225; Best, 1983: 49; Aune, 1993: 172, 392; Weaver, 1990: 84.

5.

5.1. The main thrust of this saying

Jesus could command his disciples to proclaim the imminent coming of the kingdom and to heal the sick. Their proclamation accompanied by healing and driving out devils could spread to all parts of Israel. As a result the Jewish people who heard this eschatological message could respond according to their understanding. It is unlikely that Jesus called a group of people together with the limited purpose of forming a particular sect or community. Jesus called the twelve to go to all Israel. Further, Jesus promised his disciples a particular role, to judge Israel (Matt 19:28; Luke 22:30) which could follow their proclamation of the kingdom. Accordingly, it is convincing that Jesus commissions his disciples for a particular task, to call the Israelites to repent by proclaiming the imminent coming of the kingdom (Joel 3:12). Jesus could command his disciples to go first to the lost sheep of Israel not because the Gentiles are excluded from salvation, but because Jesus attempts to restore at least Israel by calling for their repentance. The urgent need of bringing back at least Israel could lead Jesus to command them to go only to Israel. To sum up, Jesus could have sent his disciples to proclaim the imminent coming of the kingdom [Jeremias, 1971: 95 (ET)]. Repentance,

---

[74] Schweizer suspects that Matt 10:5-6 goes back to a group within the primitive Jewish Christian community. However Schweizer also admits the possibility that Jesus could once have spoken to Matt 10:5-6 during his ministry.

is specifically mentioned in Mark 6:12; it could well be implied in more of these traditions.

5.2. The bearing on the forgiveness of sins

Contrary to what Sanders argues [1985:104], Jesus clearly commands his disciples to go to Israel only. The message "the kingdom is at hand" could trigger national repentance. Jesus' disciples are chosen for this particular purpose. Hardly any other reason could be conceived except this aim. They were commanded to spread the urgent message as far as possible in Israel.

D. Did Jesus call for national repentance in Matt 11:16-19; Luke 7:31-35?

1. The conjectured original text

Matt 11:16 Τίνι δὲ ὁμοιώσω τὴν γενεὰν ταύτην; ὁμοία ἐστὶν παιδίοις καθημένοις ἐν ταῖς ἀγοραῖς ἅ προσφωνοῦντα τοῖς ἑτέροις 17 λέγουσιν,

ηὐλήσαμεν ὑμῖν καὶ οὐκ ὠρχήσασθε,
ἐθρηνήσαμεν καὶ οὐκ ἐκόψασθε.

18 ἦλθεν γὰρ Ἰωάννης μήτε ἐσθίων μήτε πίνων, καὶ λέγουσιν, δαιμόνιον ἔχει. 19 ἦλθεν ὁ υἱὸς τοῦ ἀνθρώπου ἐσθίων καὶ πίνων, καὶ λέγουσιν ἰδοὺ ἄνθρωπος φάγος καὶ οἰνοπότης, τελωνῶν φίλος καὶ ἁμαρτωλῶν. καὶ ἐδικαιώθη ἡ σοφία ἀπὸ τῶν ἔργων αὐτῆς.

2. Arguments concerning the excluded part

There are, no excluded parts. The Lucan variants are usually translation variants. Although some scholars argue that in general Luke preserves the more original text than Matthew [Koester, 1990: 133-135] the Matthean text seems more near to the original text as a whole in this passage.

3. Arguments against 1.

3.1. The parable (Matt 11: 16-17; Luke 7:31-32) was originally isolated [Bultmann, 1931:172 (ET); Fiedler, 1976: 138], and Matt 11:18-19; Luke 7:33-35 is secondary [Bultmann, 1931: 165 (ET); Luehrmann, 1969: 29-30; Schulz, 1972: 381-386]. This interpretative part reflects the situation of the early church. The following are the reasons.

a. This pericope was originally independent of the preceding oldest tradition [Bultmann, 1931: 165, 172[75] (ET)]. No clear connection between "this parable" and "John and Jesus" is envisaged [Bultmann, 1931: 199 (ET): Luehrmann, 1969: 29; Schultz, 1972, 381[76]].

b. This part reflects the polemical situation of the early church [Luehrmann, 1969: 29-31[77]; Schulz, 1972: 381-386]. The extension of polemic against all Israel with the term "this generation" is well known [Schulz, 1972: 381].

c. John and Jesus were deliberately placed here in parallel [Schulz, 1972: 386; Fiedler, 1976: 145] to reflect the polemical situation of the (hypothetical) Q community [Schulz, 1972: 386]. This part Matt 11: 18-19; Luke, 7:33 34 is a verdict passed upon John and Jesus after the completion of their lives and ministries.[78]

d. ὁ υἱὸς τοῦ ἀνθρώπου indicates the post-Easter feature of this saying [Bultmann, 1931: 165 (ET)].

---

[75] "This application of the similitude to Jesus and the Baptist [Matt 11:18-19; Luke 7:33-35] at any rate in its present form, cannot belong to the oldest tradition ... though the form shows that the similitude itself is an ancient piece of the tradition." "Matt 11:16f. could very well be a picture of a capricious people, though whether the reference to Jesus and the Baptist is original remains doubtful." [Bultmann, 1931: 199 (ET)].

[76] Schulz puts forward the following reasons. 1) The allegorical interpretation of the parable. 2) The change of the order of dance and mourning (cf. Ps 30:11). 3) The inadequate parallel correspondence between the two parts. 4) The reference to Sophia.

[77] The contrast between "John and Jesus" on the one hand and "this generation" on the other hand is also the contrast between the Q community and Israel.

[78] An expansion of Marshall's summary of Bultmann's argument on ἐλήλυθεν (ἦλθεν).

e. ἦλθεν[79] hints at the secondary nature of this saying [Bultmann, 1931: 165 (ET)].

4. Arguments against 3.

4.1. Contrary to (3.1.a) Matt 11: 16-17; Luke 7:31-32 and Matt 11: 18-19; Luke 7:33-35 form a unitary sayings[80] This introductory parable lucidly illustrates the capriciousness of the Jewish people on which the following saying focuses. Their culpability is exposed. As a result they are destined to face judgment. Their possible justification, not to have noticed any warnings of the prophets concerning the coming judgment, is completely rejected.

4.2.a. (3.1.a) seems to derive from a tendentious interpretation. Does the application of this parable (Matt 11:18-19; Luke 7:33-34) make this parable an allegory [Dibelius, 1933: 246 (ET); Schulz, 1972: 381]? That is not necessarily so.[81] Not every saying comprised of a descriptive parable and the following explanation lends itself to the suspicion of secondary application. When a saying consisted of a preceding parable and a following saying it might be seen as an allegorical interpretation. However the authenticity of this whole type of parable need not to be

---

[79] All sayings which speak of ἐλθεῖν of Jesus are under suspicion of being Church products because this terminology seems to be the means of its looking back to the historical appearance of Jesus as a whole [Bultmann, 1931: 155 (ET)].

[80] There seems scholarly consensus on the authenticity of this parable [Bultmann, 1931: 165 (ET); Jeremias, 1962: 160-162 (ET); Marshall, 1978: 297-298; Fitzmyer, 1981: 677]. Luehrmann also assumes that it is not impossible to trace this parable back to Jesus [1969: 29]. However Fiedler casts doubt on whether this parable has been transferred to the post-Easter church without experiencing alteration [1972: 137].

[81] Perrin regards this passage as not an allegory [1967: 86].

called into question.[82] Sometimes a descriptive parable could precede a saying which it illustrates. The parable of two sons in Matt 21:28-32 takes the same shape. The meaning of this parable (Matt 11:17; Luke 7:32) would have remained enigmatic or an embarrassment unless a proper explanation was given (Matt 11:18-19; Luke 7:33-34). Otherwise hardly any meaning could emerge from this parable. The audience could not properly understand what is wrong with this generation for saying the words in the parable Matt 11:16-17; Luke 7:32; children can easily blame their playmates when playing a game. The unity of the two parts is clearly manifested. The parable illustrates clearly how the stubborn Israelites, depicted as unresponsive children (Matt 11:17; Luke 7:32), excuse themselves from repentance by denigrating John and Jesus (Mart 11:18-19; Luke 7:33-34).

4.2.b. (3.1.b) seems to be a much too tendentious interpretation. Luehrmann argues extensively for the polemic use of τὴν γενεὰν ταύτην. He argues that this term refers to "Jesus' contemporaries" and, at the same time, to "all the human race" who are asked to accept the proclamation of the kingdom [Luehrmann, 1969: 29-31]. According to Luehrmann Matt 12:40-42; Luke 11:30-32 points to "all the human race" [1969: 31]; Matt 11:6; Luke 7:23 is drawn on to support his argument. However γενεά points to only Jesus' contemporaries, not to the human race in general [Buechsel, 1933: 663[83]; Graesser, 1957: 128-129; Kuemmel, 1956: 61 (ET)]. Thus Luehrmann's argument remains unconvincing. The examples he cites turn against his argument. τὴν

---

[82] Although Jesus' parables are usually not provided with an application Perrin regards this parable as authentic and as an exception, different from ordinary parables [1967: 86].

[83] "In NT it mostly denotes 'generation' in the sense of contemporaries". "In the role played by γενεά in the sayings of Jesus we can see this comprehensive purpose — He is aiming at the whole people and not at individuals — and His view of Solidarity in sin."

γενεὰν ταύτην indicates a specific group of people, “this” generation (Deut 32:5:“...a perverse and crooked generation” ; Ps 78:4:“the coming generation”), not the “human race”. Matt 1:17 also stresses the division :between each generation. Matt 12:41-42; Luke 11:31-32, upon which Luehrmann rests his case substantially, clearly refers to Jesus' contemporaries. Moreover ταύτην also confines the audience of this word to Jesus' contemporaries. The early church would not have made up sayings with the term “generation” which refer to only one generation, their contemporaries. They would have wished to encompass “all the unbelieving people”, as the audience of this saying, including future generations, for the polemic reason Luehrmann and Schulz stress. The Palestinian church would have used an expression like οἱ ἄνθρωποι (τῆς γενεᾶς ταύτης) rather than τῆς γενεᾶς ταύτης.

4.2.c. Luehrmann's argument in (3.1.c) seems not quite convincing. The figure in whom the Q community put faith is Jesus.[84] Hence they would hardly have any need to bring the scurrilous description of John the Baptist into this conflict which emerged over the issue of the acceptance or rejection of Jesus. They would have intended to focus on describing Jesus.

Similarly Schulz argues that the Q community expects John and Jesus to be judges of the unbelieving Jews [1972: 383, 386]. That argument is unconvincing.[85] Christians would hardly have expected John

---

[84] Luehrmann argues that the conflict between John and Jesus is missing probably because both of them stand against Israel [1969: 31]. He claims that putting John the Baptist as a person against Israel is a characteristic of Q [ibid]. Schulz concurs with Luehrmann [1972: 386].

[85] Although Luehrmann and Schulz argue that the Q community uses the description on John and Jesus for polemical purpose against the people of Israel they do not explain the source of this description. The Q community could have used a genuine tradition on John and Jesus for polemical use later. Q could have contained Jesus' sayings [Harnack, 1907: 249-250 (ET); T. W. Manson, 1948:12-13:

as their judge: only (God) and Jesus are the judge in his coming (John 5:30; 8:16; 8:50; 12:48; 1 Cor 11:31; 11:32; 2 Tim 4: 1; Heb 10:30; Heb 13:4). Saints (1 Cor 6:2) and Christians (1 Cor 6:3) judge, but not John the Baptist.

Luehrmann traces Matt 11:7b-9; Luke 7:24b-26 (27) back to Jesus because of this passage's positive description of John the Baptist [1969: 27]. If we follow that logic it would be reasonable to accept the authenticity of Matt 11:18-19; Luke 7:34- 35 because Jesus recognizes John positively in this saying.[86]

The unique feature in Matt 11:18-19; Luke 7:33-34, the absence of rivalry between John and Jesus[87] could affirm its primitiveness, hence support the authenticity.[88] Jesus' placing John on an equality with himself whereas the primitive Church always emphasized the subordination of John could support the authenticity of Matt 11:18-19; Luke 7:34-35 [Jeremias, 1962: 160 (ET); 1971: 46-49 (ET); Perrin, 1967: 120].[89] Accounts in John and Acts describe the rivalry between the disciples of

---

Bornkamm, 1958: 759, Toedt, 1963: 247-249]. Luehrmann dates Q around A.D. 50 to 60 [1969: 88], the time parallel to the beginning, of the Gentile mission of the early church.

86 Contrary to Schulz this saying seems not to reflect how the Q community understands Israel's rejection of their prophets, from the O.T. to John and Jesus, because Jesus differentiates John from the O.T. prophets (Matt 11:12; Luke 16:16) [Stanton, 1989: 173].

87 Bultmann [1931: 165 (ET)].

88 "The early church had an understandable tendency to subordinate the Baptist to Jesus" "All the sayings that betray such a high estimate of the Baptist are certainly authentic. The early church, which had to compete with communities of followers of John the Baptist, did not invent anything of this kind." [Jeremias, 1971: 47 (ET)].

89 However Hahn argues that the Baptist is here neither witness nor competitor of Jesus is not sufficient evidence of authenticity [1963a: 44]. Fiedler concurs with Hahn's view [1976: 417]

John the Baptist and Jesus (e.g. John 3:25-27; 4:1; Act 11:16). In the following sayings Jesus gives high regards to John the Baptist; Mark 11:30 (John's baptism is from God), Matt 21:32 (John's coming in the righteousness), Matt 11:11; Luke 7:28 (the greatest of all men). Some members of the early church in Ephesus (Hellenistic area) were baptized with the name of John the Baptist's name (Acts 19:3). Hence, the early church would have been reluctant to have even enemies describe John as possessed.

4.2.d. Contrary to Bultmann's argument (3.1.d) ὁ υἱός τοῦ ἀνθρώπου is hardly secondary. Jesus could have referred to himself with ὁ υἱός τοῦ ἀνθρώπου.[90] Bultmann also wavers.[91] Following Vielhauer [1965: 125-127] Schulz vigorously opposes this argument: this Son of Man title does not deliver the power of the earthly Jesus [Schulz, 1972: 383 n 40]. Hoffmann also argues that Q ascribes the power of Jesus to that of the Son of Man in almost all cases [1969: 135]. However that feature draws attention to something characteristic of Jesus. Jesus could have used this term because of his utmost modest attitude, identifying himself with ordinary people, and his intention, not to reveal his greatness (Messiahship). This term captures his intention. At the same time the idiom "son of man" could also echo the determination of a prophet who

---

[90] T. W. Manson, 1948: 70-71; Kuemmel, 1956: 39, 46 (ET); Schniewind 1954:146; Jeremias, 1962: 160 (ET); Fuller, 1965: 128; Vermes, 1967: 314; 1973: 182, 260 n 77; Marshall, 1978: 302-303; O'Neill, 1980; 104, 107, 112]. Perrin directs attention to Gen. Rab. 7. 2, 3 [1967: 120]. See Freedman's translation [1939: 50]. O'Neill directs attention to y. Ber. 1:2. See Zahavy's translation of Jerusalem Talmud [1989: 35].

[91] "There is no *a priori* objection against the possibility that Jesus should have spoken of himself and his coming in the first person. After all, that would accord with his prophetic selfconsciousness." [Bultmann, 1931: 153 (ET)]. "Yet as individual sayings they rouse a number of suspicions." [ibid].

wants to fulfil the solemn responsibility of calling Israel to repentance despite all anticipated sufferings. "The son of man" in this passage seems like one of the best cases in which Jesus refers to himself. Contrary to Schulz the son of man in this text is not painted with any apocalyptic feature. Hence this term does not fit the category Schulz intends to put it in.[92] The use of this term seems to be perfectly natural. Obviously Schulz does not cover the research on the "son of man" done after Vielhauer [Schulz, 1972: 382]. However even if we do not take into account recent developments, the "son of man" in this passage is peculiar in its non-apocalyptic and non-doctrinal features: one nicknamed a glutton and a drunkard, a friend of tax collectors and sinners. The theme of the rejection of the son of man could shed new light on this enquiry. Bayer [1985: 212] lists sayings on the rejection of the son of man: in Luke 6:22 "mankind" rejects, in 7:34 the "generation" does (v. 31), in 9:22 "Jewish authorities" do, in 9:58 "the world" does and in 11:29, 30 again "this generation" does. Among them "Jewish authorities" in Luke 9:22 could refer to the contemporary Jewish authorities at the time of Jesus. What rejects Jesus in Luke 9:58 is not "the world"; but he takes on the destiny of a fully determined faithful traveling prophet who wants to share the suffering of his people willingly. This list seems to comprise two intrinsically different types of sayings. "Generation" in Luke 7:34; 11:29, 30 is distinguished from "mankind", people in general, in Luke 6:22. The former could have come from Jesus, the latter from the early church. The son of man in Matt 11; 18; Luke 7:34 seems to belong to the former.

---

[92] In light of Bultmann's argument Schulz assumes that only the apocalyptic Son of Man can be traced back to the historic earthly Jesus. Against the earlier material the title "Son of Man" here in Q is not apocalyptic, henceforth, hardly ascribed to the earthly Jesus [Schulz, 1972: 382]. At this point Schulz argues that this passage stems from the Hellenistic Jewish Church which awaits the imminent end. The exalted (- present) Jesus, the coming Sort of Man, is ascribed to this old Palestinian Q community. The Hellenistic-Jewish Christian community ascribes the apocalyptic Son of Man title to the earthly Jesus.

4.2.e. Bultmann's argument on ἦλθεν seems unconvincing[93] because ἐλήλυθεν (Matt ἦλθεν) is also used to describe John the Baptist's coming (Luke 7:33; Matt 11:18). Bultmann also admits that it could have come from an Aramaic equivalent which refers to "I come" or "I am there" [1931: 156 (ET)].[94] Further ἦλθεν could not only mean "come" but also "appear, come before the public" [BAGD: 310-311]. Jesus could have said "I came before the public eating and drinking; then they say, 'Behold this man is a glutton and drunkard, friend of tax collectors and sinners'".

4.3. Jesus' consorting with sinners and tax collectors in Matt 11:19; Luke 7:34 coheres with Mark 2:13-17 and par. Schulz also recognizes the close relation between this passage and Mark 2:15-17; Matt 10-13; Luke 5:29-32 [1972: 384]. Nevertheless Schulz stresses the fundamental difference in the traditions between Q and the Marcan text [1972: 384]. But this view turns against his main argument. Jesus' consorting with sinners,[95] multiply attested in mutually independent traditions, support the

---

[93] Marshall [1978: 302] directs our attention to Colpe [1969: 431 n 238]. Fuller affirms that Jesus could have spoken of himself and his coming in the first person (ἦλθον) (cf Luke 12:49; Mark 2:17; Matt 15:24) [1965: 127-128].

[94] Bultmann states that "Naturally it is always possible to ask whether such a phrase were possible to Jesus himself" while remaining sceptical of this possibility. See Montefiore on 5:17 [1927: vol. 2: 47].

[95] T. W. Manson affirms that "Friend of publicans and sinners" was true enough. But the quality of the friendship was determined by Jesus and not by the publicans and sinners: it raised them without lowering him [1948: 71]. Further Schulz correctly points out that "Sinners and tax collectors" still assumes the Palestinian setting: no law-free mission to the Gentiles [1972: 383]. Braun also affirm the authenticity of Jesus' consorting with sinners: "Behold, a glutton and a drunkard, a friend of tax collectors and sinners" (Matt 11:19 par., RSV), is surely not a formulation by the community but an early tradition, Jesus did live as a friend of religious and social outcasts." [1969: 114 (ET)].

authenticity.

4.4. In conclusion, Matt 11:18-19; Luke 7:33-35 contains Jesus' advocacy of John the Baptist, not the understanding of the Q community on the judgment of the hostile Jewish people who never responded to the call of John and Jesus. Matt 11:18-19; Luke 7:33-35 coheres with the preceding saying Matt 11:11-15; Luke 7:28-30, 16:16, Jesus' advocacy of the authority of his colleague prophet John the Baptist. A similar idea is also attested in Mark 11:27-32. This double attestation in mutually independent traditions, Q and Mark, could support the authenticity,

5.

5.1. The main thrust of this saying

The parable of children's game (Matt 11:16-17; Luke 7:31-32) already implies the national repentance of Israel. τὴν γενεὰν ταύτην (Matt 11:16; Luke 7:31) could refer to all Israelites. And this term has a pejorative connotation (cf. Luke 9:41; 11:29-32, 50-51; Act 2:40) [Fitzmyer, 1981: 679]. Children are supposed to be naive, they are supposed to accept the Kingdom of God gladly with a pure mind (Mark 10:15). But here they are depicted as indifferent like the Israelites who need repentance. Accordingly this saying refers to the national repentance of Israel. The children calling their colleagues represent the unrepentant passive Jewish people at the time of Jesus who just sit and watch to see the more strenuous performance of their playmates [Bishop, 1955: 104; Jeremias, 1962: 161 (ET)]. What is worse is that they blame their playmates because they did not act according to what they initiated. They could be like people who always make their decisions first and then insist that others follow. They simply judge upon the basis of their narrow subjective superficial observation and interpretation without a sympathetic attitude and careful attention to the activities of their colleagues. In this passage Israelites are like them. John and Jesus are depicted as their playmates [Jeremias, 1962: 161]. They did not carefully enquire what John's ascetic life and Jesus' sympathetic attitude toward sinners symbolize. When John the Baptist fasts they want to make him eat: when Jesus eats with sinners they want to make him quit. Constantly the Israelites expose their capriciousness; whether they eat or do not eat John and Jesus are destined to be criticized. Their criteria is their capriciousness. Hence this saying implies that the Israelites must repent

5.2. The bearing on the forgiveness of sins

Sanders regards this passage as having a ring of authenticity [1985: 179], but he does not think the present passage is a *verbatim* account. However Sanders concurs with the idea that Jesus associated with the wicked and was criticized for it. It is noteworthy that Sanders assumes close agreement of John and Jesus on the main task [1985: 92]. Sanders does not specify the nature of the main task of these two men. However in the preceding sentence within the same paragraph he casts "no doubt on the depiction of John as an eschatological preacher" [1985: 92]. From this sentence it can be conjectured that Sanders indirectly admits Jesus was also doing the same task, as John, the calling of repentance. The authenticity of this passage seems to be firm. Sanders puts forward Matt 21:32; 11:18 as grounds for distinction on the question of repentance and sinners between John's message from Jesus' message [1985: 206]. However these two passages do not seem to provide the conclusion Sanders wants to draw. Certainly many other passages give different picture of the role of Jesus. Jesus' saying on John's coming in the way of righteousness (Matt 21:31-32) does not count against the view that Jesus proclaimed the same message as John. "John the preacher of repentance, was not accused on the grounds that Jesus was" [Sanders, 1985: 206] does not prove that Jesus was different from John. Sanders has not produced good reasons for his conclusion that John was "the spokesman for repentance and righteousness ordinarily understood" and that Jesus was "the proclaimer of the inclusion of the wicked who heeded him" [1985: 206]. "The message of Jesus is not only the proclamation of salvation, but also the announcement of judgment, a cry of warning and a call to repentance in view of the terrible, urgency of the crisis." [Jeremias, 1962: 160 (ET)]. To sum up, Jesus calls for the national repentance of Israel with this saying.

E. Did Jesus call for national repentance in Matt 11:21-23a; Luke 10:13-15?

1. The conjectured original text

Matt 11:21 Οὐαί σοι, Χοραζίν, οὐαί σοι, Βηθσαϊδά· ὅτι εἰ ἐν Τύρῳ καὶ Σιδῶνι ἐγένοντο αἱ δυνάμεις αἱ γενόμεναι ἐν ὑμῖν, πάλαι ἂν ἐν σάκκῳ καὶ σποδῷ μετενόησαν. 22 πλὴν λέγω ὑμῖν, Τύρῳ καὶ Σιδῶνι ἀνεκτότερον ἔσται ἐν ἡμέρᾳ κρίσεως ἢ ὑμῖν. 23a καὶ σύ, Καφαρναούμ, μὴ ἕως οὐρανοῦ ὑψωθήσῃ; ἕως ᾅδου καταβήσῃ·

Luke 10:13 Οὐαί σοι, Χοραζίν, οὐαί σοι, Βηθσαϊδά ὅτι εἰ ἐν Τύρῳ καὶ Σιδῶνι ἐγενήθησαν αἱ δυνάμεις αἱ γενόμεναι ἐν ὑμῖν, πάλαι ἂν ἐν σάκκῳ καὶ σποδῷ καθήμενοι μετενόησαν. 14 πλὴν Τύρῳ καὶ Σιδῶνι ἀνεκτότερον ἔσται ἐν τῇ κρίσει ἢ ὑμῖν. 15 καὶ σύ, Καφαρναούμ, μὴ ἕως οὐρανοῦ ὑψωθήσῃ; ἕως τοῦ ᾅδου καταβήσῃ.

2. Arguments concerning the excluded parts.

The variants between the two versions are, small and unimportant. The complete saying is taken to be authentic.

ἐγενήθησαν] Luke could have had a translation variant of the word

λέγω ὑμῖν] Luke could have avoided the redundant use of this phrase (Luke 11:12)

ἐν τῇ κρίσει] Luke could have had a translation variant of ἐν ἡμέρᾳ κρίσεως[96]

τοῦ] Luke could have a translation variant.

ὅτι εἰ ἐν Σοδόμοις ἐγενήθησαν αἱ δυνάμεις αἱ γενόμεναι ἐν σοί, ἔμεινεν ἂν μέχρι τῆς σήμερον] Matthew could have added this part in light of v. 24 [Marshall, 1978: 427].

πλὴν λέγω ὑμῖν ὅτι γῇ Σοδόμων ἀνεκτότερον ἔσται ἐν ἡμέρᾳ κρίσεως ἢ σοί] Matthew could have put this floating saying in v. 24 while Luke could have shifted it to v. 12 in a slightly different form.

3. Arguments against the authenticity of 1.

3.1. The authenticity of this passage is suspected "because the condemnation of Israel and praise of Gentiles makes one suspect the activity of the later church (Matt 11:21-24; 12:41f)." [Sanders, 1985: 117].

3.2. Some scholars claim this passage as a community formulation, since the saying looks back on Jesus' activity as something already completed, and presupposes the failure of the Christian preaching in Capernaum [Bultmann, 1931: 112, 151 (ET); Luehrmann, 1969: 62, 64].

3.3. "... the impression is given that both passages have been constructed according to "a scheme of early Christian polemic" [Bultmann, 1931:

---

96 Matt 12:41 has ἐν τῇ κρίσει too. But Kuemmel argues that Matthew with his mention of the day of judgment preserved the more primitive saying [1956: 36 (ET)]. Marshall regards the Lucan text as original [1978: 425; Schulz, 1972; 360-361].

113[97] (ET); Luehrmann, 1969: 63-64; Schulz, 1972: 366].

3.4. The fact that the similar form of Matt 11:22, 24 occurs again in Matt 10:15 only in a slightly modified form could support its spuriousness [Kaesemann, 1965: 95 (ET)]. The scepticism on the authenticity of this passage arises from the point: "...fixed forms of speech are being used to bring to the hearers' consciousness the terrors of the last judgment, like the saying concerning waiting and gnashing of teeth in Gehenna..." (Matt 8:12; 13:42, 50; 22:13; 24:51) [Kaesemann, 1965: 95 (ET)].

3.5. "The reference to the many mighty works which have been done in these towns recalls 7:22f, and the failure which was nevertheless experienced there justifies a saying so clearly in the prophetic vein as 8: 11f...".[Kaesemann, 1965: 100 (ET)].

3.6. The following hypothesis is put forward to argue for the inauthenticity of this saying: the judgment saying against Israel belongs to the later tradition in Q [Schulz, 1972: 362]. This hypothesis seems to be extended from the hypothesis "a scheme of early Christian polemic" [Bultmann, 1931: 113 (ET)]. οὐαί is a clearly prophetic-apocalyptic introduction form; unlike the, old Q-materials, this passage is against the three cities in Galilee [Schulz, 1972: 362]. So this extension of the polemic belongs to the late Q tradition [362] (italics mine). Although the oldest polemical Q tradition against the Pharisees stands in the foreground of the conflict, the later Q tradition stresses the opposition against all

---

[97] "In both cases Gentiles are contrasted with unrepentant Israel, which has refused to have faith in the κήρυγμα or δυνάμεις of Jesus. The structure of the two passages is the same, in that each accusing contrast has two parallel members, and after each of them there is a refrain-like repetition of the reproach: Matt. 12.41, 42: καὶ ἰδοὺ πλεῖον...ὧδε, Matt. 11:22, 24: πλὴν λέγω...ὑμῖν...ἀνεκτότερον ἔσται...."

Israel; "this generation" extends the Polemic [Schulz, 1972: 362[98], 362 n 261; Luehrmann, 1969: 93-94, 93 n 4].

3.7. Jesus would hardly have imagined Capernaum to be exalted to heaven by his activity [Bultmann, 1931; 112 (ET); Wellhausen, 1914: 54[99].].

3.8. The Hellenistic Palestinian church derived ἐν σάκκῳ καὶ σποδῷ from a Jewish idea on repentance (cf. Isa 58:5; Jonah 3:6, Job 2:8; 42:6; Jdt 4:11; 1 Macc 3:47; Pss. Sol. 2:20) [Schulz, 1972: 364].

3.9. Arguments against the authenticity are claimed by some other scholars with or without any additional reasons [Wellhausen, 1904: 54-55[100]; Klostermann, 1927: 100[101]].

4. Arguments against 3.

The authenticity or historicity of this saying depends upon its point of view. Was the fall of Israel seen as an incident that had already occurred or an event coming very soon that had not yet occurred. If the former case is true, this passage could be an inauthentic saying. If the

---

[98] Schulz's argument is supported by Luehrmann [1969: 47]: It must be noted that the apocalyptic curse is directed to warn the Pharisees, not to all Israel.

[99] Wellhausen claims that Capernaum could have been exalted to heaven by Jesus' stay there; but is difficult to think that Jesus felt that.

[100] Wellhausen argues for the inauthenticity on the basis of his hypothesis: according to Mark Jesus failed to draw followers only in Nazareth. In Capernaum Jesus attracted a large following. Hence this Q passage could not have come from the experience of Jesus in Galilee. Probably this saying arose in the post apostolic period.

[101] Klostermann regards this passage as the creation of the early church which presupposes the failure of the Christian preaching in Capernaum.

latter case is true, this passage could be an authentic saying of Jesus. In other words if this passage looks back on the basis of the fall of Israel as having already occurred, this passage was made up on the basis of that past incident by the early church. If this passage looks forward to the coming fall of Israel as an imminent event that could have been avoided Jesus could have said it. After all Fiedler leaves the authenticity of this saying as an open question [1976: 240].

4.1. However the interpretation (3.1) does not take into account of the literary character of this saying. Jesus does not condemn Israel in order to praise the Gentiles. What Jesus intended seems to be to admonish the unrepentant Galileans in his distress over their destiny; Jesus vents his sorrow at their unrepentant attitude by saying that Gentile cities would have repented given the advantages his fellow Jews had enjoyed. One of the ways of expressing love is in affectionate admonition and persuasion aimed at leading sinners into repentance and correction. Sometimes ethics stands upon that foundation, rather than on the foundation of unconditional grace and mercy.

4.2. Contrary to the assumption of (3.2) it is hardly likely that Jesus' disciples or even the missionaries of the early church declared "woe" to the Galileans. Jesus' disciples seems not to have upbraided these Jewish cities in their mission. Their utter disappointment was hardly turned into bitter condemnation. They seem to continue to entreat their fellow Jews to repent and believe in Christ even under persecution (Acts 4:30; 5:41).

4.3. It is much more unlikely that missionaries from the early church condemned Jews in the Galilean cities orally when the residents did not repent. The early church's mission hardly ended up with the curse of the cities, an expression of their frustration. The disciple of Jesus were commanded at most to cast off the dust from their sandals as a sign of the absence of their repentance (Acts 13:51). Accordingly it is hardly likely that the missionaries of the early church upbraided the Galilean cities because the missionaries would not go further than their predecessors, the apostles had done (Matt 10:14; Luke 10:11). Accordingly, it is very likely that only Jesus could utter οὐαὶ and could proclaim these words. "Woe to..." seems to stem from the prophetic rhetoric in the O.T. (e.g. Isa 5:8-22).

4.4. What life setting of the early church does (3.3) presuppose? There seems to be no clear reason to make up this saying in retrospect of the failure of the early church's mission. It is hardly likely that for a simple polemic reason the church would need to make up this saying. What is usually implied by the polemic reason is the assumption that when the early Jewish mission of the early church failed they took it as a reason to reach out to the Gentiles. But the insistence on imposing the Jewish way of repentance on the Gentile cities, ἐν σάκκῳ καὶ σποδῷ μετενόησαν, implies that they still did not completely abandon the Jews: they were still keen on calling their fellow Jews to repent. The lingering adherence to the Jewish way of repentance shows that they still aspire to see the repentance of Israel, even in their comparison of the Jewish cities with those of the Gentiles. Hence this passage does not yet justify the polemic of the early Palestinian church's turning away from the Jews and going to the Gentiles.

4.5 (3.4) seems to be hardly convincing. Kaesemann does not seem to take into account the possibility that Matt 10:15, Matt 11:22, 24 (Luke 10:12, 14) could have been transmitted as an isolated saying of Jesus.[102]

4.6. Contrary to Kaesemann's argument this passage seems to be

[102] The minor textual variation could have occurred at the time of translation from Aramaic. In view of the argument that one of the unique features of Jesus' saying is their brevity this hypothesis could be reasonable.

distinctively different from a refrain in Matt 6:4, 8, 18 where the eschatological *jus talionis is* again proclaimed [Kaesemann, 1965; 95 (ET)]. Kaesemann's claim that "Only a false conception of inspiration as resulting in an uncontrolled outburst of feeling can enter this in evidence against the presence of prophecy here" seems to be overcritical [Kaesemann, 1965: 95 (ET)].

4.7. It is not reasonable to exclude every possibility that proclamations of a judgmental character in the synoptic gospels could have come from the pre-Easter Jesus. Jesus could have proclaimed judgment and punishment in many parts of his sayings. Kaesemann's statement "From the point of view of the N.T., even the use of the concept "poetical" is thoroughly inappropriate"[Kaesemann, 1965: 95 (ET)] seems also to be overdone.[103] Certainly the N.T. is not a book of poems. However in view of the fact that parallelism is one of the literary forms in the Jewish Hellenistic literature and in the O.T. Jesus could have used this literary form.

4.8. What Kaesemann implies in his argument (3.5) is that Jesus could have spoken this passage if the authenticity of Matt 8:11f is confirmed.[104] There seems to be scholarly consensus on the authenticity of this passage. Luehrmann also confirms its authenticity [1969: 93 n 4]. Thus this passage could be regarded as capturing the prophetic vein of Jesus' proclamation. Kaesemann's reluctant conclusion sufficiently illustrates how keenly he feels about the force of the opposite argument: "This is genuine apocalyptic which, without throwing any doubt on the seriousness with which Jesus himself preached judgment, we ought nevertheless to ascribe rather to the community after Easter." [1965: 100

[103] Burney [1925: 77, 83; Jeremias, 1971: 14-15 (ET)]. Contrary to Kaesemann Jeremias counts parallelism for the evidence of authenticity.

[104] Bultmann thinks that it is difficult to reach a firm conclusion on Matt 8:11f [1931: 128 (ET)].

(ET)] (italics mine).

4.9. Contrary to (3.6) this passage seems not to have emerged from the catechetical need of the early church [Davies, 1964: 386] or the concern over the rules of behaviour [Toedt, 1963: 246-247 (ET)]. It is very plausible that the so called common source in Matthew and Luke could contain sayings of the historical Jesus. Contrary to Schulz [1976: 362] the non-Marcan material commonly appearing in Matt and Luke could contain sayings of the historical Jesus [Davies, 1966: 383[105]; 1966: 126-129].

4.10. Just the opposite of (3.6) seems to be the case.[106] One of the criteria of distinguishing an authentic saying of Jesus from that of the early church is to check whether a saying has an eschatological connotation [Bultmann, 1931: 205 (ET)]. Thus the eschatological feature in ἐν ἡμέρᾳ κρίσεως (ἐν τῇ κρίσει) could support authenticity.

4.11. The early church could have collected eschatological sayings of

---

[105] "It seems clear from Q that, before and apart from the catechetical usage of the primitive Church, which did draw upon the words of Jesus along with other material for its purposes, the Church had preserved a tradition of the ethical teaching of Jesus which it regarded as in itself part of the crisis wrought in his coming.... Q sets the ethical teaching of Jesus in its utterly radical or critical context as part of the drawing near of the kingdom, that is, that teaching is not primarily a catechetical necessity or an addendum to the Gospel but itself part of the Gospel... the ethical teaching of Jesus in Q was preserved not merely as catechetically useful, and not only as a radical demand, but as revelatory: *it illumines the nature and meaning of the coming of the Kingdom as demand, which is concomitant of the coming Kingdom as grace*." (italics mine). cf. Stanton [1973: 40].

[106] Schrage [1982: 122 (ET)] clarifies the complicated issue correctly. "But there were collections of Jesus' sayings at a very early date. This is documented above all by the Q source used by Matthew and Luke, which represents a collection of sayings and saying complexes."

Jesus. The purpose of this collection could be to give ethical teachings appropriate to members in their life setting in the course of reshaping the preserved sayings of the historical Jesus. Accordingly, a flat rejection of the possibility of a collection of sayings of the historical Jesus seems to be off the target. It is much more likely that Jesus' eschatological sayings would be collected as traditions.

4.12. It is generally agreed that there are accounts where the early church ascribes the conflict situation to the Pharisee or Sadduccees. On the contrary there seems to be hardly any case of the sayings being made up about the opposition or warning against all Israel or "this generation". Accordingly, it would be more reasonable to say that the sayings of the historical Jesus against all Israel or this generation, which call for national repentance, could be in the oldest layer in the material commonly embedded in Matt and Luke. It is possible that the early church repeated[107] what the historical Jesus proclaimed for their situation, for the exhortation of the members [Toedt, 1963: 247; Uro, 1987: 162-168].

4.13. Contrary to the assumption in (3.7), what Matt 11:21 points out seems to be the unrepentant haughty attitude of the people in Capernaum; there seems to be no sign that Jesus meant to exalt this arrogant city to heaven by his presence.

4.14. Tyre and Sidon are Israel's enemies (Isa 23:1-13; Jer 25:22, 27; 27:3-6; 47:4; Ezek 26-27; 28:20-23; Zech 9:3-4; 1 Macc 5:15; Jdt 2:28; Sib. Or. Book 4. 90). They sold Jews to Greeks (Joel 3:4-8). Therefore

---

[107] Schrage [1982: 122 (ET)]: "...the word of the earthly Jesus were obviously collected because they were felt to provide binding guidelines for Christian living," "The crucial element is *the eschatological motivation of the sayings since Q is concerned primarily to continue preaching the eschatological message of Jesus.*" [123] (italics mine). Bultmann also assumes that the early church collected and reshaped the synoptic tradition [1948: 33 (ET)].

the early church would have been very reluctant to describe these Gentiles cities as exalted over the Jewish cities, Chorazin, Bethsaida and Capernaum, even in an imaginary setting. Prophets alone could have foretold the future of Israel in comparison with the Gentile nations (Jer 25:8-9). Hence this kind of prophetic message could hardly have been expected from others but only from a prophetic figure, like Jesus.[108]

4.15. One of the most convincing counter arguments against Bultmann seems to be made by Dunn [1975: 70-71]. Dunn puts forward four reasons as evidence of authenticity: Firstly, "The tradition of Jesus' miraculous activity in the area of the Sea of Galilee is too firmly established in the traditions" because "Jesus' reputation as a miracle worker comes to us in explicitly charismatic terms and is clearly present in our earliest sources" (Acts 2:22; 10:38; Mark 6:2, 5, 14; cf. I Cor 12:10, 28f, Gal 3:5; 2 Cor 12:12). Accordingly δυνάμεις could echo Jesus' miraculous activity in Galilee. Secondly, this passage is the only place which shows Jesus himself describing his ministry in terms of his mighty works. Thirdly, this passage "is hardly inconsistent with Jesus' other apocalyptic utterances". Fourthly, seemingly the most important reason, there are hardly any accounts where the early Christian mission claimed the performance of δυνάμεις as the reason for prophetic judgment. Dunn argues that these arguments show how deeply this reputation of Jesus as a charismatic miracle-worker is rooted in the earliest tradition of Jesus: "...Jesus saw himself as a Spirit-inspired exorcist and healer if the words of Matt 11:21 go back to Jesus, as seem most probable. They confirm that Jesus saw himself as a charismatic, a

---

[108] Hahn's argument seems to be convincing: "Thus the places that have been condemned as godless according to Old Testament judgment will fare better than the townships of Israel that have experienced Jesus's words and works, but have rejected him. Such an antithetical reference to the Old Testament is intelligible only in the mouth of Jesus himself..." [1965: 34]. I do not quite agree with Hahn's term "antithetical"; however I agree with his main thesis.

worker of miracles." [cf. Vermes 1973: 79].

4.16. It is noteworthy that this passage does not mention faith in Jesus, upon which the early Christian mission would base judgment or blessing. To put it more forcefully, the missionaries of the early Church would upbraid Jewish cities when they did not believe in Christ who had risen, not because of the absence of repentance after having seen the miracles done. In this passage Jesus does not ask the Galileans to believe in him, Thus this argument could support the view that the early church is unlikely to have made up this saying.

4.17. (3.8) remains unconvincing. It is unlikely that the Hellenistic church made up this saying because, the use of terms drawn from the Jewish way of repentance; they would not describe the people in Tyre and Sidon as repenting in ἐν σάκκῳ and σποδῷ. It must be noted that the Jerusalem council tried to avoid putting a yoke upon the neck of the Gentiles as much as possible (Acts 15:10). Peter said that God cleansed the Gentiles' heart by faith (Acts 15:9). There is no account that the Jerusalem Council decided the Gentiles had to follow the Jewish way of repentance; it does not stipulate the way of doing repentance (Acts 15:29). For the Gentiles, only faith would be required as the sign of repentance.

4.18. (3.9) seems to be unlikely. The Hellenistic Palestinian church would hardly have wished to irritate either the Hellenistic or Jewish faction of their church with this imaginary description.

4.19. Further, it is more likely that even in the Hellenistic Jewish church Jewish ideas still dominates their religious life. If they were so committed to the Jewish way, enough to describe the Gentiles as following their way of repentance, they would not put the Jewish cities βεθσαϊδα and Χοραζίν to shame by contrast with the Gentile cities like Τύρῳ and Σιδῶνι, the enemy of Israel.

4.20. The account that many people came to Jesus from Tyre and Sidon (Mark 3:8; Luke 6:17) or Jesus' trip to these cities (Matt 15:21; Mark 7:24; 31) could support its authenticity.

4.21. The mention of Capernaum could also support the authenticity. This city is an important place where Jesus taught and healed (Matt 8:5; Luke 7:1; Matt 17:24; Mark 1:21; Luke, 4:31; Mark 2:1, 9:33; Luke 4:23; John 2:12, 4:46; 6:17, 24, 59). Jesus lived in Capernaum (Matt 4:13). Jesus entered Capernaum and healed the servant of the centurion and the mother-in-law of Peter (Matt 8:5-13, 14-17; Luke 7:1-10). People in Capernaum were amazed at Jesus' reaching of authority (Mark 1:21-22; Luke 4:31-37). Jesus cast out the unclean spirit from the possessed man (Mark 1:23-28). Jesus also healed the paralytic assisted by his friends (Mark 2:1-12). Jesus foretold what the people in Nazareth would ask him to do, what he did in Capernaum (Luke 4:23). Luke 4:23 affirms the success of Jesus' activities in Capernaum. All these accounts seems to confirm how Capernaum has a close connection with Jesus. Accordingly this passage could be rooted in an earlier tradition and could well have been the basis of an admonition of the historical Jesus to the Galilean cities.

4.22. Χοραζίν appears only here in the N.T. Hence it could hint its early tradition. Although the name of the region Χοραζίν is not known with certainty, this does not necessarily indicate that it is an editorial addition because the pre-Lucan tradition could have passed on this saying including the local reference. Moreover, Χοραζίν does not figure elsewhere in the early Jesus-tradition; thus it may be a good evidence for attributing these woes to Jesus himself [Jeremias, 1956: 50 n 1 (ET); Fitzmyer, 1996: 852]. Χοραζίν, βηθσαϊδά, Καφαρναούμ seem to have come as a fixed ideal tradition.[109]

4.23. The Aramaism in ἕως οὐρανοῦ ὑψωθήσῃ [Wellhausen, 1914: 55; Jeremias, 1956: 50 (ET)] could also support the authenticity of this passage.

4.24. After reading the arguments for and against the authenticity of this saying carefully Cabraja concludes that this saying seemingly arises from the reaction of Jesus to success as a result of his powerful activities and the rejection of his work by the people in the Galilean towns [1985: 47].

4.25. In contrast to (3.9) some scholars regard this passage as authentic saying of Jesus with or without putting forward significant reasons [J. Weiss, 1917: 308; Dodd, 1930: 61[110]; W. Manson, 1930: 124; 1943: 36; J. M. Robinson, 1959: 109-110; Fenton, 1963: 182; Caird, 1963: 143; Toedt, 1963: 246 (ET); Kuemmel, 1972: 32[111], 43, 62 (ET); H. B. Green, 1975: 118-119; Maish, 1975: 31; Schweizer, 1973: 266[112] (ET); Marshall, 1979: 427; B. Meyer, 1979; 158[113]; Mussner, 1979: 213 (ET);

---

109 Bultmann, [1931: 65 (ET)]: "... it is still not impossible for the early tradition itself to have passed on this or the other apophthegm complete with localization."

110 Dodd accepts Matt 11:23; Luke10:17 as the eschatological proclamation of Jesus.

111 "Nevertheless we have enough of Jesus' individual sayings which show that he announced God's severe judgment:" " On the day of judgment it will be more tolerable for Tyre and Sidon than for you" (Matt 11:22 par.)".

112 Schweizer argues that Jesus might well have said only 21-22. However, there seem to be no clear reason excluding v 23a.

113 "Moreover, the two panel schemes is typical of Jesus."

Grundmann, 1981: 211; Davies, 1964: 383; Fitzmyer, 1986: 850[114], 852; Schrage, 1982: 23, 41[115] (ET); Uro, 1989: 163-168; Schnackenburg, 1985: 103-104; Gnilka, 1986: 427, 430[116]].

5.

5.1. The main thrust of this saying

Jesus could have performed mighty works (δυνάμεις) to lead the Galileans to repent: The mighty works include miracles. The eschatological healer could ask for ethical reformation.[117] What the Galileans failed to perceive from Jesus' mighty works was that his mighty works are the sign of the coming eschatological kingdom which asks for

---

[114] "...the Woes are hardly pertinent to the work expected of the disciples in the mission charge."

[115] "Although the coming of God's kingdom is the real motive for repentance, even Jesus can call to repentance in the context of threatened judgment, although the judgment is not so much the motive for repentance as the consequence of refusing to repent (in addition to Mark 13: lff., see Matt. 11:20ff., the series of woes over the cities that did not repent)."

[116] Gnilka states that the call of "woe" (21f) and "judgment" presupposes the work of the historical Jesus [1986: 430]. Further, contrary to Bultmann, he thinks that the judgment is aimed at the cities which refused Jesus' work, not to the later Christian mission.

[117] H. C. Kee [1986: 1251:"Although *the primary importance of a miracle* in the New Testament is that of eschatological sign....This leads to a second observation: the role of Jesus as healer was by no means an accommodation of an itinerant preacher-prophet to Hellenistic culture, but was in *direct continuity with O.T. prophetic understanding of what God was going to do in the New Age,* for the salvation of his people and for the healing of the nations." "One of the basic images *for the divine renewal of the creation* is, in keeping with the O.T. tradition, *healing* (1 Enoch 10:7)." [72]. "...the plan of Yahweh the Healer is being achieved through the *signs* that God's agent perform. The first paradigmatic agent is Jesus then, by the power, he bestows his followers as well." [Kee, 1986: 126] (italics mine).

repentance of the individuals and the whole of Israel.[118] But in these towns they resisted accepting this solemn sign; as a result the Galileans were to meet the judgment of God. In face of this disastrous negligence Jesus could proclaim this saying to rescue them from the destined judgment. As a Jew who read the O.T. with piety Jesus could have said these words, standing in the prophetic tradition (Amos 6:4-7; Mic 2:1 Hab 2:6-7; Zeph 2:5).

5.2. The bearing on the forgiveness of sin

To sum up, contrary to the way Sanders reads the passage, Matt 11:21-23a (Luke 10:13-15) could be a genuine saying of Jesus calling for the repentance of the Galileans; this call is almost equivalent to the call for the national repentance of Israel.

---

[118] Caird [1963: 143]: "The judgment of Jesus is pronounced against whole towns and cities, which implies that he is looking for a *corporate* rather than an individual response to the gospel message." Fenton [1963: 183]: "The miracles were evidence that the kingdom was coming, so the response to the miracles should have been the same as the response which is called for by the preaching of the kingdom...." [italics mine].

F. What did Jesus want to teach in Matt 18:12-14; Luke 15:4-7?

1. The conjectured original text

Matt 18:12 Τί ὑμῖν δοκεῖ; ἐὰν γένηταί τινι ἀνθρώπῳ ἑκατὸν πρόβατα καὶ πλανηθῇ ἓν ἐξ αὐτῶν, οὐχὶ ἀφήσει τὰ ἐνενήκοντα ἐννέα ἐπὶ τὰ ὄρη καὶ πορευθεὶς ζητεῖ τὸ πλανώμενον; 13 καὶ ἐὰν γένηταί εὑρεὶν αὐτό, ἀμὴν λέγω ὑμῖν ὅτι χαίρει ἐπ' αὐτῷ μᾶλλον ἢ ἐπὶ τοῖς ἐνενήκοντα ἐννέα τοῖς μὴ πεπλανημένοις.

Matt 18:14 οὕτως οὐκ ἔστιν θέλημα ἔμπροσθεν τοῦ πατρὸς ὑμῶν τοῦ ἐν οὐρανοῖς ἵνα ἀπόληται ἓν τῶν μικρῶν τούτων.

Luke 15:4 Τίς ἄνθρωπος ἐξ ὑμῶν ἔχων ἑκατὸν πρόβατα καὶ ἀπολέσας ἐξ αὐτῶν ἓν οὐ καταλείπει τὰ ἐνενήκοντα ἐννέα ἐν τῇ ἐρήμῳ καὶ πορεύεται ἐπὶ τὸ ἀπολωλὸς ἕως εὕρῃ αὐτό; 5 καὶ εὑρὼν ἐπιτίθησιν ἐπὶ τοὺς ὤμους αὐτοῦ χαίρων 6 καὶ ἐλθὼν εἰς τὸν οἶκον συγκαλεῖ τοὺς φίλους καὶ τοὺς γείτονας λέγων αὐτοῖς Συγχάρητέ μοι, ὅτι εὗρον τὸ πρόβατόν μου τὸ ἀπολωλός.

Luke 15:7 λέγω ὑμῖν ὅτι οὕτως χαρὰ ἐν τῷ οὐρανῷ ἔσται ἐπὶ ἑνὶ ἁμαρτωλῷ μετανοοῦντι ἢ ἐπὶ ἐνενήκοντα ἐννέα δικαίοις οἵτινες οὐ χρείαν ἔχουσιν μετανοίας.

2. Arguments concerning the excluded parts

Nothing is excluded. In regards to the original text two opposite arguments contend with each other. The Matthean text, more primitive in its vocabulary and structure, is the original against the Lucan text [Harnack, 1907: 92-93 (ET); Bultmann, 1931: 171[119] (ET); Klostermann,

[119] "Luke's fuller form seems secondary to me, and the force of the parable gains nothing by the filling out."

1929: 156; Braun, 1957, vol. 2: 34 n 3; Linnemann, 1969: 67-68 (ET); Petersen, 1981: 142-144; Fitzmyer, 1986: 1074]. On the contrary the Lucan text is claimed to be original [Montefiore, 1927, vol 2: 679; Derrett, 1979: 59; Jeremias, 1962: 40 (ET); Schweizer, 1973: 366 (FT)].

However it would be a more cogent to say that the marked difference between the Matthean and Lucan text comes from two independent traditions [Streeter, 1927: 185, 265; T. W. Manson, 1948: 208[120]; W. L. Knox, 1957: 89[121]; Marshall, 1978: 600-601[122]].

3. Arguments against the authenticity of 1.

Some scholars regard Luke 15:7; Matt 18:14 as secondary with or without particular arguments.

3.1. "But admittedly the application in Matt. 18.14 is also secondary for it narrows down the original meaning in saying that no member of the Christian community will be lost, and gives no expression to the joy over finding the lost, which is nevertheless the essential feature of the similitude." [Bultmann, 1931: 171 (ET)].

3.2. a. Luke 15:7 is secondary [Juelicher, 1899: 323; Braun, 1957: 34 n 3; Conzelmann, 1957: 111 (ET); Linnemann, 1964: 17[123], 68 (ET);

---

120 T. W. Manson argues that the independent saying Luke 15:7 is different and perhaps more original [1948: 209].

121 "the wording differs as widely as it could.... This might suggest that Matthew is following a different source, especially as he omits the parable of the lost coin."

122 "..it is on the whole more likely that Luke has preserved the original ending of the parable and the Matthew has abbreviated it in order to introduce his v. 14."

123 Linnemann reads Luke 15:7 as an application of the parable.

Fiedler, 1976: 220-222; Schweizer, 1982: 245 (ET)[124]; Sanders, 1985: 175[125], 179, 203].

b. Luke 15:7 is secondary: "...one is driven to the conclusion that the application in Lk. 15.7 is also a secondary formulation, echoing the original ending (Matt. 18.13b)." [Bultmann, 1931: 171 (ET)]. Somewhat differently Schottroff regards Luke 15:7 as a later addition for the following reasons.

c. The focus in Luke 15:4-6, which primarily lies in the shepherd's action to seek the lost sheep, does not go with that of v. 7, the repentance of the sinner [Schottroff, 1971: 33]. The tension between the parable and its application lead to a conclusion that two intrinsically different pericopes stem from different authors [Schottroff, 1971: 33].

d. Luke generalized the Jesus tradition in Mark 2:17b into Luke 15:7 according to his theological framework (e.g. 5:32f) where he brought in his idea of salvation by repentance [Schottroff, 1971: 34].

e. Luke 15:7 belongs to the same category of editorial asides in which Luke criticizes the self-righteous attitude (Luke 10:29; 16:15; 18:9; 20:20) [Schottroff, 1971:34-35].[126] ἤ has the exclusive meaning [Schottroff, 1971:34-35].

4. Arguments against 3.

---

124 Luke 15:7 hardly belongs to the parable for its lack of coherency.

125 "One may also note as dubious Luke's conclusion to the Parable of the Lost Sheep (joy over one sinner who repents, Luke 15.7), which is an edifying remark not present in the Matthean parallel (Matt 18.10-14)."

126 The ninety-nine appear righteous, but in fact they never think of repentance as necessary.

There seems to be scholarly consensus on the authenticity of Matt 18:12-13; Luke 15:4-6 [T. W. Manson, 1948: 282-283; Derrett, 1979-80: 37, 60; Charlesworth, 1982: 472; Jeremias, 1962: 38-40 (ET); Linnemann, 1964: 69-73 (ET); Weder, 1978: 173; Braun, 1969: 49 (ET)[127]; Cabraja, 1985: 136, 135].[128] Bultmann and Sanders do not deal with authenticity of this passage [Bultmann, 1931: 171[129] (ET); Sanders, 1985: 111, 115].

4.1. (3.1) is not quite convincing. Contrary to what Bultmann presupposes Matt 8:14 need not be a conclusion of Matt 18:12-13. Matt 18:13b already encapsulates the main thrust of the preceding parable correctly. Rejoice over finding the lost is not highlighted here. However it would be best to read this verse as an isolated saying uttered in a different context.[130]

4.2. (3.2.a) is unlikely to have happened. The early church would have been reluctant to make up a saying, "ninety-nine" righteous, which contradicts their belief: "None is righteous, no not one" (Rom 3:10). By the same token a phrase like οὐ χρείαν ἔχουσιν μετανοίας would

---

127 Braun affirms that Luke 15:7, although secondary, correctly reproduces Jesus' intention.

128 Cabraja counts the harmony of Jesus' word and action in seeking out the sinners as evidence of the authenticity of this passage.

129 Bultmann simply raises a question. "Were the parables about the lost in Lk. 15:4-10 originally meant as comfort and invitation, or as pure polemic?" [1931: 199 (ET)]. Luehrmann and Schulz also do not deal with the authenticity of Matt 18:12-13; Luke 15:4-6 [1969: 114-115]. Schulz merely states that this text belongs to the Hellenistic Traditions layer in Q [1972: 389].

130 Matt 18:14 seems to have followed Matt 18:10 originally. This verse, need not be ascribed to the early church. μικρῶν need not have to refer to the disciples of the early church. Jesus could have referred to sinners with the term μικρῶν which could mean "humble" or "the ones of least importance." [BAGD, 521]

hardly have emerged in the early church when the conversion of the non-believer was set at the centre of their mission.

4.3. Bultmann's argument (3.2.b) is based upon the hypothesis that Luke altered the Matthean text. Even if Luke 15:7 was derived from Matthew 18:13 it does not affect the authenticity of this saying: Luke's editorial work on some parts of text, probably putting the word "repentance" to make this into a saying on repentance, presupposes the existence of somewhat equivalent saying to Matthew 18:13 in the Lucan passage; at most an alteration, not an entirely new construction.[131] Further Jesus could have said this saying. Jesus' endeavour to bring sinners back to Israel, attested in his proclamation and parable, sufficiently confirms the possibility that Jesus said a saying similar to Luke 15:7 repeatedly. Luke could have put Luke 15:7 in a quite fitting place. A similar saying recurs in Luke 15:10. It is difficult to know which of the two sayings was original, Luke 15:7 having ἢ ἐπὶ ἐνενήκοντα ἐννέα δικαίοις οἵτινες οὐ χρείαν ἔχουσιν μετανοίας or Luke 15:10 the short saying? However the authenticity of Matt 18:13b ἢ ἐπὶ τοῖς ἐνενήκοντα ἐννέα τοῖς μὴ πεπλανημένοις and the order of arrangement of Luke 15:7 and Luke 15:10 support the former. The Aramaism in Matt 18:12-13; Luke 15:7 (χαρὰ ἐν τῷ οὐρανῷ ἔσται ἐπὶ ἑνὶ ἁμαρτωλῷ μετανοοῦντι) [Black, 1967: 184-185][132] could also support the authenticity.

4.4. (3.2.c) is based upon the assumption that the whole passage Luke 15:4-7 arose from a single unitary tradition. If that was the case Schottroff is right in pointing out the tension between the parable and its

---

[131] Marshall correctly summarizes Schottroff's argument and points out why her argument is not convincing: only the motif of repentance is Lucan and Luke 15:7 does nor spring purely from the parabolic situation [1978: 602].

[132] The parallelism in both verses, which is a characteristic of the sayings of Jesus, also could support its authenticity. Dodd gave a similar argument on the basis of Hebraic parallelism [1936: 94].

application.[133] However a multiple source hypothesis could save the need of complicated explanations on the relationship between the main parable and the following conclusive saying. Luke 15:7 could have come from an isolated saying of Jesus. Matt 18:14; Luke 15:7 could have been put together with the preceding parables and other pericopes because of the thematic connection of repentance. The alleged tension seems to stem from this reason.

4.5. (3.2.d) seems to derive from a presupposition about the Lucan theology. It is unlikely that Luke generalizes Mark 2:13-17 to make Luke 15:7. Luke 5:32, which would rather fit as the parallel text of Mark 2:17 and reduces the possibility of the editorial reconstruction which Schottroff assumes. The independent tradition represented by Matt 18:14 and Luke 15:7 hardly allows μετανοοῦντι or μετανοὶας in Luke 15:7 to be simply an addition to Matt 18:13.[134]

On the contrary Mark 2:13-17 supports the historicity and authenticity of Luke 15:7. Both verses elucidate the focus of Jesus' historical ministry: God's joy over the repentant sinners and the need of Jesus' reaching out to the sinners. Luke 15:7 (cf Matt 18:14), following a parable which justifies the need of an initiative to approach sinners (Matt 18:12-13; Luke 15:4-6; also reflected in Mark 2:13-16), parallels Mark 2:17 in the point: God who has sought out sinners strenuously now awaits their repentance.

---

133 However Luke 15:7's stemming from a different source does not indicate its secondary character.

134 Jeremias argues that "μετάνοια occurs on the lips of the earthly Jesus only at Luke 15.7" [1971: 152 n 5 (ET)]. It is noteworthy that after exhaustive examination of arguments tied to this passage Fiedler still admits the possibility that Luke 15:7 in its independence from the parable could be traced back to Jesus [1976: 222]. This verse is an isolated saying of Jesus [Perrin, 1967: 99; Marshall, 1978: 602].

4.6. (3.2.c) seems to arise too much from a forced interpretation. Contrary to Schottroff, Luke 15:7 seems to be distinguished from these asides in its location at the end of a parable: all these asides are placed before the intended saying. Further the particular comparison of one to ninety-nine counts against the generalization Schottroff assumes.

Contrary to Schottroffs argument ἤ in Luke 15:7 has the comparative, not exclusive meaning [BAGD: 342].[135] Hence it could follow that the repentant sinner is regarded as equally righteous in this passage [Montefiore, 1927, vol. 2: 521]. Sanders argues that "repentant sinners are more highly regarded than those who are always righteous (Luke 15:3-7; Luke 15:8-10; 15:11-32)." [1985: 150]. The fact that joy over finding a lost sheep is greater than having ninety-nine righteous in Luke 15:7 does not mean that the righteousness of the ninety-nine were entirely rejected. The point of the parable is but to express the incomparable utmost joy at finding the lost [Jeremias, 1962: 135 (ET)]. μᾶλλον in Matt 18:13 also could go with this interpretation. This word could mean not only "more than" but also "instead of" [BAGD: 489] [Marshall, 1978: 602]. "Rather" (Rom 8:34; Gal 4:9) seems to be the most proper meaning in this verse. Hence it does not exclude the ninety-nine sheep.

4.7. Luke 15:7 does not reject the ninety nine righteous. The implication could be that you all are the lost sheep.[136] Montefiore also argues in the

---

[135] Lagrange, 1927: 418; Schulz, 1972; 390. ἤ could have both meanings, comparative and exclusive [Jeremias, 1962: 141-142 (ET); Baumbach, 1963: 147]. Baumbach criticizes Jeremias for arguing for the comparative meaning of ἤ in Luke 15:7 while arguing for the exclusive meaning in 18:14a inconsistently [1963: 147].

[136] In Mark 2:17 Jesus could ask the Jewish people to repent with this implication: I come to call the sick not the healthy, (By the way, do you think that there is any righteous? No, unfortunately, there is none! All are sinners!). Dodd argues that the reference to the righteous is open to the objection which arose in regard to Mark 2:17 (Did Jesus really teach that there were righteous persons who

same way; "he (Jesus) supposes that many of his hearers, strict and rigidly moral Jews, may stand well with God; what he asserts is that sinners converted by his ministry...procure for heaven a joy like that of the shepherd who finds his lost sheep." [Montefiore, 1927, vol. 2: 521; Loisy, 1908: vol. 2: 140].

4.8. Jesus' seeking out the lost is attested many times over in different literary forms, the parable (Matt 18:12-14; Luke 15:4-7), the discourse (Mark 2:13-17), the mission discourse (Matt 10:6). Thus this feature could also support the authenticity of this passage. Further, τὸ ἀπολωλὸς ζητήσω and τὸ πλανώμενον ἐπιστρέφω which are both in Ezek 34:16, could support the argument that Jesus could use the forerunner in Luke 15:4-7, and use the latter in Matt 18:12-14. Jesus could have spoken Matt 18:12; Luke 15:4-7 in the spirit of Ezek 34:16, Ps 119: 176. It would be reasonable to assume that Jesus could often have spoken this type of identical saying during his ministry to defend his consorting with sinners and to rescue them through the call for repentance.

4.9. If the early church made up this parable they would probably have made it up to admonish members to seek out the lost member. If that is the case they would have been reluctant to make up a saying like Luke 15:7 which could have given an impression that the members of the church who were not astray are comparatively less important than the one unbeliever.

4.10. Other similar accounts, Gos. Thomas 1. 107; Gen. Rabbah 86.6

---

needed no repentance?). However, W. L. Knox [1957: 89] clarifies that Dodd "seems to fail to recognize a note of satire which is quite in keeping with the methods of Jesus and the O.T. prophets."

[Neusner's translation, 1985, vol. 3: 223][137] could support the authenticity of this parable. To sum up Matt 18:12-14; Luke 15:4-7 could be a genuine of Jesus parable consisting of two independent sayings, Matt 18: 12-13 and Matt 18:14, Luke 15:4-6 and Luke 15:7.

5 .

5.1. The main thrust of this saying

Jesus seems to have maintained a special strategy in his approach to isolated groups of sinners: persuading them without provoking their anger and their self-accusations. Sinners, who knew how they were regarded in their society, would have preferred to remain in the corner condemning themselves and others in isolation. Hence they would have unlikely to have come out before Jesus who was calling for repentance in public. This reason could have driven Jesus to approach and meet them specially. In this situation parables could best fit a peaceful but powerful educational aim. Sitting at a table with them Jesus could draw picture of the nature of God who endeavours to rescue lost sinners. Sinners' understanding of God's mind could arouse them to react with a corresponding initiative, to turn to God who is so pleased to see the repentant sinner.

The point of the interpretation of this parable lies in the comprehension of two questions, how the audience perceives this parable and what sort of impact this parable makes on the audience. To put it another way, it would be wise to find how this passage would inspire the audience to respond implicitly, rather than what this passage directs them

---

137 Bultmann [1931: 202 (ET)]:"Lk. 15.4-7//Matt. 18.12-16: cp. GnR 86 (55b) in Strack-B. I, 785: a cattle drover, one of whose twelve beasts has run away, leaves the eleven behind and goes after the lost". A modern translation of Neusner on Genesis Rabbah is available [1985: 223]. However Schottroff does not concur with the adequacy of this reference [1973: 451].

to do explicitly. Accordingly, it becomes important to ask what kind of idea and motivation would have emerged in the mind of the audience. This passage contains significant aspects of Jesus' ministry in microcosm. Jesus is likely to have chosen to teach using this parable precisely because he hoped for a variety of responses. Anyone who, like Sanders, insists on only one interpretation (individual repentance) could make an error of missing other important points of this parable. Hence it is reasonable to suppose that the impact of this parable could have evoked three types of response as follows.

Firstly, the Jewish audience who have heard this parable would have recollected their acquaintance with O.T. passages such as Ps 119:176, Is 53:6[138], Ezek 34:10,11,16,22 which portray God's determination to seek out the lost sheep. As a result they would have identified the lost sheep with Israel. Therefore they would naturally have grasped the point, all Israelites are asked to repent because "the concept of the Jewish people as lost sheep who have gone astray is commonplace (Ps 11 9:176; Isa 53:6)" [Derrett, 1980: 37; Chilton, 1980: 2; Braun, 1959: 242-243 (ET); Schulz, 1972: 389]. The judgmental reference in Ps 119:176: "I have gone astray like a lost sheep; seek thy servant, for I do not forget thy commandments" (lamentation over the sin in repentance), Ezek 34:16 (I will watch over the fat and strong) and Ezek 34:20-21 (the judgment of fat sheep) could have lead the Jewish audience naturally to understand this parable as calling for the repentance of the whole of Israel.[139]

---

[138] "All we *like sheep gone astray;* we have turned every one to his own way" (Isa 53:6) hints that the lost sheep could indicate that all Israelites have strayed from God's way. (italics mine)

[139] Conzelmann [1957: 227 (ET)] assumes that the imminent coming of the Kingdom evokes the call of repentance. He also assumes that the call to repentance and conversion was motivated by Judgement. In the call to repentance to Jews we see the continuity with the message of the O.T. and of John the Baptist; Conzelmann assumes implicitly that the judgmental character embedded in the call to repentance

At the same time the audience would naturally have been reminded of the implicit message that you are counted: God would not let you off, so do not try to run off from God, rather return to God, The hearers of the first parable could hardly fail to be reminded of the familiar O.T. imagery of God and his flock [Dodd, 1936: 119 n 21]

Secondly, the shepherd's rejoicing at finding the lost certainly symbolizes God's joy over finding sinners. Hence as a proclaimer of the will of God Jesus could have defended the need of his reaching out to sinners properly in this parable: God wishes to search for and bring back the lost sheep (Ezek 34:11, 16), which refers to both the whole of Israel and the lost people of Israel, the sinners of Israel.[140] At the same time the parable of this sort could fit as an answer to the question of some people, Pharisees in particular, who would have disapproved his consorting with people living outside the Law.

Thirdly, a revealing meaning could arise. This parable could encourage sinners to go after the one thing needed. The picture of this parable stresses to the audience the need to copy the joy of the shepherd who discovers the most precious and urgent in contrast to things to be less cherished and less urgent. This verse stresses the joy over finding a single sheep so strongly that ninety-nine could be seen pushed to the periphery. This expression hardly indicates the impact of the "reversal of value" as Sanders claims [1985: 150]. The audience of this parable are faced with some sort of shock which leads them to acknowledge their dangerous complacency (cf. Luke 12:16-21); they also need to repent.[141]

---

by John and Jesus could have motivated people to repentance.

[140] Jeremias assumes that, "The disciples are sent to the lost sheep of the house of Israel (Matt. 10.6)—presumably as shepherds, for so at least Matt 18.12-14 understood their function." [1962: 216 (ET)].

[141] Schottroff points out the irony that the righteous ninety nine is rejected in favour of the unrighteous one [1971: 34-35].

5.2. The bearing on the forgiveness of sins

Sanders seems to show inconsistency in his argument. He argues that Luke 15:3-6, the parable about God's seeking the lost, once the Lucan conclusion is removed (v.7), is seen to be focused not on repentance, but on God's action [1985: 109, 203]. Later Sanders also admits that God's action may imply repentance [1985: 203]. But in other places he argues differently: "Matt. 18.12f. does not have to do with repentance, but apparently individual repentance." [1985: 111] (italics mine). All these unconvincing arguments seem to arise from Sanders' failure to see the collective meaning of "a lost sheep". Further, individual repentance could be extended to national repentance.[142]

With regards to the relationship between the God's action to search for the lost and the repentance of the lost, Sanders seems to stress only one part of this two-sided relationship. Bornkamm also argues that "all talk of the conditions which man must fulfil before grace is accorded him in here silenced." [1959: 84 (ET)]. Both of them seem to go too far. This sort of sweeping interpretation seems to arise from the way of reading this parable as a doctrinal instruction declaring to sinners the forgiveness of their sins, rather than reading the parable the way a Jewish audience would understand it and in the way they would respond when motivated to act by the parable.[143] The speaker says this parable with an expectation of the due response of the audience. Hence the ideal interpretation needs to start from the side of the audience.

God's grace precedes the repentance of the sinner. However a genuine forgiveness occurs only when the sinner agrees to respond.

---

[142] Horsley [1987: 196] argues for the inadequacy of dividing, into two kinds of repentance, national and individual.

[143] Hence the argument that repentance of sinners has nothing to do with the parable since the sheep (unlike the son in Luke 15:20) has not "returned" [Schweizer, 1982: 244 (ET)] remains unconvincing.

Otherwise it is bound to fail. This principle works the same way in this parable. "There was in the Pharisaism of all ages a real anxiety to make the return of the sinner easy. *It was inclined to leave the initiative to the sinner, except that it always maintained God's readiness to take the first step. Jesus in his attitude towards sin and sinners was more inclined to take the initiative.*" [Abrahams, 1917: 59] (italics mine). Montefiore concurs at this point. The three parables in this chapter all illustrate the interest which God (including therefore, in God's service, Jesus) takes in the sinner, and His constant desire that he should *"return" and "be found."* [1927, vol. 2: 520][144] (italics mine). What is common to these scholars is that the action of God and sinners work together for forgiveness; an endeavour on one side alone does not bear fruit. In short in this parable Jesus could implicitly ask the Jewish people to respond with repentance to God's never ending search for the lost.

[144] "we must also note that although repentance and conversion are necessary conditions, they are not thought of as an "achievement"" [Conzelmann, 1957: 229 (ET)].

G. Did Jesus call for national repentance in his lament over Jerusalem; Matt 23:37-39; Luke 13:34-35?

1. A conjectured original text

Matt 23:37 Ἰερουσαλὴμ Ἰερουσαλὴμ, ἡ ἀποκτείνουσα τοὺς προφήτας καὶ λιθοβολοῦσα τοὺς ἀπεσταλμένους πρὸς αὐτήν, ποσάκις ἠθέλησα ἐπισυναγαγεῖν τὰ τέκνα σου, ὃν τρόπον ὄρνις ἐπισυνάγει τὰ νοσσία αὐτῆς ὑπὸ τὰς πτέρυγας, καὶ οὐκ ἠθέλησατε. 38 ἰδοὺ ἀφίεται ὑμῖν ὁ οἶκος ὑμῶν ἔρημος. 39 λέγω γὰρ ὑμῖν, οὐ μή με ἴδητε ἀπ' ἄρτι ἕως ἂν εἴπητε, Εὐλογημένος ὁ ἐρχόμενος ἐν ὀνόματι κυρίου.

Luke 13:34 Ἰερουσαλὴμ Ἰερουσαλὴμ, ἡ ἀποκτείνουσα τοὺς προφήτας καὶ λιθοβολοῦσα τοὺς ἀπεσταλμένους πρὸς αὐτήν ποσάκις ἠθέλησα ἐπισυνάξαι τὰ τέκνα σου, ὃν τρόπον ὄρνις τὴν ἑαυτῆς νοσσιὰν ὑπὸ τὰς πτέρυγας, καὶ οὐκ ἠθελήσατε. 35 ἰδοὺ ἀφίεται ὑμῖν ὁ οἶκος ὑμῶν. λέγω δὲ ὑμῖν, οὐ μὴ ἴδητέ με ἕως ἥξει ὅτε εἴπητε, Εὐλογημένος ὁ ἐρχόμενος ἐν ὀνόματι κυρίου.

2. Both versions are in general authentic

ἔρημος] B L ff^{2} sy^{s} sa bo^{pt} omit this word. Matthew or a scribe could have added this word [McNeile, 1915: 342; Bultmann, 1931: 115 (ET)[145]]

ἀπ' ἄρτι] The Lucan text does not have this word. It could have been added to stress the responsibility of the Jews for not responding to Jesus' call [Kuemmel, 1956: 81 (ET); Gnilka, 1988: 299].

---

[145] It is not good Greek. But Burney [1925: 146] argues that this word is the essential in the rhythm of an old Hebrew elegy. Matthew seems to keep the original text.

3. Arguments against 1.

3.1. A supra historical entity, namely wisdom, which has just spoken in Matt 23:34-36; Luke 11:49-51, is the speaker of this passage [Bultmann, 1931, 114-115 (ET)]. The sender is Wisdom (Prov 1:20; Enoch 42; Bar 3:14) [Bultmann, 1931: 114-115 (ET); Gnilka, 1988: 302, 306].

3.2. This saying was originally a Jewish prophecy. It was proclaimed at the time before the fall of Jerusalem (A.D. 66-70) [Steck, 1967: 57, 238].[146]

3.3. The early church made up this Jewish wisdom saying from the Jewish wisdom material to reflect their life setting [Schulz, 1972: 346-360 (349)], the polemical reasons of the Q community [Braun, 1957, vol. 2: 63 n 5; 1966: vol. 1: 50[147], Schulz, 1972: 357-359 (349)[148]]. The Q community intends to express the idea that Israel's rejection of Jesus, the final prophetic Wisdom, results in punishment, the desolation of Jerusalem [Schulz, 1972: 357-359; Miller, 1988: 238-2391.

3.4. This passage does not reflect the historical event. It merely describes the general eschatological interpretation of Q [Schulz, 1972: 357-359]. The eschatological judgment in Q was described as a punishment for the Jewish people's failure to accept the crucified Jesus as the prophetic

---

[146] Steck cites *Jewish War* 6.299-300; 2 *Apoc. Bar.* 9:1-2; *Jewish War 5.412*; *Jewish Antiquities* 20.166; *Jewish Antiquities* 2.539; 5.19; Forty years of fasting of R, Zadoqs before the distinction of Jerusalem (b. Gitt 56a); y. Joma 6.43c, 61 (Johannan b. Zacchai); *Jewish War* 6.288-311; 2. 454f; 6. 109f; *Jewish War* 6.300-309; αἰαὶ 'Ιερουσολύμοις (*Jewish War* 6.304, 306).

[147] Braun reads this episode as *vaticinium ex eventu*.

[148] When their mission to Israel failed the Q community interpreted the destruction of Jerusalem as the punishment for Israel's rejection of Jesus, the last prophetic messengers of Wisdom [1972: 359].

Wisdom sent by God [Schulz, 1972: 3531. Hence this eschatological sayings in no way reflects Jesus' condemnation of the Jewish people [ibid].

3.5. ἀφίεται indicates that Jerusalem is already desolate, not yet to be desolate [Wellhausen, 1914: 115; Bultmann, 1931: 115 (ET)]. ἀφίεται in Matt 24:41 does not force us to take the meaning of this word as referring to the future [Wellhausen, 1914: 115].

3.6. Matt 23:39; Luke 13:35b is a secondary addition [Haenchen, 1951: 56-57[149]; Wilkens, 1964: 515 n 350; Hoffmann, 1971: 176-177; Gnilka, 1988: 307].[150]

3.7. Some scholars argue against the authenticity of Matt 23:37-39; Luke 13:34-35 without any additional reasons [Wellhausen, 1914: 115; Dibelius, 1933: 245; 285 (ET)].

4. Arguments against 3.

4.1. Is (3.1) convincing? Bultmann's argument hinges upon the hypothesis that Matt 23:34-36 and Matt 23:37-39 originally belonged together in Q [Bultmann, 1931: 115 (ET)]. However this argument remains unconvincing because Luke 13:34-35 is not preceded by the parallel passage of Matt 23:34-35. Matt 23:37-38 is not really a continuation of Matt 23:34-36, but a related idea associated with the same theme [T. W. Manson, 1948: 126, Kuemmel, 1956: 80 (ET)]. ἀποστέλλω (v. 34: present tense) and ἀπεσταλμένους (v. 37: past and passive) also

---

[149] A Christian addition to a Jewish formulation.

[150] However Bultmann argues that Matt 23:39; Luke 13:35b belongs to the main saying and has to be understood in the light of the myth of divine Wisdom [1931: 115 (ET)].

suggest different origins of the two passages. Jesus could speak like the Wisdom of God [Fitzmyer, 1986: 1034]. But Jesus is not Wisdom.

4.2. Q could hardly include the logion within a collection of the sayings of Jesus without making the identification between the speaker of the saying and Jesus [Dunn, 1989: 203; cf. Wilkens, 1964; 515 (ET)].[151] Even if it is actually highly probable that Matthew has preserved the order of sections in Q [Bultmann, 1931:114-115 (ET)] this may not affect the authenticity of Matt 23:37-39; Luke 13-34-35.

4.3. There is no authority anywhere for connecting the Wisdom myth with the expectation of the coming Messiah (Matt 23:39) [Kuemmel, 1956: 81 (ET)].

4.4. The early church would hardly have identified Jesus with Wisdom (Prov 1:28). They would have described Jesus as the representative of Wisdom. "God made Jesus Christ our wisdom" (1 Cor 1:30) or "...in whom are hid all the treasures of wisdom and knowledge" (Col 2:3) mean that wisdom is given to Jesus by God, Wisdom itself, not that Jesus is Wisdom.

---

[151] Certainly the speaker of Matt 23:34-35; Luke 11:49-51 is distinguished from the speaker of Matt 23:37-39; Luke 13:34-35. However Matt 23:34-36; Luke 11:49-51could be an authentic saying of Jesus because the teachers of the early church are unlikely to have called the messengers wise men or scribes [O'Neill, 1980: 50]. Wisdom does not normally speak of "this generation" [ibid]. Marshall puts forward the possibility that Jesus could have spoken Matt 23:34f as a comment on the present situation [1978: 573]. Hence Jesus could have used a wisdom saying which originally stemmed from Jewish prophecy. Further Bultmann also leaves it open that Jesus could have quoted originally a Jewish prophetic saying [1931: 114 (ET)]. Further, "Luke, of course, is not aware of any identification of Jesus and Sophia. cf. 11.49; Sophia is pre-existent, but not Jesus." [Conzelmann, 1957: 110 n 1 (ET)]. Hence, Jesus could speak in this way after his ministry in Jerusalem.

4.5. The description of the world as a οἶκος [Bultmann, 1931: 115 (ET)] does not confirm the view that the saying derives from myth. The city Ἰερουσαλήμ is personified in this passage. So, τὰ τέκνα σου indicates Jerusalemites. οἶκος could mean both the city of Jerusalem (T. Levi 10:5) and the Temple (1 Enoch 89:50, 54, 56; Jer 26:6; 2 Bar 8:2). Accordingly, the house of Jerusalem does not have a mythical meaning as Bultmann argues [1931: 115 n 4 (ET)].[152]

4.6. A more convincing evidence of this passage's independence would be that the mother bird imagery fundamentally differs from the Wisdom imagery. Wisdom commands the prophets and the sage and the scribes (v. 34), but in vv. 37-39 the speaker himself acts like a hen gathering her brood.

4.7. The rhetorical feature could support the authenticity of this saying. The twice repeated call of "Jerusalem" already implies the desire of a proclaimer who strives to rescue his people from impending desolation (cf. Gen 22:11, Abraham; Exod 3:4 Moses). "Oh Galilee Galilee" (y. Shab. 16.15d) [Steck, 1967: 59 n 1], "O altar altar!" (1 Kings 13:2), "Ho Ariel Ariel" (Isa 29:1)), "Simon, Simon" (Luke 22:31) demonstrate the urgency of calling people from impending disaster.[153]

4.8. As a prophet Jesus could have called for the repentance of Israel [O'Neill, 1980:44-58] in his lament over Jerusalem. Jesus clearly describes himself as a prophet (Mark 6:4; Luke 13:33).[154] This prophetic

---

[152] Schulz remains unconvinced by Bultmann's argument [1972: 356 n 230].

[153] The simile of the bird suggests something more intimate and urgent [McNeile, 1915: 341].

[154] Stanton argues that Luke 13:33 "is not a proverb because there is no sign of an expectation in Judaism that a prophet should expect to perish in Jerusalem." [1989: 179].

saying indicates that Jesus regarded his own fate as linked with that of the ancient prophets [Stanton, 1989: 179].[155]

4.9. Wisdom would hardly have spoken in the style of Matt 23:38; Luke 13:35a. The similarity with Jer 22:5 already implies this verse's prophetic, not wisdom origin. Jesus could have spoken as an eschatological prophet.

4.10. (3.2) remains not entirely convincing. It is not certain whether Jesus himself quoted it or whether the early Church ascribed it to him [Bultmann, 1931: 114-115 (ET)]. Further the possibility that the prophets in the later Judaism or in the early church could copy or reshape or derive these sayings of Jesus from their tradition is fairly strong. There seems to be no compelling reason to date the prediction of the destruction of the temple to the time of the Jewish war around A.D. 70. Jesus could have already proclaimed eschatological sayings in a like manner. Some scholars also confirm that its literary dependence cannot be proved [Bultmann, 1931: 115 n 3 (ET); cf. Montefiore, 1909, vol. 2: 305;: Dibelius, 1933: 245 (ET)].

4.11. Jesus could know well about the persecution of prophets. The possible implication in the saying of more visits to Jerusalem than the last one need not limit Jesus' central concern for the imminent destiny of

---

[155] Aune summarizes what Schulz argues "Jesus identifies himself with a long series of messengers who have been sent in vain to Israel" [1983: 158]. "The Q community recognized John the Baptist and particularly Jesus as prophets in the ancient tradition who shared the fate of their predecessors. The prophetic messengers of the Q community, though their existence and activities can only be inferred, also regarded themselves as sharing the fate of the ancient prophets and Jesus." But Kloppenborg [1986: 235], along with Luehrmann [1969: 87-88], assumes that "Q's mission to Israel ("this generation") has ended in failure". Koester [1990: 135] concurs with Kloppenborg. But the wisdom elements in some of Q hardly requires the rejection of the eschatological character of other sayings in Q.

Jerusalem.[156] Jesus could have tried to gather Jerusalemites repeatedly (ποσάκις) even during a single stay in Jerusalem. Jesus could have spoken of Jerusalem as ἡ ἀποκτείνουσα τοὺς προφήτας καὶ λιθοβολοῦσα τοὺς ἀπεσταλμένους πρὸς αὐτήν from his historical consciousness (Neh 9:26; 2 Chr 24:17-22).

4.12. Jesus' prediction of the fall of Jerusalem temple in Mark 13:2 is coherent with this passage. The account on Jesus' address to the wailing daughters of Jerusalem (Luke 23:27-31) and Jesus' weeping over Jerusalem's future in Luke 19:41-44 could also support the authenticity of this saying.[157]

4.13. Matt 23:37-39; Luke 13:34-35 has only a few textual variants. Thus it may come from a common source.

4.14. The poetical parallelism in Matt 23:37; Luke 13:34 [Burney, 1925: 146] is a piece of the evidence for its independence from Luke 11:49-51 [T. W. Manson, 1964: 126].

4.15. The single occurrence, of the Aramaic form Ἰερουσαλήμ in Matt 23:37; Luke 13:34 [Wellhausen, 1914: 115], distinguished from Ἱεροσόλυμα which is frequently used in the synoptic gospels, could support the antiquity [McNeile, 1915: 341; Jeremias, 1980: 235][158] and uniqueness of this passage.

---

[156] T. W. Manson reads this into "How often have I longed" [1948: 127]. Borg sets Jerusalem's fall as a historical fact; as a prophetic figure Jesus was most likely to call for repentance before this imminent danger [1987: 162-163].

[157] "....there is no compelling reason for denying the original version [Luke 19:41-44] of this oracle to Jesus." [Aune, 1983: 176].

[158] cf. [BAGD: 373]. However Wellhausen states that no certain conclusions can be drawn concerning the use of the two forms of the name.

4.16. Another Semitism πρὸς αὐτήν (πρός σε) [Wellhausen, 1914: 115] also supports this argument.

4.17. Contrary to (3.3), the desolation of Jerusalem does not fit the punishment of unbelieving Jews as the early church conceived it. The early church would hardly have described Jerusalem's destruction as the punishment of their unbelief. For the early church the punishment upon unbelief seems to be individual, not collective (John 3:18; 8:24). The destruction of Jerusalem fits as the punishment of the Jewish people who never repented at the urgent prophetic message.

4.18. The early church would have been reluctant to have Jesus condemn Jerusalem because of following reason. They seem to have shifted their interests from "the earthly Jerusalem" to "the heavenly new Jerusalem" (Gal 4:25; Heb 12:22; Rev 3:12; 21:2; 21:10).

4.19. If the early church made up Matt 23:37-39; Luke 13:34-35 to reflect the Jewish persecution or rejection of their missionaries they would hardly have put vv. 37-38 along with v. 39, the account which could illustrate Jesus' coming again. In Matt 23:39; Luke 13:35b Jerusalemites (You, οὐ μὴ ἴδητε) are seemingly described as destined to see the Messianic figure in Jerusalem at the parousia. However the early church would hardly have the Jerusalemites, punished for the unbelief of Christ, see the coming Messiah in their Jerusalem. εὐλογημένος ὁ ἐρχόμενος ἐν ὀνόματι κυρίου (Ps 118:26) indicates the coming of the glorified Messiah to the awaiting people.

4.20. The conversion of three thousand in Acts 2:37-42 could hardly have escaped the attention of the early church. Further this account does not fully agree with the text "you did not want" (ἠθελήσατε).

4.21. The early church would hardly have made Jesus foretell the desolation of "Jerusalem". The early church tended to address "the inhabitants of Jerusalem" (Acts 4:16) not personified Jerusalem itself. Peter addresses to the "Men of Judaea and all who dwell in Jerusalem" (Acts 2:14). Addressing the personified name, of countries or cities is very much the way of the, O.T. prophets: Deut 6:4 (Israel!); Isa 44:21 (Jacob, Israel); Isa 52:1 (Zion); Isa 47:1 (Babylon). The urgency embedded in the double calling of Jerusalem could imply the prophetic character of this saying. In his prophetic lament over the imminent fate of Jerusalem Jesus could have wished to evoke the repentance of Jerusalemites and the whole nation.

4.22. If the early church made up this passage the προφήτας must be the prophets from the early church, not prophets before the church because this phrase was put together with the account λιθοβολοῦσα τοὺς ἀπεσταλμένους πρὸς αὐτήν which could have referred to the stoning of Stephen (Acts 7:59). However hardly any other incident of Jerusalem's killing of "prophets" from the early church is known except this single incident. Agabus who predicted the famine seems to have survived persecution in Jerusalem (Acts 11:19) with other prophets of the early church (Acts 11:27-28). The shedding of the blood of Zechariah (Luke 11:51), even if it may portray a historical incident, seems not to refer to someone who was regarded as a prophet from the early church.

4.23. The early church would hardly have made up Matt 23:37-38; Luke 13:34. They still seem to think that the Jews would be punished only temporarily. They did not abandon or condemn the Jews once and for all. Otherwise they would not have made up a passage which seems to allow Jerusalemites to see the return of Messiah (Matt 23:39; Luke 13:35). On the contrary the early church seems to understand the punishment of the unbeliever as bound to last forever.

4.24. Contrary to what Schulz argues in (3.3) the destruction of Jerusalem would hardly have been regarded as the punishment of the unbelieving Jews and the vindication of the activity (failure of the mission) of Q community. The punishment of the unbelieving Jews would be an once and for all event. But Matt 23:39; Luke 13:35 states that the desolation of Jerusalem would be followed by the parousia.

4.25. The early church would hardly have thought that Jesus would come again to Jerusalem (Matt 23:39; Luke 13:35). "Your" house (οἶκος ὑμῶν) implies Jerusalem or the Jerusalemites. Then the. early church would hardly have described Jerusalemites as destined to see Jesus (ἴδητε) when he comes in glory (v. 39).

4.26. The early church still regards Jerusalem as an important place in its religious role in their history. Hence they would have been reluctant to make up a saying with the specific name Jerusalem. The early church still respects the Jerusalem Temple.

4.27. The early church would not have used the mother hen imagery. If they made it up the mother hen would represent the early church and the brood would represent the Jerusalemites or the unbelieving Jews. The early church was supposed to gather the Jewish people who confess Jesus as Messiah (Acts 2:36-38; 5:30-32). Hence gathering is selective, However the mother-hen is portrayed as gathering her brood indiscriminately,

4.28. Further the mother hen imagery could have been derived from the O.T. (Deut 32:11; Ruth 2:12; Ps 17:8; 36:7; 57:1; 61:4; 63:7; 91:4; Isa 31:5) rather than from a relatively less familiar apocryphal wisdom saying.

4.29.ὃν τρόπον (Matt 23:37; Luke 13:34) frequently used in LXX, in preference to ὡς used in other literature, also indicates that Matt 23:37-

38; Luke 13:34 could have come from the O.T. rather than from a Wisdom source.

4.30. (3.4) remains unconvincing. Despite Schulz's vigorous emphasis [1972: 351-352], hardly any evidence seems to support the argument that eschatological sayings in Q were made up at a relatively late stage, later than the other teaching material. "But the community which preserved Q material for us, concentrating its attention almost exclusively on Jesus' teaching, was convinced that Jesus' pointing to the coming of God's reign has not lost its meaning in the post Easter situation, but must be proclaimed anew." [Toedt, 1963: 249 (ET)]. Q is composed of the pre--Easter and post-Easter prophetic saying materials. Thus Matt 23:37-39; Luke 13:34-35 could have come from the pre-Easter sayings of Jesus.

4.31. (3.5) is not entirely convincing because the prophetic future ἀφίεται (BDF: 323) could point to the future event. The killing of prophets and stoning of messengers could indicate a historical incident (2 Chr 35:25; the death of Josiah; Jer 26:20ff; 1 Kings 18; 4, 13, 19: 10).

4.32. (3.6) correctly points out somewhat awkward continuity between these verses.[159] Originally Matt 23:39; Luke 13:35b does not seem to belong to Matt 23:37-38; Luke 13:34-35a. It could be an isolated saying of Jesus that was put in this place at a later times. Jesus could have said this somewhat ambiguous saying in Galilee before his departure for Jerusalem to express his personal wish to come to Galilee again when a figure in the name of Lord, probably Messiah, comes.[160] However Jesus

---

159 "It is hardly likely that in the wisdom saying, widsom suddenly changes into the figure of the Messiah." [Wilkens, 1964: 515 n 350 (ET)].

160 W. L. Knox [1957: 82-83] argues that Jesus could have said this saying while he was still in Galilee with the anxiety over the already desolate situation of Jerusalem (possibly because under Roman dominion).

does not identify himself with the Messiah.[161] The audience is left puzzled.[162]

4.33. This implicit messianic saying goes well with Matt 23:37-38; Luke 13:34-35a. The gathering of scattered people into Jerusalem is one of reiterated themes of Messianic expectation (e.g. Isa 60:4, Zech 10:6-10)[Caird, 1963: 173].

4.34. If Matt 23:39; Luke 13:35b refer to Ascension and Parousia, that would hardly go with Matt 23:37-38; Luke 13:34-35a. The account which seemingly illustrates Ascension (around A.D. 33) could hardly precede the account on the desolation of Jerusalem in A.D. 70.

4.35. In contrast to (3.7) some scholars argue that Jesus spoke this passage with or without any additional reasons [McNeill, 1915: 341; Dodd, 1936; 62- 63; T. W. Manson, 1948: 126-128; A. J. Cadoux, 1941: 256; Wilkens, 1964: 515 (ET); Jeremias, 1971: 78, 177, 294 (ET); O'Neill, 1980: 26, 51[163]; Aune, 1983: 175; Schweizer, 1982: 231-232 (ET); Fitzmyer, 1986: 1034, 1036; Uro, 1987: 236- 237[164]].

---

161 O'Neill [1990: 55]: "Jesus characteristically neither explicitly accepts nor explicitly denies the measianic ascription."

162 Marshall [1978: 574], along with Kuemmel [1953: 91-82], argues that the cryptic nature of this saying could suggest its origin from Jesus.

163 O'Neill seems to mean, Jesus is speaking as a prophet in the name of the Lord. He is trying to avoid the charge that this saying assumes the speaker is the Messiah.

164 "It is obvious to me that Jesus, who is in the context of Q is obviously the speaker of the saying, appears in Lk 13.34 more than simply as a "messenger" of Wisdom (cf. Lk 11.49-51)." Uro also does not exclude the possibilities that Luke 13:34 in some form goes back to the teaching of Jesus." [1987: 238 n 143, 239].

5.

5.1. The main thrust of this saying

Jesus could speak using an imagery which vividly portrays a prophets lament over the future of his people. He could ask all Jerusalemites and Jews to repent in the face of imminent judgment. This passage could include two opposite meanings, judgment and salvation. "The children of Jerusalem" could mean all Israelites who live in the influence of Jerusalem religiously and politically. Isa 31:5 and Ps 36:7 are similar to this passage in their main thrust, the protection and rescue of Jerusalem from the imminent danger. The meaning of Matt 23:38; Luke 13:35a is this, "Behold! the Jerusalem that you see now will be forsaken and desolate". Matt 23:39; Luke 13:35b could mean, "because you reject my repeated endeavour to gather you, I will be absent until the Messiah comes and judges you". Jer 12:7 has a similar message.

5.2. The bearing for the forgiveness of sins

Sanders does not deal with this passage [1985: 114].[165] These two verses imply a final call for the national repentance of Israel. Further, it is noteworthy that Jesus' prophecy of his absence until the Messiah comes implies that this saying is set in an eschatological setting and indicates judgment [Gnilka, 1988: 305]. This absence is considered as a punishment. And this saying implies that Jesus comes as judge but then it will be too late to repent [T. W. Manson, 1948: 128]. To sum up, Jesus could ask for the national repentance of Israel in his lament over Jerusalem.

---

[165] However Sanders argues that Matt 23:34-36; Luke 11:49-51 could reflect Jewish rejection of the gospel.

CHAPTER IV

The Special Matthean Passages

A. Did Jesus command sinners to be reconciled with those who had been offended before offering a worthy sacrifice (Matt 5:23-24; cf. 6:14; Mark 11:25)?

1. A conjectured original text

Matt 5:23 ἐὰν οὖν προσφέρῃς τὸ δῶρόν σου ἐπὶ τὸ θυσιαστήριον κἀκεῖμνησθῇς ὅτι ὁ ἀδελφός σου ἔχει τι κατὰ σοῦ 24 ἄφες ἐκεῖ τὸ δῶρόν σου ἔμπροσθεν τοῦ θυσιαστηρίου καὶ ὕπαγε πρῶτον διαλλάγηθι τῷ ἀδελφῷ σου, καὶ τότε ἐλθὼν πρόσφερε τὸ δῶρόν σου.

Mark 6:14 ἐὰν γὰρ ἀφῆτε τοῖς ἀνθρώποις τὰ παραπτώματα αὐτῶν, ἀφήσει καὶ ὑμῖν ὁ πατὴρ ὑμῶν ὁ οὐράνιος.

Mark 11:25 καὶ ὅταν στήκετε προσευχόμενοι, ἀφίετε εἴ τι ἔχετε κατά τινος, ἵνα καὶ ὁ πατὴρ ὑμῶν ὁ ἐν τοῖς οὐρανοῖς ἀφῇ ὑμῖν τὰ παραπτώματα ὑμῶν.

2. Arguments concerning the excluded parts

Nothing is excluded. Matt 5:23-24 is entirely independent from

Mark 11:25. Mark 11:25 and Matt 6:14 seem to be translation variants of the original Aramaic text.[1]

3. Arguments against 1.

3.1. Matt 5:23-24 was made up by the early Church.

a. Mark 11:25 was transformed into Matt 5:23-24 [Wellhausen, 1914: 20]. Matthew transformed Mark 11:25 (the case of the offended) into Matt 5:24 (the case of the offender) in order to harmonize with the following Matthean passage, Matt 5:25-26 [Wellhausen, 1914: 20].

b. Matt 5:23 is perhaps a Christian construction [Bultmann, 1931: 147 (ET); Gnilka, 1986: 151]. It is one of the "Rules of Piety" by which the Church was conscious of its characteristic piety in distinction from that of Judaism [Bultmann, 1931: 146[2] (ET); Braun, 1969: 58 (ET); Schrage, 1982: 71 (ET)[3]; Strecker, 1985: 68[4](ET)].

---

[1] What is the relationship between Mark 11:25 and Matt 6:14? Some scholars argue that Matt 6:14f is the commentary on Mark 11:25 [Bultmann, 1931: 132 (ET)], or a development of Mark 11:25b [Brooks, 1987: 46]. However two sayings could be the different translations of the same Aramaic saying [Boring, 1982: 207].

[2] "Sayings formulated in legal style are mostly older, having received their form essentially in the Church, but with whose content the Church and the brotherhood within the Church had nothing to do, like Matt. 6.2-18, 5.23f, 23.16-22; Mk. 11.25, Lk. 17.3f." "I want to call these Rules of piety. In them the Church was conscious, not of its churchly duties but of its characteristic piety in distinction from that of Judaism"[Ibid]. "Matt. 5.23f. could have been taken over from Jewish tradition...." [1931: 411 (ET)].

[3] "Unfortunately this passage cannot be claimed as historical evidence for the precedence of reconciliation over the cult in Jesus' teaching. It is a response to the Jewish Christian interpretation of the first antithesis and probably reflects a rule of the early Christian Community."

[4] "This community rule presupposes the existence of the second temple and an unbroken relationship to the cult of offering in the early Christian Community in

c. Jesus could not have said Matt 5:23-24 because this saying does not fit the Galileans to whom he was speaking. This passage stems from the vicinity of the Jerusalem church and is comprehensible only when assuming that the sacrificial service in the Temple was ongoing [Wellhausen, 1911: 62 n 1].

4. Arguments against 3.

4.1. Contrary to (3.1.a) Matt 5:23-24 hardly suits the alleged case Wellhausen assumes. One significant reason why this argument is not convincing is that if that kind of transformation occurred, Matt 6:14 (15) would have been more similar to the alleged form. The wordings of Mark 11:25 and Matt 6:14 are remarkably identical compared with Matt 5:23-24. Further it is hardly likely that Matthew changed the Marcan passage and at the same time modified it into a form which is harmonized with the following passages (Matt 5:25-26). This kind of double modification seems to have occurred rarely. Further "the forgiveness in and outside of the Temple" (Matt 5:23-4) and "Make reconciliation on the way to court" (Matt 5:25, 26) are distinctively different contexts. Thus it would be reasonable to argue that Matt 5:23-24 is a more original form than Mark 11:25.[5]

4.2. Further, the two sayings are intrinsically different, being directed to quite different cases. In Matt 5:23-24 the offender is asked to be reconciled to the offended. But in Mark 11:25 the offended is asked to forgive the offender. Hence it is possible to assume that two sets of

---

Jerusalem."

[5] Bultmann arrives at the same conclusion from a different perspective. Matt 5:23-24 "is in any case a variant to Mk. 11:25. and indeed most probably a more original form, which presupposes the existence of the sacrificial system in Jerusalem." [1931: 132 (ET)].

sayings on forgiveness would have existed from the beginning, the one directed to the offender (Matt 5:23-24), the other one to the offended (Matt 6:14, Mark 11:25).[6]

4.3. Bultmann's argument (3.1. b) remains unconvincing. It is noteworthy that Bultmann wavers significantly. In his later work, *Theology of the New Testament,* published in English in 1952 (translated by K. Groebel from the one of the German editions published in 1948, 1951) he concurs with the authenticity of this saying: "In Matt 5:23f, participation in the temple is taken for granted without misgiving. It may well be a *genuine saying of Jesus*." [Bultmann, 1948: 17 (ET)] (italics mine),

4.4. Bultmann claims that this saying has no connection with the Church.[7] This claim may be turned against his suspicion of the authenticity. If a saying is not from the early church it may have come from Jesus.[8]

4.5. Contrary to the way Bultmann argues this saying does not seem to show a piety distinctive from Judaism. The need of making reconciliation

---

[6] However Bultmann argues that Mark 11:25, Matt 6:14 are also perhaps a Christian construction [1931: 132 (FT)]. For Bultmann Matt 5:23-24 and Mark 11:25 are suspected as inauthentic for the same reasons, their distinctive piety from Judaism [1931: 146 (ET)].

[7] "In the same way, between and alongside such passages there have been in introduced logia which originally had no connection at all with the Church. The exhortation to be reconciled in Matt. 5:23f, is followed by a passage in 25f. which is part of a *parable* of the Parousia turned into a *rule* of piety." [1931: 149 (ET)].

[8] According to Bultmann's criteria, a saying can be authentic when it is distinguished from the Jewish morality and piety at the time of Jesus' day and from the features of the early Christian elements at the same time [1931: 205 (ET)]. Faced with the dilemma that this saying fits his criteria, Bultmann seems to put forward a rather strange third argument: the early church made up a saying which is distinguished from Jewish morality and piety.

before giving an offering on the altar is clearly stressed in Yoma 8.9[9] (t. Yoma 4.9[10]). A right offering is stressed in Prov 15:8; 21:3, 27; Sir 7:9; Amos 4:4-5; Jer 6:20, 7:3. Further even the early Palestinian church does not seem to have had any inevitable reason for heightening its distinctive piety against Judaism. What they would have intended to show could only be that they continued to attend Jewish worship while confessing the risen Jesus as the Messiah. They seem to have had no reason to be more rigorous than contemporary Judaism. Hence they need scarcely have made up a saying in which they intended to show their piety as distinctive from that of contemporary Judaism.

4.6. εἶ ὁ ἀδελφός σου ἔχει τι κατά σοῦ πρῶτον διαλλάγηθι τῷ ἀδελφῷ σου could have been sufficient if the early church made up this saying to teach Christians to have a sound relationship with their fellow Christians or with non-believing Jews. The remaining part would hardly have been necessary.

4.7. If the early church made up Matt 5:23-24 they would have done it to

---

[9] Grundmann [1968: 157] and Schweizer [1973: 119 (ET)] argues that a sacrifice could be interrupted only for ritual reasons: The need of reconciliation hardly interrupts the ongoing sacrifice. Both of these scholars seems to refer to b. Qam. 110a-110b and t. Pesch. 4.1."If one brought his guilt offering, but did not bring that which he had stolen [to make restitution], one should not stir the guilt-offering until he restores that which he stole." (Neusner's translation [1981: 130]). The point is that when the stolen goods are not returned the sacrifice for sin-offering could be interrupted. However a more general rule m. Yoma 8.9 seems to override these two more specific rules.

[10] "Sin offering and guilt offering and death and the Day of Atonement, all of them together do not expiate sin without repentance." (t. Yoma 4.9). However on the effect of death opinions differ. In the following part of the same t. Yoma 4.9 death was regarded as of being tantamount to an act of repentance: "Repentance effects atonement with death." The same idea appears in Isa 22:14. On the whole it would be reasonable to conclude that repentance was clearly stressed until the time of death.

solve such problems as that some members making their offerings in the Temple without being reconciled with the offended. However, hardly any account suggests that such a problem arose in the life setting of the early church.

4.8. Schrage's argument remains unconvincing. Matt 5:21-22 hardly arose from the Jewish-Christian Church because they would hardly have brought their cases to Council (Sanhedrin): Paul discouraged Christians' going to (civil) law (1 Cor 6:1). Further the early church would have been reluctant to appeal to Sanhedrin which indirectly led to the stoning of Stephen (Acts 6:9-15; 7:54-58).

4.9. The Syriac variant ἔχει τι and Aramaism ὕπαγε [Black, 1967: 263, 270] could also support the authenticity of Matt 5:23-24.

4.10. Further Did. 14:2 and 15:3 also stress the reconciliation between the offended and the offender through the offender's initiative. If they have been handed down separately from Matt 5:23-24, that could support the authenticity of this saying. Indeed there are some differences. Did. 14:2 has a much strong colour of a "rule", e.g. "let none who has a quarrel with his fellow join..." than Matt 5:23-24. If the early church made up Matt 5:23-24 they would have made it up into a saying which has the strong character of "ruling" like Did. 14:2.

4.11. Sanders is in favour of rejecting the authenticity of Matt 5:23-24 [1985: 263]; "Since negatives are so difficult to prove, I do not wish to argue that we can know that Jesus said none of the things attributed to him in the sections under consideration. I am inclined to reject the entire section, Matt 5.17-6.18, except for the prayer (Matt 6:9-13)."[1985: 263].[11] At this point it is important to advise readers of Sanders' work

---

[11] Sanders correctly points out the underlying dilemma. Matt 5:23-24 becomes inexplicable in view of Matt 9:13, 12:7, a quotation of the O.T, passage Hos 6:6,

Jewish Law from Jesus to the Mishnah not to be misled by an idea that Sanders regards Matt 5:23-24 (and Mark 1:40-44 and par.) as authentic sayings of Jesus. The following passages could lead readers to gain the impression that Sanders sees Jesus as a strictly law-abiding Jew in matters of repentance and restitution. "The synoptic Jesus lived as a law-abiding Jew." He (the synoptic Jesus) accepts the sacrificial system both as atoning (Matt. 5.23f.) and purifying (Mark 1.40-44). In common with other teachers, he cautioned his followers not to sacrifice until wrongdoing had been rectified and grievance assuaged. [1990: 90]. "Thus when Jesus said that the one who presents an offering, and who remembers that another person has been wronged (implying that it was a guilt offering), should first reconcile the brother (Matt 5:23f), he was in agreement with a long line of people who had made the same point about the relationship between justice and laws of sacrifice." [Sanders, 1990: 43]. After all, it becomes clear that Sanders rejects the authenticity of this saying because in the heading of this book he states: "For the purpose of this study I shall for the most part work on the basis of two assumptions which I do not actually hold: that all the material which is attributed to Jesus in fact goes back to Jesus..." [1990: 1]. (italics mine)

4.12. A sharp point raised in (3.1.c) deserves careful attention but remains unconvincing because of two main reasons.

Firstly, Jesus could have spoken this saying in Judaea [McNeile, 1915: 63]. The references to the location before a collection of sayings, e.g. Jerusalem or Galilee, do not necessarily mean that the entire part was spoken exactly in those places. For example Jesus was set on the pinnacle of the Temple (Matt 4:5) although he was led up by the Spirit to be tempted in the wilderness of the Galilee (Matt 4:1; cf. Matt 3:13). Luke 11:50-52, 13:34-35 are described as spoken in the Judaea while Matt

---

which Sanders regards as hardly authentic: "If he actually explicitly opposed one of the main institutions of Judaism, he kept it secret from his disciples." [1985: 67].

23:34-35, 37-39 are described as spoken in Jerusalem (Matt 21: 1). Luke 18:9-14, an ideal teaching if spoken before the Jerusalem Temple, is described as having been spoken in Judaea. The synoptic evangelists could have put traditions in an ideal place according to their theological perspectives.

Secondly, the Galileans could have returned from Jerusalem to Galilee to make reconciliation with the offended. If the aim of going to the Jerusalem Temple is the forgiveness of sins, the described double trip between Galilee and Jerusalem would have been worth making for the assurance of forgiveness.

4.13. Some scholars regard this sayings as authentic with additional reasons; Grundmann, 1968: 157[12]; Bornkamm, 1956: 114[13] (ET); Jeremias, 1971: 207[14] (Ef); Goppelt, 1975: 107[15] (ET); Luz, 1985: 281, 289[16] (ET); Davies, 1988: 516; 1974: 349 n 45; Flusser, 1988: 494.

---

[12] This saying stems from Jesus' combination of the commandments on the love of God and the love of neighbour.

[13] Bornkamm reads reconciliation with the offended as a condition of receiving God's forgiveness: "For God is prepared to wait, and does not want to come to him alone, unreconciled. Reconciliation to him without a readiness to be reconciled to your brother is impossible."

[14] "Forgiveness—one's own readiness to forgive and a request for forgiveness where one has committed an offence—is the presupposition for the prayer of Jesus' disciples." [Jeremias, 1971, 193 (ET)].

[15] "He did not admonish generally to practice reconciliation, but challenged the one who was about to offer a prayer to think about his relationship to his brother (Mt. 5:23)." However, contrary to Goppelt's argument, reconciliation and repentance and restitution are interlocked in Jesus teaching [O'Neill, 1980: 58].

[16] "As often with Jesus, so we have here a categorical, hyperbolically sharpened exemplary demand which aims at a new basic attitude to the fellow human and as such, enjoins more than its literal fulfillment."

5.

5.1. The main thrust of this saying

Jesus could have asked his followers to demonstrate distinctive morality in the way they behaved in making sacrifices in the Temple. He could have put forward this command in light of sharp teachings on restitution and reconciliation easily comprehensible to the Jewish people of his time. The idea on the imminent end also seems to quicken the urgency of this command, to be equally sensitive to the damage done to neighbours and to the fulfilment of cultic commands. This important command could have led his followers to scrutinize themselves before departing to make a Temple offering: they would need to be sensitive and rigorous in examining their sins and offences inflicted upon others in order to avoid double trips to the Temple.

5.2. The bearing on the forgiveness of sins

Some scholars, while accepting the authenticity of this passage, raise a question whether Jesus deprecates the cultic obligation while emphasizing the love of neighbour [Lohmeyer, 1942: 61[17] (ET)]. Some scholars even argue that Jesus openly declared war on the cult [Hahn, 1970: 25[18] (ET)]. But these scholars seem to go too far. Contrary to their

[17] "From this conscious disregard of current cultic usage one might argue for a fundamental remoteness in Jesus' connexion with it rather than the reverse." Some scholars follow this line of argument although suspecting or rejecting the authenticity of this saying [Moule, 1981: 81, 84; Schrage, 1982: 89 (ET)].

[18] Some scholars follow this strong argument: Schweizer [1973: 119 (ET); Theissen, 1977: 72 (ET)]. However some scholars argue that Jesus did not challenge the authority of the Temple and cult [Grundmann, 1968: 157; Hill, 1972: 122, 175; Goppelt, 1975: 96 (ET); Gnilka, 1986: 156; Ashby, 1988: 50]. Jeremias' argument is most illuminating: "This saying is not meant, say, to devalue sacrifice in favour of

arguments, the command to complete the offering at the altar after a temporary suspension in Matt 5:24 clearly counts against these arguments. The need of offering was not rejected. This saying rather teaches the need to render a perfect offering which includes a due restoration of personal relationships through restitution and reconciliation.

---

fellowship (sacrifice is unimportant, a man's relationship to his brother is the only thing that matters); on the contrary, it is meant to take sacrifice with the utmost seriousness." [1971: 193 (ET)]. Luz draws our attention to the importance of the unity of the ethics and cult embedded in wisdom tradition [1985: 289 (ET)].

B. Did Jesus stress repentance and forgiveness in Matt 18:23-35?

1. The conjectured text

Matt 18:23 Διὰ τοῦτο ὡμοιώθη ἡ βασιλεία τῶν οὐρανῶν ἀνθρώπῳ
βασιλεῖ, ὃς ἠθέλησεν συνᾶραι λόγον μετὰ τῶν δούλων αὐτοῦ.
24 ἀρξαμένου δὲ αὐτοῦ συναίρειν προσηνέχθη αὐτῷ εἷς
ὀφειλέτης μυρίων ταλάντων. 25 μὴ ἔχοντος δὲ αὐτοῦ ἀποδοῦναι
ἐκέλευσεν αὐτὸν ὁ κύριος πραθῆναι καὶ τὴν γυναῖκα καὶ τὰ
τέκνα καὶ πάντα ὅσα ἔχει, καὶ ἀποδοθῆναι. 26 πεσὼν οὖν ὁ
δοῦλος προσεκύνει αὐτῷ λέγων, Μακροθύμησον ἐπ' ἐμοί, καὶ
πάντα ἀποδώσω σοι. 27 σπλαγχνισθεὶς δὲ ὁ κύριος τοῦ δούλου
ἐκείνου ἀπέλυσεν αὐτον καὶ τὸ δάνειον ἀφῆκεν αὐτῷ. 28
ἐξελθὼν δὲ ὁ δοῦλος ἐκεῖνος εὗρεν ἕνα τῶν συνδούλων αὐτοῦ
ὃς ὤφειλεν αὐτῷ ἑκατὸν δηνάρια, καὶ κρατήσας αὐτὸν ἔπνιγεν
λέγων, ἀπόδος εἴ τι ὀφείλεις. 29 πεσὼν οὖν ὁ σύνδουλος αὐτοῦ
παρεκάλει αὐτον λέγων Μακροθύμησον ἐπ' ἐμοί, καὶ ἀποδώσω
σοι.

30 ὁ δὲ οὐκ ἤθελεν ἀλλὰ ἀπελθὼν ἔβαλεν αὐτον εἰς φυλακὴν
ἕως ἀποδῷ τὸ ὀφειλόμενον 31 ἰδόντες οὖν οἱ σύνδουλοι αὐτοῦ
τὰ γενόμενα ἐλυπήθησαν σφόδρα καὶ ἐλθόντες διεσάφησαν τῷ
κυρίῳ ἑαυτῶν πάντα τὰ γενόμενα. 32 τότε προσκαλεσάμενος
αὐτὸν ὁ κύριος αὐτοῦ λέγει αὐτῷ, Δοῦλε πονηρέ, πᾶσαν τὴν
ὀφειλὴν ἐκείνην ἀφῆκά σοι, ἐπεὶ παρεκάλεσάς με· 33 οὐκ ἔδει
καὶ σὲ ἐλεῆσαι τὸν σύνδουλόν σου, ὡς κἀγὼ σὲ ἠλέησα; 34 καὶ
ὀργισθεὶς ὁ κύριος αὐτοῦ παρέδωκεν αὐτὸν τοῖς βασανισταῖς
ἕως οὗ ἀποδῷ πᾶν τὸ ὀφειλόμενον.

2. Arguments concerning the excluded parts

I accept the substantial authenticity of the parable as printed. My only hesitation is about whether or not v.35 originally belonged to the parable.

V. 35 οὕτως καὶ ὁ πατήρ μου ὁ οὐράνιος ποιήσει ὑμῖν, ἐὰν μὴ ἀφῆτε ἕκαστος τῷ ἀδελφῷ αὐτοῦ ἀπὸ τῶν καρδιῶν ὑμῶν] Perhaps an isolated saying was put here at a later stage.[19]

3. Arguments against 1

3.1. The entire parable is made up by the early church to stress the need for forgiveness between Christians [Hirsch, 1951: 321].

3.2. Some scholars argue that vv. 30-34 is a secondary episode made up by the early church [Fiedler, 1976: 197-204; Weder, 1978: 211-212, 217].[20] Vv. 30-34 are unnecessary, even cause a misunderstanding [Fiedler, 1976: 204; Weder 1978: 211-212].

3.3. The following arguments are put forward in support of the claim that later hands have added to the parable.

---

[19] This argument is supported by the following scholars [Jeremias, 1962: 109 (ET); Linnemann, 1964: 107 (ET); Grundmann, 1968: 422-423; Perrin, 1967: 125; deBoer, 1988: 228]. Bultmann argues for its construction by Matthew [1931: 177 (ET)]. Kilpatrick read it as: "...an interpretative addition apparently derived from Mark xi.25." [1950: 29].

[20] Gnilka, rejecting the two alleged intrinsically different segments theory of Weder or Fiedler, argues that vv. 23-33 is the original parable of Jesus [1989: 144, 148]. Perrin also regards v. 34 as a possible Matthean addition which "converts the original challenge of this parable into a warning" [1967: 125]. However this argument is unconvincing. The threatening tone already emerges in vv. 23-30 (the command to sell the family and to go to prison). The only difference is the "reprieved" and "executed" command.

a. The un-Jewish feature in this parable could indicate its secondary nature.[21] "A man is sold as a Hebrew slave, but a woman is not sold as a Hebrew slave." (t. Sota 2.9)[22] [Jeremias, 1962: 211 (ET); Linnemann, 1964: 109 n g (ET); Gnilka, 1988: 146]. Scholars differ as to whether they take these vestiges as evidence that Jesus did not tell the parable or as evidence of secondary embellishments which can be removed to leave behind an authentic parable.

b. The inconsistent use of "king" (v. 23) and "lord" (v. 25, 27, 32, 34), contrary to the consistency of using "king" in the Marriage Feast (22:1-14), could hint at its secondary nature [deBoer, 1988: 225-227; cf. Michaelis, 1956: 191].

c. God could hardly have reversed his decree of forgiveness: for an oriental monarch to rescind a decree would have been a serious matter.[23]

d. Some parts of this parable show vestiges of a later hand, e.g. μυρίων ταλάντων, προσκυνέω [deBoer, 1988: 222-223, 227-229].

4. Arguments against 3

---

[21] Hirsch [1951: 321] already points out that this parable describes circumstance unknown to Jesus. Linnemann argues that there was no slavery for debt in Israel and no allowance of torture in Jewish law. However βασανισταῖς could mean "jailers" [BAGD: 134].

[22] Neusner's translation of the *Tosefta vol. 3* [1979].

[23] A similar account appears in b. Famid 32a-32b: "Behold I will slay you by royal decree. They replied: Power is in the hands of the king, but it beseems not a king to be false." A story of a king who agonized over the change of his decree [Braude, 1959, vol. 1: 96-97]. The king Alexander was told not to change his previous oath: *Plutarch's Lives* in Perrin's translation [1919: column 64].

4.1. Is (3.1) convincing? Hirsch gives an impression that the entire parable vv. 23-34 was made up by the early church to stress the mutual forgiveness between themselves [1951: 320-321]. He argues that "king" ("lord") and "his servants" are allegorical descriptions of "the risen Christ" and "his community" [1951: 321].[24] This argument seems forced. Even if Hirsch's argument is right it is seriously defective as a Christian allegory. If the early Church describes the king as God, and the first servant (singular) as Christians (plural) who are forgiven, why would they have made up "the paying back of everything (v. 26, 29 ("I will pay you")) (the return of all debt to God)." The early church would scarcely have thought that they could pay back God's forgiveness completely by doing some sort of a corresponding action.

4.2. Neither Fiedler nor Weder suspects the authenticity of the first segment. Both of them affirm that vv. 23-30 could have come from Jesus [1976: 195-197, 200, 204; 1978: 211-212]. On the contrary, (3.2) vv. 31-34 need to be interpreted differently. There seems to be no hard evidence of the secondary nature of vv. 31-34.[25] The early church would hardly have made up vv. 31-34, a passage stressing the reversal of forgiveness and an ensuing judgment. The pervasive underlying assumption of Fiedler's argument is that the God whom Jesus proclaimed is the God of forgiveness, not of judgment [1978: 204]. Therefore Fiedler dismisses vv. 3lb-34 as secondary due to its judgmental features, e.g. the imprisonment and renewed claim of debt (v. 30b, 34). However even Fiedler would agree on one point: judgmental features, which he assumes to emerge only

---

[24] The description "fellow servant" (συνδούλων) (vv.28-29) or "fellow servants" (αύνδούλοι) (v. 31) depicts the close internal relationship within the Christian church.

[25] Fiedler dismisses the authenticity of v.30b. He concedes that it is possible to ascribe this parable (vv. 23-30a) to the context of Jesus' proclamation [1976: 201-204].

in vv. 30b-34, already appear in vv. 23-30: the command to pay the debt even by becoming a slave family (v. 25). Further it is noteworthy that Fiedler does not put forward any more decisive evidence of its secondary nature. The God Jesus proclaimed is certainly the God of forgiveness, but at the same time, the God of judgment[26]: forgiveness and judgment are two sides of the same coin.

4.3. Weder argues that vv. 32-34 gives an impression that it is an interpretation of the preceding parable (vv. 23-30) [1978: 211]. Weder fails to see the intrinsic difference between vv. 23-30 and vv. 31-34. The people who hear vv. 23-30 may have grasped the point quickly, but at the same time there is a danger: They could have ended up with a wrong interpretation, e.g. there are merciless people (in prestigious positions) who defraud only the powerless and poor. Only by hearing the reminder (vv. 30-34), the emphasis on God's judgment to a person who failed to forgive others the audience would have become aware of the point. At this point the role of vv. 30-34 seems to be unique. Hence unless there was a guarantee that Jesus' audience could have grasped the point of vv.

[26] Fiedler argues that a Jew could see his existence in God's forgiveness is natural and as not to be doubted [203]. Fiedler thinks that God's forgiveness is not conditional: God is bound to forgive [ibid]. In order to prove his argument Fiedler cites Sifre Deut 21:8 along with Sifre zuta Num 27:17: "Ruler of the world, you did not bring out Israel from Egypt under the condition, that you, when they sinned, would wish to make demands on them, but under the condition, that you, when they sinned, would wish to forgive them." [Fiedler, 203]. Fiedler argues that Jesus and his hearers built their basis upon this assurance [203]. Weder, along with Fiedler, stress only the love side of God's character [1978: 216-217]. The absense of any reference to the need for repentance in this rabbinic saying does not, of course, mean that the writer thought God's forgiveness was granted whatever Israel did and even if they did not repent.

23-30 this sort of interpretation would have been necessary.[27]

4.4. Fiedler argues that vv. 32-34 are unnecessary,[28] because vv. 23-30a already contains what Jesus intended to express, or even misleading, because Jesus' hearers might have doubted God's wholesome mercy which overwhelms any barrier against the forgiveness of sins [1976: 204].[29] One of the reasons why Fiedler dismisses vv. 32-34 as secondary is that compared with the enormous mercy and forgiveness of God, the demand to forgive the culpable neighbour is almost unnecessary [1976: 204]. However the point of the matter is not the astonishing magnitude of forgiveness to the first servant, but the clear stress on the need to forgive others. "The ordinance of mercy" [Linnemann, 1964: 112 (ET)] or "No abuse of God's mercy" [Fuchs, 1960: 153 (ET)] shows that the forgiveness of others is firmly set as a necessary condition. This is the binding force in this parable. The claim and punishment commanded in vv. 32-34 hardly contradict the mercy and forgiveness shown in vv. 23-30a. The emphasis on the responsibility to forgive fellow servants is hardly insignificant or invalid compared with the mercy and forgiveness of God in vv. 23-30a. Scripture clearly stresses God's love and judgment equally. God rules the world by the two measures, mercy and judgment, but at the last judgment God uses only the measure of judgment; compassion shall pass away (2 Esdras 7:33-34; cf 1 Enoch 13:1-4, 14:4-7). God's forgiveness does not dispense with the need for forgiving a

---

[27] Jesus spoke in the milieu of the audience who would have needed a full interpretation.

[28] Fiedler already dismisses v. 30b-31 as secondary [1976: 197-199].

[29] Fiedler argues that the sin of not forgiving the neighbour is already absorbed in God's forgiveness. This interpretation is hardly correct. Each forgiveness has its own domain. Further this parable clearly captures the spirit of judgment or what Fuchs calls the "threatening tone" [1960: 153 (ET)].

neighbour's sin[30] (cf. Matt 13:24-30; the parable of the Tares; Matt 13:47-50: the parable of net). Hence this parable could echo the Jewish conception of forgiveness embedded in Jesus' teaching.

4.5. Further the early church would have been reluctant to make up this passage which teaches that the forgiveness made in the crucifixion of Jesus would have been rescinded as a result of their unmerciful behaviour to their fellow Christians (v. 34).[31] For the same reason a clause like "(I forgave you all that debt) because you besought me" (v. 32) would have been unnecessary to the early church for the purpose of allegorization. The criteria of judgment at the end taken by the early church would have been belief in the risen Jesus as Messiah, not the behaviour of Christians.

4.6. Contrary to (3.3.a), a different view could emerge. Selling of children is attested: Amos 2:6-7, 8:6, Sifre Deut iii. 23. 26 (70a), 2 Kings 4:1 (children seized by creditors), Isa 50: 1, Neh 5:5 (parents selling their children). V. 25 seems not to refer to the sale of a wife as an isolated case, as Jeremias assumes "... his lord ordered him to be sold, with his wife and children and all that he had" (v. 25) could mean that the first servant is ordered to be sold to another owner as a whole slave family with their belongings to pay the debt (within many years to come). Maccoby correctly notes that only a limited form of slavery was allowed to cover a case of bankruptcy so that, by selling himself, a person could pay his debts and achieve a kind of livelihood [1989: 125]. If the aim of

---

[30] "The point of the parable is the miracle of the justice of God.... But God insists upon the dignity of his mercy. As God was merciful, he wants his mercy to he respected.... The action of God is similar to that of nature. Nature lets itself be used, but not abused. He who abuses it, will be punished." [Fuchs, 1959: 493].

[31] Only those who commit apostasy, or fall away (παραπεσόντας) (Heb 6:6) are described as having no chance of repentance.

the sale was not to get a gradual payment of debt from the earnings of labour the king need hardly have allowed them to go with πάντα ὅσα ἔχει, which could be confiscated, but which were seemingly essential for survival and labour. Thus this account has a fair ground to be regarded as a genuine story.

4.7. (3.3.b) deserves a careful consideration. Has Matthew introduced βασιλεῖ in v. 3 to turn this parable into an allegory about a king [Michaelis, 1956: 191; Jeremias, 1962: 28 (ET); Weiser, 1971: 75; deBoer, 1988: 225-227, 229]? On the contrary, the majority of manuscripts witness that the original parable has βασιλεῖ in its text.[32] Further, the Aramaism of ἀνθρώπῳ βασιλεῖ [Dalman, 1898: 64], is a sign of primitiveness. Manuscripts 472*, g omit ἀνθρώπῳ, perhaps a deliberate removal of the Aramaism. Rather ὁ βασιλεύς is omitted in Matt 22:13 (ff^1) and in Luke 10:24 (P^{25} pc sa^{ms} bo^{ms}).

deBoer's argument seems to arise because after v. 23 only ὁ κύριος follows consistently (v. 25, 27, 31, 32, 34). But Jesus could have alternated between "king" and "Lord". Certainly sometimes ὁ κύριος was used consistently (Luke 14:15-24) (V. 21, 22, 23). Matt 21:1-11 has "lord" (v. 3), "king" (v. 5) and "lord" (v. 9). Likewise, Matt 25:31-46 starts with "the Son of Man" which is replaced by "king" (v. 34, 40) and "lord" (v. 37, 44). All these cases indicate that the alleged change from "lord" to the "king" in Matt 18:23 did not happen. Further no manuscript witnesses the addition of ὁ κύριος in 23-30 and vv. 31-34.

The "king" fits this context because the large sums of money hints at a royal situation.[33] Accordingly, it is convincing that the dialogue

---

[32] B. T. D. Smith [1937: 217], Grundmann [1968: 422] also affirm that this parable originally refers to a "king."

[33] Via [1967: 138 n 60] ; Jeremias [1962: 210-211 (ET)]; Linnemann [1964: 108, 175 n 8 (ET)].

between ὁ κύριος and δοῦλος elucidates the hierarchy between the two persons. Further, in the parable of the Last Judgment (Matt 24:31-46), the Son of man (v. 31) and king (v. 34, 40) are replaced by the "lord" (v. 37, 44) and "he" (v. 45, the king) without spoiling the consistency. Hence, it is not convincing to argue that "king" (v. 23) is altered to "lord" by Matthew.

4.8. (3.3.c) is an argument of significance. However God is described as having repented when his holy work was abused by wicked human behaviour (Jer 18:10; 1 Sam 15:11; cf. Mark 13:20). In some cases God withholds his hand, and cancels an unfavourable decree (Gen 18:20-30; Exod 32:7-14; 1 King 21:19, 29; Jonah 3:10). In Luke 13:6-9 the decision to cut down a tree (v. 7) is reprieved for one year. Thus, it is biblical to state that even divine decrees are sometimes revocable for the repentance of the people. If a king can revoke a pardon granted, it testifies to the conditional character of God's forgiveness.

4.9. On (3.3.d) some scholars argue that, when compared with the parable of the Talents (Matt 25:16-28; Luke 19:11-27), the astonishing discrepancy in the amount of debt hints at Matthew's inflation, who wants to maximize the difference of amount.[34] Others argue that this extraordinary amount arose from the incorrect copying of scribes[35] of originally 10 talents [T. W. Manson, 1948: 213] or ten thousands denarii [deboer, 1988: 227-229]. These arguments does not seem compelling. There are records which witness vast amount of money (Josephus, *Jewish*

[34] B. T. D. Smith suspects that "Matthew has multiplied the debt in order to heighten the contrast between the two sums involved and to emphasize the moral of the story." [1937: 218]. Jeremias [1962: 210-211 (ET)].

[35] On the amount of debt, Aleph* Origen, co has πολλῶν instead of μυρίων ταλάντων (v. 24).

Antiquities 12.175-176).[36] Moreover, in Luke 12:1, Acts 21: 20, Heb 12:22 and other texts, μυρίων is used for describing "innumerable, countless" [BAGD: 529].[37]Hence Matthew does not seem to be responsible for conflating the amount of the servant's debt.

4.10. Is προσεκύνει (v. 26) Matthew's editorial work? [deBoer, 1988: 222-223; Linnemann, 1964: 109 n 1].[38] deBoer argue for this case because προσεκύνει often describes the worship of Jesus (Matt 2:2, 8, 11; 8:2; 9:18; 14:33; 15:25; 20:20; 28:9, 17; 4:10 (worship to God); 4:9 (worship to Satan)) and παρεκάλει in v. 29 better fits the context. However προσεκύνει does not carry the same meaning of "worship" in all other instances in Matthew. Sometimes both προσεκύνει and παρεκάλει describe the desperation of the entreating sick or sinners (9:18; 14:33; 15:25), as in this parable (v. 26). Joseph and Asenath 5:10 depicts "utmost respect to another person", not worship of a divine figure. Moreover, the need to describe a hierarchical relationship between creditor and debtor, the king and the first servant, and the first servant and the second servant, could have led to the use of different verbs. deBoer elaborates an argument that the structure of v.26 demonstrates a Matthean pattern (8:2; 9:18; 15:25, cf 20:20-21): (a) the imperfect προσεκύνει preceded (b) by the aorist participle of attendant circumstances προσελθὼν and followed (c) by the participle λέγων that introduces (d) a request for assistance [deBoer, 222]. This theory deserves careful attention. But the point is that v. 26 has πεσὼν not προσελθὼν which has an identical meaning. In Matthew these words stand in different order when describing the same scene "falling on knees to Jesus" (λέγων...

---

[36] Derrett [1970: 36].

[37] It is a parable, not a narrative.

[38] deBoer, 1988: 222; Linnemann, 1964: 109, n 1. [BAGD: 716: the first meaning].

προσελθοῦσαι... προσεκύνησαν) (Matt 28:9) and (προσεκύνησαν... προσελθὼν... λέγων) (Matt 28:17-18). Hence the theory, this pattern is used to describe the worship of God, the heavenly father or the earthly Jesus, not the behaviour of ordinary people, remains not compelling. Rather it would be more convincing that the verb and the pattern (προσελθὼν...προσεκύνει...λέγων) is used to demonstrate an approach in desperate need and respect to a mighty figure. It must be noted that deBoer's theory does not distinguish the heavenly God from the earthly Jesus.

4.11. deBoer argues that ὡμοιώθη ἡ βασιλεία τῶν οὐρανῶν is the formulation of Matthew, indicative of Matthew's orientation toward the final judgement, because it is unique in Matt [1988: 225].[39] But it is not clear whether this formulation was from Matthew or from the pre-Matthean tradition available to him. deBoer himself also is not sure of his theory [1988: 225]. In Matt parables start with various ways of introductory formulae (in present, past and future tense). It must be noted that the present verb in the parable characterizes a typical recurrent episode, and the historic tense characterizes a particular affair treated as typical [Dodd, 1936: 18]. Accordingly the argument which supports the formulation of Matt 18:23 loses its force.

4.12. Some scholars regard this parable as authentic with or without additional reasons; Juelicher, 1899: 305; J. Weiss, 1917: 340[40];

---

[39] "I thus think it likely that the introduction to the parable of the Unforgiving, Servant is redactional, though it is impossible to be sure."

[40] J. Weiss merely suspects that the original idea in Jesus parable of the Talents (Matt 25:14-30; Luke 19:11-27) was substantially reworked later.

Montefiore, 1927, vol. 2: 256[41]; Klostemann, 1927: 153[42]; Bultmann, 1931: 177 (ET)[43]; Linnemann, 1964: 177 (ET); Perrin, 1967: 126[44]; Grundmann, 1968: 423[45]; Gnilka, 1988: 148.

5.

5.1. The main thrust of this saying

Jesus could have underscored the need of forgiveness and repentance in this parable. Matthew could have put this saying in its present position to reflect the life setting of his church.[46] The debate on

---

[41] "There is no reason why it should not be authentic. The moral is clear, and wholly in accordance with Rabbinic teaching."

[42] Klostermann leaves the authenticity of v. 35 open: a pre-Matthean tradition or a saying repeatedly spoken by Jesus. He seems to regard vv. 23-34 as an authentic saying of Jesus [1927: 153].

[43] "To this parable, began again with (διὰ τοῦτο) ὡμοιώθη ἡ βασιλεία τ οὐρ. and continuing. thence forward entirely in narrative form, an application is added by the phrase οὕτως καὶ ὁ πατήρ... ποιήσει ὑμῖν, which rightly expresses its meaning, though admittedly this does not establish its original character." Bultmann regards v. 35 as secondary. He seems not suspects the authenticity of the main body (vv. 23-34).

[44] Perrin takes this story's context, which corresponds the Palestine (except the sale of a wife), as evidence of authenticity.

[45] Grundmann states that Jesus was described as asking forgiveness and reconciliation between peoples which springs from their hearts (ἀπὸ τῶν καρδιῶν ὑμῶν) [1968: 425].

[46] Hill rightly points how the early church used this saying in describing their life setting: "Just as the merciful king and the heavenly Father have to be severe in their judgment on the unforgiving, so the Church, though ready to pardon, is forced to judge sternly those who jeopardize the fellowship by their lack of mercy towards others." [1972: 277].

the original parable does not affect the core teachings of this parable. Both the longer version (vv. 23-35) and the short version (vv. 23-30) clearly teach two points. Firstly, sinners should repent. The first servant was forgiven only after admitting his debt and asking for patience (v. 26). Likewise the second servant shows a clear sign of repentance (v. 29). Secondly, true repentance requires a willingness to forgive others. Jesus' listeners perhaps could arrive at a similar point in their meditation on the meaning of this shorter version. The longer version directly stresses this point.

5.2. The bearing on the forgiveness of sin

Sanders does not deal with this significant passage. This parable is one of important passages which teach the conditional nature of forgiveness: repentance accompanied by the willingness to forgive others must precede the entreaty for the forgiveness of sins.[47]

---

[47] T. W. Manson: "The parable itself emphasizes a characteristic feature in the teaching of Jesus that only a forgiving spirit can receive forgiveness, that a mean and revengeful disposition shuts out God's forgiveness..." [1948: 213]. Beasley-Murray [1986: 154].

CHAPTER V

The Special Lucan Passages

A. Did Jesus call for national repentance in Luke 13:1-5?

1. The conjectured original text?

Luke 13:1 Παρῆσαν δέ τινες ἐν αὐτῷ τῷ καιρῷ ἀπαγγέλλοντες αὐτῷ περὶ τῶν Γαλιλαίων ὧν τὸ αἷμα Πιλᾶτος ἔμιξεν μετὰ τῶν θυσιῶν αὐτῶν. 2 καὶ ἀποκριθεὶς εἶπεν αὐτοῖς, δοκεῖτε ὅτι οἱ Γαλιλαῖοι οὗτοι ἁμαρτωλοὶ παρὰ πάντας τοὺς Γαλιλαίους ἐγένοντο, ὅτι ταῦτα πεπόνθασιν; 3 οὐχί, λέγω ὑμῖν, ἀλλ' ἐὰν μὴ μετανοῆτε πάντες ὁμοίως ἀπολεῖσθε. 4 ἢ ἐκεῖνοι οἱ δεκαοκτὼ ἐφ' οὓς ἔπεσεν ὁ πύργος ἐν τῷ Σιλωὰμ καὶ ἀπέκτεινεν αὐτούς, δοκεῖτε ὅτι αὐτοὶ ὀφειλέται ἐγένοντο παρὰ πάντας τοὺς ἀνθρώπους τοὺς κατοικοῦντας Ἰερουσαλήμ; 5 οὐχί, λέγω ὑμῖν, ἀλλ' ἐὰν μὴ μετανοῆτε πάντες ὡσαύτως ἀπολεῖσθε.

2. Arguments concerning the authenticity of the excluded parts

Nothing is excluded. It seems unnecessary to argue that περὶ τῶν Γαλιλαίων ὧν τὸ αἷμα Πιλᾶτος ἔμιξεν μετὰ τῶν θυσιῶν αὐτῶν was shifted from its original location after οἱ Γαλιλαῖοι οὗτοι (v. 2) to the present position in order to explain the historical background of vv 2-5 [Evans, 1990: 546]. A similar argument was put forward: ἐκεινοι οἱ

Γαλιλαίοι instead of περὶ τῶν Γαλιλαίων [G. Schwarz, 1969: 123]. The speaker could comment about the slaying after having heard about the incident from the informants.

3. Arguments against the authenticity of 1.

3.1. This passage is not authentic because the account in Luke 13:1-5 is not paralleled outside the N.T.. Josephus could have hardly missed noticing this incident [Wellhausen, 1904: 71[1]; Klostermann, 1929: 142].

3.2. Luke could have constructed this saying on the basis of Josephus' account in *Jewish Antiquities* 18. 85-87 [Bultmann 1931: 110, 23, 54-55, 64 (ET); Sanders, 1985: 110[2]].

3.3. Some scholars argue against the authenticity of this saying on the basis of the fact that in v. 3, 5 Jesus is portrayed as rejecting the traditional Jewish idea of the relationship between punishment and sins: earthly disaster demonstrates the punishment of particular sins [Fiedler, 1976: 110]. The denial of this generally accepted understanding about the

---

[1] Wellhausen' point could be summarized as follows [1904: 71]. 1) If this happened in Jerusalem, Josephus would have reported it. 2) Galileans could only make sacrifices in Jerusalem. 3) So this refers to the Samaritans (Josephus, *Jewish Antiquities* 18-85). 4) This event led to Pilate's deposition from office. 5) If this event occurred after Easter 35 Jesus would not have referred to it; Easter 35 is the latest date for his crucifixion. 6) Luke clearly did not use Josephus. To sum up, Wellhausen supposes that the rebels murdered at the altar could not be Galileans; the murder of the Samaritans (Josephus, *Antiquities* 18: 85-87) cited by Josephus was probably mentioned here. Nevertheless it is important to notice Wellhausen's position; Luke clearly did not know Josephus' work [1904: 71].

[2] Sanders concurs with Bultmann who argues for Luke's dependency on Josephus, *Jewish Antiquities* 18. 87 [1931: 55 (ET)]. There is a fundamental difference between Wellhausen and Bultmann on the view over the historicity of the account in Luke 13:1-5. Wellhausen argues for Luke's independence of Josephus. On the contrary Bultmann argues for Luke's dependence on the Josephus account.

sequence between a sinful act and the following punishment could probably be regarded as a special Christian idea [Fiedler, 1976: 266-267[3]].

3.4. The motive for repentance is not the newly proclaimed salvation but fear of judgment and this contradicts Jesus' standard approach [cf. Fiedler, 1976: 267[4]].

3.5. The account of Archaelaus' massacre of the Jewish people was wrongly attributed to Pilate (*Jewish Antiquities,* 17. 213-218).

3.6. Luke 13:4 could be inauthentic because Aboth Rabbi Nathan 35 states that no structures ever collapsed in Jerusalem.

4. The counter arguments against 3.

4.1. Contrary to the assumption taken in the hypothesis (3.1) Luke could be more reliable than Josephus. Luke 13:1-2, although not paralleled in Josephus, could be firm because Luke probably did not use Josephus as a source.[5] In addition there is no guarantee that Josephus wrote about

---

[3] Fiedler at first does not give reasons for authenticity. He merely states that it is out of question to trace this saying back to Jesus [1976: 110]. But he holds this probable Christian element to be a piece of the evidence of inauthenticity [1976: 266-267].

[4] Fiedler cites J. Becker [1972: 89]. Becker summarizes his point in his conclusion. He seems to grasp the double nature of the coming kingdom correctly. The imminent judgment and the kingdom of God are chronologically understood [1972: 105].

[5] Concerning the historicity of two figures in Acts 5:36-37, Hemer argues that "it is generally agreed that Luke did not use Josephus as a source. It is possible that Josephus rather than Luke is wrong." [1989: 162]. "The fact that Luke's background information can so often be corroborated may suggest that it is wiser to leave this particular matter open rather than condemn Luke of a blunder." [163].

every incident that occurred in Israel. Josephus could have ignored the incident of Pilate's mingling of the blood of the Galileans with their sacrifices (vv. 1-2) for the following reason. Compared with thousands of people murdered in other incidents of which he wrote, a small number of people was slaughtered. The number of the victims "eighteen" in v. 4 could hint at a relatively small number of the massacred in the incident in vv. 1-2. Further, why would the early church make up this passage from a vacuum when they could have drawn a similar account from Josephus' work?

4.2. Josephus would have concealed by all means the fact that the Roman prefect Pilate allowed his soldiers to slaughter some Galileans during one of the special Jewish festivals.[6] The report on the massacre followed by the mingling of their blood with their sacrifices at the center of the Jewish religion could have led to a great outcry against the Romans. The plea of maintaining security inside the Temple could not justify the mingling of the blood of worshipers with the blood of their sacrifices. Even the Roman reader would have condemned this horrible triple sin committed in the shadow of the *Pax Romana.*

4.3. Josephus could have been reluctant to portray Galileans, whom he, describes as ληστάς, brigands or revolutionaries, from his experience in Galilee (*The life,* 28-30. 175), as religiously faithful to the Temple sacrifice.

4.4. The absence of a parallel account in Josephus could hardly affect the authenticity of Luke 13:1-5. Josephus' account of Pilate's career could be incomplete [W. L. Knox, 1957: 75[7]; Marshall, 1978: 553]. Josephus

---

[6] Blinzler strongly defends the historicity and authenticity of two incidents recorded in Luke 13:1-5 [1958: 24-49]. Grundmann, 1981: 275-277.

[7] "But the massacre of a few Galileans during a riot at the Passover or some similar occasion might well be too small a matter to excite any particular interest,

gives as the reason for the withdrawal of the effigies from Jerusalem the bravery of the Jews (*Jewish War* 2.169-174; *Jewish Antiquities* 18.55-59). However Philo gives as the reason Pilate's concern over the letter of petition to Tiberius *(Legato Ad Gaium* 299-305).

4.5. The hypothesis (3.2) is not entirely convincing. This hypothesis could give a partial answer about the source of Luke 13:1-2. It does not give an answer about the source of the account in Luke 13:4. Josephus has no similar account of the Fall of the Tower of Siloam described in Luke 13:4. Further Josephus need not have mentioned the accident in Luke 13:4 because it is not a political affair and because it presupposes the knowledge of the hearers of the local history of Jerusalem [cf. Wellhausen, 1904: 71-72; Klostermann, 1929: 143]. This accident could have escaped the attention of the secular historian Josephus [T. W. Manson, 1948: 74].[8] Thus it would be more convincing to argue that Luke was independent of Josephus.[9]

---

especially if they belonged to the disaffected element in the population which Josephus habitually writes off as brigands." Zeitlin points out the clear contradiction between the account in Josephus' *The Life* 7-8 (28-39) and *Jewish War* 2. 569-576 [1973: 192]. Zeitlin argues that Josephus played a double role in Galilee.

[8] "It has no significance for the secular historian." According to W. L. Knox the water draining was repeated daily for seven days of the feast [1957: 76]. This heavy use of water during the Festival season and the uncertain location of the Tower could, as Finegan [1969: 114] hints, support the likelihood of this accident.

[9] W. L. Knox rightly points out the possibility of a minor turbulence during the Passover and the following slaying of some Galileans: "The natural occasion for such an incident would be one of the great festivals, Passover, Weeks or Tabernacles, when there were large crowds of Galileans in Jerusalem, and a disturbance would easily arise which might lead to the massacre. We cannot rule out the possibility of a disturbance at the feast of Tabernacles" [1957: 76]. The festivals were likely to be occasion of disturbance (Josephus, *Jewish War* 1. 88) [1953: 118]; the disturbance at the feast of Tabernacles (*Jewish Antiquities.* 13. 372). However O. Betz argues that this incident occurred during the Passover, the only festival at which lay people could bring sacrifices to the Temple [1990: 244].

4.6. It is hardly likely that the early church or Luke made up a fake story with "eighteen", the number of casualties. If they did, they would not have specified the number of victims. They would have not included a specific number unless it is a historical source. It does not goes with Luke's policy of discretion in 1:1-3.

4.7. Did the early church change the massacre of the Samaritans in Josephus' *Jewish Antiquities* 18.86-87 into a story about Galileans? That could hardly be the case. The two incidents seem distinctively different. A simple embellishment would not have narrowed the fundamental difference: The identification of the victim (The Samaritans vs. the Galileans), the place of the incident (Mount Gerizim in Samaria vs. the Jerusalem temple), the way of disposing the corpse (the mingling of the blood vs. the absence of such account). Moreover, the early church would have had no reason to make up an account by substituting "the Galileans" for "the Samaritans". If they made up this passage they would have preferred to put the Jerusalemites or the Jews, a group of people in general, rather than the Galileans, a particular group of people.

4.8. The hypothesis (3.3) seems to take hold of the wrong end of the stick. What Fiedler puts forward as evidence for inauthenticity could rather support authenticity ironically. Fiedler assumes the denial of the idea of the sequence whereby the sinful act followed by punishment is evidence of its Christian origin [1976: 266-277]. In the course of this argument he cites Kuemmel and Jeremias [1971: 110]. What Fiedler neglects to consider is that these two scholars affirm the authenticity of this saying in their arguments.[10] Against the argument Fiedler puts forward, the point

---

[10] " The tendency to regard earthly misfortune as punishment for special guilt is therefore just as much rejected by Jesus" [Kuemmel, 1972: 56 (ET)]. "In Luke 13:1-5 Jesus expressly attacks the dogma that misfortune is a punishment for the definite sins of particular people." [Jeremias, 1971: 183 (ET)] (Job 4:7; 8:20; 22:3-5; John 5:14; 9:1-3). However both scholars seems not to state the main point of this passage. "Jesus does not criticize or deny the prevailing doctrine of the time that

Jesus stresses in Luke 13:1-5 is not the outright denial of the connection between fate and guilt but the urgency of repentance in view of the imminent end (cf. Bornkamm [1959: 87[11] (ET)]).

4.9. Contrary to (3.4) the eschatological feature of this saying [Jeremias, 1971: 134 (ET)] could support its authenticity. The offering of salvation and the warning of rejection are two sides of the same coin. Both sides are equally important. Fiedler seems to fail to capture the judgmental character of the coming kingdom [see my general argument in Chapter 1.C.2 b].

4.10. The episode on Archaelaus' slaughter (3.5) is similar to Luke 13:1-5 in some points. Jerusalem is the place of the incident, the Jewish people were slaughtered while busy offering sacrifices. However, this incident took place some thirty years earlier at the time of a different ruler. This number of massacred (three thousand) is hardly comparable with the number of victims (eighteen) in v. 4 [Marshall, 1978: 553]. παρῆσαν (v. 1) hints that Jesus was told of a contemporary incident. This hypothesis (3.5) leaves the source of Luke 13:4-5 unanswered.

---

suffering denoted guilt." [Montefiore, 1927, vol. 2: 500]. Further, Jeremias notes that "suffering. is a call to repentance, a call which goes out to all." [183].

[11] "Thus he (Jesus) puts an end to the question of God's justice in relation to this catastrophe and that turns it into a new question to his questioners, facing them with themselves and the future of God." However "The point of the passage is not that the men who suffered were not guilty, but they were not *specially* guilty." [Montefiore, 1927, vol. 2: 500]. Schmid also affirms that Jesus does not reject the connection between suffering and sin [1960: 228]. Conzelmann lucidly sums up the point of this saying: Jesus seemed not to have developed any idea of judgment. The focus is rather that of judgment in the world to come [1968: 114 (ET)]. "The Old Testament idea of guilt and retribution is taken up (Luke 13.1 ff.). But the dominant idea is that of judgment in the world to come." [114]. "Penitence is required, and in return man receives forgiveness" [1968: 115 (ET)]. Luke xiii.2 (s) is addressed to all, not in the Pauline sense of being inescapable, but on the contrary as an appeal to individual initiative." [Conzelmann. 1960: 227 (ET)].

4.11. The text used in the hypothesis (3.6) seems not to count against the historicity of the Fall of Tower in Siloam. Scholars date this text to A.D. 300 [Goldin, 1955: xxi]. Hence it could have hardly affected the Gospel of Luke. There are two versions of Aboth Rabbi Nathan, A and B. Goldin [1955: 143] translates the version A, Saldarini [1975] version B. The shorter version B does not have the reference that would exclude the collapse of the tower. The statement on the collapse in version A seems to reflect the wishful thinking on Jerusalem, how the ideal Jerusalem should be in the past and in the future, rather than the historical Jerusalem. The neighbouring verses in the same chapter 35 seem to confirm this observation. The Roman occupation of Jerusalem and Judaea contradicts "No place is made available there for a resident alien". The prophecy of the O.T. prophets goes against a saying that affirms, "It (Jerusalem) is not to be declared a condemned city."

4.12. οὐχί λέγω ὑμῖν, the primitive form of ἀμὴν λέγω ὑμῖν, supports its authenticity.[12]

4.13. ὀφειλέται the Aramaic form of ἁμαρτωλοὶ could echo its primitiveness and authenticity [Black, 1967: 140].

4.14. ὧν τὸ αἷμα Πιλᾶτος ἔμιξεν μετὰ τῶν θυσιῶν αὐτῶν could hint at an awkward Semitic construction [W. L. Knox, 1957; 76; G. Schwarz, 1969: 125]. ἐφ᾽ οὓς ἔπεσεν ὁ πύργος ἐν τῷ Σιλωὰμ καὶ ἀπέκτεινεν αὐτούς points to a Semitic origin [W. L. Knox, 1957: 76]. παρὰ a rendering of the Aramaic comparative preposition *min* could be a Semitism [Jeremias, 1962: 141 (ET)]. This Semitism could support the authenticity of this saying.

---

[12] Jeremias, 1953: 90. Jeremias claims that ναί λέγω ὑμῖν could have shown the Matthean tendency of strengthening the possible original word of Jesus. Luke 13:5 has a similar word (οὐχὶ).

4.15. The early church would have not needed to make up this kind of a fake story. This passage does not seem to reflect any of the life settings of the early church. They would not have wanted to bear the blame for distorting secular history.

4.16. The early church would hardly have made up a story using terms like Πιλᾶτος, θυσιῶν, Γαλιλαῖοι, πύργος ἐν τῷ Σιλωὰμ, κατοικοῦντας Ἰερουσαλήμ which have a historical connection with Jesus. They would have been reluctant to include the name Pilate in their made-up story, who was clearly involved in the historical crucifixion of their Lord Jesus. They could be aware of the danger that this kind of arbitrary inclusion could downgrade the historicity of the crucifixion event. By the same token the Hellenistic church would hardly have made up a story with many Jewish venues.

4.17. The early church would hardly have made up this periscope because of the absence of manifestly Christian elements [Cabraja, 1985: 128].

4.18. Pilates' callousness portrayed in this passage is coherent with Josephus' other accounts in his work (The massacre of the Samaritans, *Jewish Antiquities* 18. 86-87; The dispute over the use of temple treasury funds, *Jewish War* 2.175-177, *Jewish Antiquities* 18.60-62).

4.19. The revolutionary nature of some of the Galileans could also support the likelihood of the incident in Luke 13:1-2 (Josephus, *The Life* 28-30) [Zeitlin, 1973: 196-197, 200].

4.20. This passage is coherent with Jesus' distressed call for national repentance in face of the coming fate of Jerusalem in Luke 13:34-35; Matt 23:37-39.

4.21. Luke 13:1-5 seems to bear the marks of historical veracity [Dodd,

1936: 65].[13]

5.

5.1. The main thrust of the saying

According to Luke 13:1-5 the wise are those who warn others and examine themselves in light of national disasters. Unraveling the calamity could lead them to repentance. On the contrary the unwise are those who make fuss over the disaster of a nation but make no change in themselves. The danger of the Jewish people lies in their self righteousness. This latent attitude was not challenged even by the disasters of their fellow Jews. In his revealing question δοκεῖτε ὅτι οἱ Γαλιλαῖοι οὗτοι ἁ μαρτωλοὶ παρὰ πάντας τοὺς Γαλιλαίους ἐγένοντο, ὅτι ταῦτα πεπόνθασιν Jesus reveals their self righteousness. Jesus sharply criticized their catastrophic complacency which rested upon their self righteousness. They tend to think that they are less sinful than the victims of disaster. οὐχί, λέγω ὑμῖν (v.3, 5) strongly rejects their logic of complacency. πάντες ὁμοίως clearly points to the universal character of judgment and the need for urgent repentance. Jesus took the imminent end as the pivotal reason for his call to repentance. It is now time to ask why disasters happened to some and not the others. The essential question was not the causal relationship between sin and punishment but between sin and the imminent end. This end did not leave room for them to be complacent about this disaster. In light of the imminent end the entire Galileans were no better than the massacred Galileans. Likewise the Jerusalemites were no better than the victims of the fallen Tower. All would perish unless they repented.

---

[13] Scholars confirm the authenticity of this saying: T. W. Manson, 1948: 273-274; W. L. Knox. 1957: 75-76; Schmid, 1960: 228-229 (ET); Trautmann, 1980: 163; Fitzmyer, 1996: 1004; Evans 1990: 547-548. Braun states that Luke 13:1-5 could have come from Jesus or the early church [1969: 66 (ET)].

Did Jesus give the impression that he did not mind what happened to his nation because he did not show the kind of response anticipated by the bearer of the news? That does not seem to be the case. It is certainly true that Jesus could feel angry and anxious over the disaster of his fellow Jews. He could be distressed at their fate (cf. Matt 9:36, sheep without shepherd). Jesus was not a man living as an island, who cares only for his individual interests or for members of a small religious community separated from the Jewish nation. He was keenly attentive to every movement in his country. He does not distance himself from the fate of his nation. His only concern was to rescue his fellow Jews from the imminent judgment. These sudden disasters could only reinforce his call for national repentance. Jesus could call for national repentance as a person standing in the prophetic tradition [Dodd, 1936: 65; 1971: 86].

5.2. The bearing of the saying on the forgiveness of sins

Is it true that the authenticity of the three principal passages which call for general repentance does not look very sturdy [Sanders, 1995: 110]? The opposite seems to be the case. πάντες could include the whole of the Jewish nation. Accordingly v.3, 5 could call for the national repentance of Israel.

B. Did Jesus call for an eschatological national repentance in Luke 13:6-9?

1. The conjectured original text

6 Συκῆν εἶχέν τις πεφυτευμένην ἐν τῷ ἀμπελῶνι αὐτοῦ, καὶ ἦλθεν ζητῶν καρπὸν ἐν αὐτῇ καὶ οὐχ εὗρεν. 7 εἶπεν δὲ πρὸς τὸν ἀμπελουργόν, ἰδοὺ τρία ἔτη ἀφ᾽ οὗ ἔρχομαι ζητῶν καρπὸν ἐν τῇ συκῇ ταύτῃ καὶ οὐχ εὑρίσκω ἔκκοψον [οὖν] αὐτήν, ἱνατί καὶ τὴν γῆν καταργεῖ; 8 ὁ δὲ ἀποκριθεὶς λέγει αὐτῷ, κύριε, ἄφες αὐτὴν καὶ τοῦτο τὸ ἔτος, ἕως ὅτου σκάψω περὶ αὐτὴν καὶ βάλω κόπρια, 9 κἂν μὲν ποιήσῃ καρπὸν εἰς τὸ μέλλον· εἰ δὲ μή γε ἐκκόψεις αὐτήν..

2. Arguments concerning the excluded parts

v.6 Ἔλεγεν δὲ ταύτην τὴν παραβολήν] A pre-Lucan or Lucan introduction.

3. Arguments against 1.

3.1. The early church made up this parable.

a. The early church could have derived this passage from the story of Ahikar 8:5.[14]

b. Drury argues that this parable was derived from Mark 11: 12-14; Matthew 21:18-19 [Drury, 1985: 160].[15] Some scholars regard Mark 11:

[14] The text is in Charles's translation [1913, vol. 2: 775].

[15] Telford argues that Luke omitted Mark 11:12-14 [1990: 232-233].

12-14 as secondary [E. Schwarz, 1904: 80-84; Wellhausen, 1909: 106].[16] In that case Luke 13:6-9 becomes secondary.

4. Arguments against 3.

4.1. (3.1) deserves careful consideration but is hardly convincing. The Hellenistic church would hardly have made up this passage because fig trees and vineyards are very much features of Jewish imagery (Isa 34:4; Jer 5:17; 8:13; 24; 29:17; Hos 2:12; 9:10; Joel 1:7; Micah 4:4; Zech 3:10; m. Sota 9:9) although there are many examples of Hellenistic usage of these terms. The Palestinian church would hardly have made up the parable. If we follow the argument the fig tree symbolizes the Jews, the vinedresser Jesus, the landlord, the Palestinian church would have been reluctant to describe Jesus as a vinedresser who eventually agrees to cut the fig tree down (ἔκκοψον οὖν αὐτήν) after one year if not bearing fruit. In the perspective of the Palestinian church the cutting down of the tree (ἐκκόψον αὐτήν) symbolizes the exclusion of the unbelieving people. This portrayal of a vinedresser (Jesus) seem to be against the will of the early church's mission. They would have wished to get more people even after continued failures. Also, why is there only one year reprieve if the church made it up: if they see three years as the period of Jesus' public ministry one year for the conversion of the Jewish people would have been too short.

---

[16] Weiss argues that Jesus did not speak this part. A later people ascribe this story from a barren fig tree to Jesus [1917: 178]. Citing E. Schwarz Goguel argues that "In any case, the incident is non-historical; it is a typical example of a miracle for purposes of display only." [1932:241 (ET)]. Although Wellhausen notes that Schwarz in general expounds well there is a clear difference between two scholars' assumptions. Wellhausen assumes that originally Jesus did not curse the fig tree, but merely spoke about an already withered tree. However, Schwarz assumes that the early church entirely ascribed this saying to Jesus.

4.2. The early church or Luke would scarcely have made up this parable to explain the delay of the coming of Jesus because the delay is only one year and the eschatological imminence is still there. Rather the early Palestinian church could have put this saying of Jesus in its present position to reflect their missionary situation [Gaston, 1971: 342-343]. Although they are discouraged about the relative failure of their mission to Israel "they beg for just one last opportunity before despairing of their task as hopeless." [Gaston, 1971: 342].[17]

4.3. The opposite case of (3.1) seems to be more likely. "Luke has used preceding apophthegms as a frame for the parables" and "apophthegms developed in the tradition when independent sayings were joined" [Bultmann, 1931: 61 (ET)]. This argument already hints at the primitiveness, or even authenticity, of Luke 13:6-9. There are pre-Lucan traditions (ἰδοὺ τρία ἔτη, ἀφ᾽ οὗ, ἔρχομαι ζητῶν καρπὸν ἐν τῇ συκῇ ταύτῃ καὶ οὐχ εὑρίσκω) [Jeremias, 1980, 227]. ἀποκριθεὶς λέγει and κἂν, εἰ δὲ μή γε are not Lucan (v. 6, καὶ ἐὰν), and could be a pre-Lucan tradition [Jeremias, 1980: 227-228; Klostermann, 1929: 143] like Luke 13:1-5 which could be an authentic saying of Jesus [see my close examination on Luke 13: 1-5].

4.4. Bultmann merely notes that Luke 13:6-9 has a parallel in Ahikar's parable. He does not reject the authenticity of Luke 13:6-9.[18] Bultmann

---

[17] Gaston does not deal with the authenticity of Luke 13:6-9. However he seems to concur with the authenticity of this parable: "In the Proto-Lucan version there is still a chance for repentance, and Israel is exhorted to bear fruit before it is too late." [343].

[18] Telford [1980: 225, 246 n 95] states in his footnote that Bultmann regard this passage as secondary. However Telford notes that Bultmann, only "cautiously", assumes this parable as a Christian formulation. As far as my reading is concerned Bultmann seems not to make any clear judgment on the authenticity. Grundmann states that this parable could have come from Jesus or from the early church [1981: 275 n 3].

also affirms the possibility that "Jesus himself could have picked a floating story" [1931: 222].[19] That alleged floating story could have come from the story of Abikar, Syriac edition 8:35.

4.5. (3.1.a) is not quite convincing. The story of Ahikar 8:35 is distinguished from Luke 13:6-9 in the following points.

a. Judgment is not delayed. No eschatological urgency before the imminent End is present.

b. No mediator like the vinedresser who stands between the landlord and the tree enters on the stage.

c. The judgment of cutting down the tree is not because it bears no fruit, but because it lets all its fruit drop into the river.

d. It is unusual that a Palm tree shall bear carobs.

Hence the early church would hardly have had Jesus repeat this story in this parable. Further Jesus could have modified the Ahikar story into a parable with a different perspectives.[20]

---

[19] This translation seems to be better. Marsh translates "Jesus could himself have borrowed from some out-of-the-way tradition." [1931: 205(ET)]. But the meaning of "out-of-the way tradition" seems less clear.

[20] T. W. Manson argues that "the Syriac version of *Ahikar* may have been influenced by reminiscences of the New Testament" without giving any evidence [1948: 274]. Although the main text of Ahikar could be dated earlier than thee fifth century this part could be a later addition because of its variants. Marshall correctly points out that the story in Ahikar may be a later addition to the text because a further variant is found in Aboth Rabbi Nathan 16 (6a) (see Neusner' translation) [1986: 119]. Lindenberger who translates Ahikar in Charlesworth's edition of Pseudepigrapha claims its date the later seventh or early sixth century B.C. [1985:

4.6. (3.1.b) does not seem quite convincing. The relationship between Luke 13:6-9 and Mark 11:12-14, 20-21; Matt 21:18-20 remains an open question.[21] Drury assumes the Marcan origin of this parable. However the vice versa is also possible. The Matthean and Marcan accounts could have come from Luke 13:6-9 [Bultmann, 1931: 230-231[22] (ET)]; W. L. Knox, 1957: 77; Taylor, 1952: 459[23]; Derrett, 1973: 259]. Luke 13:6-9 is hardly derived from Mark 11:12-14 and par. Significant differences lie between them. First and most importantly, the two passages are not only dissimilar in their main thrusts, delayed judgment and declared judgment, but also fundamentally different in their literary forms; proclamation and parable. Second, the latter has pre-Marcan materials, ὁ γὰρ καιρὸς οὐκ ἦν σύκων (Mark 11:13) [Cranfield, 1959: 354-355], ἀπὸ μακρόθεν (Mark 11:13) and (Mark 11:20) [Robin, 1960-61: 27], which are not paralleled in Luke 13:6-9. συκῆν, ἐν αὐτῇ, ἦλθεν, οὗδεν, οὐχ, Luke) εὗρεν, καρπὸν (καρπὸς Matt) are the only words paralleled in these synoptic accounts. The only similar point is that in both accounts figs are sought from a tree in vain: otherwise all the features are different [Telford, 1980: 235-236]. Third, Luke 13:6-9 has no element of miracle as Mark 11:12-14, 20-21 and par. A parable could scarcely have come from a

482]. Jeremias dates this text back to the earlier than the fifth century B.C. [1962: 170 (ET)].

[21] Hirsch notes the relationship between two pericopes remains unclear [1941: 218]

[22] "It has frequently been supposed that the cursing of the fig tree in Mk. 11. 12-14, 20 has grown out of a parable (cp. Hos. 9-10, 16, Mi. 7.1)."

[23] "Probably the best explanation of the narrative is that the parable of the Fig Tree in Lk. xiii. 6-9, or a similar parable, has been *transformed into a story of a fact,* or that in a primitive Christian tradition a popular legend came to be attached to a withered fig tree on the way to Jerusalem." (italics mine). cf. Knox [1953: 90f].

miracle narrative.[24] The pericope attested in Matthew and Mark is a rare miracle story which arises out of *Jesus' own personal need.* Further it is the only miracle of destruction in the synoptic gospels [Cranfield, 1959: 354].

Some scholars argue for the Lucan omission of the original account in Mark 11:12-14 par. [Rawlinson, 1927: 154; Telford, 1980: 229-233]. Telford argues that Luke omitted the Marcan account because the judgment idea was too offensive to the Lucan church who live in a time when salvation history was replacing eschatology [1980: 231]. Telford establishes his argument on the assumption: Luke did have Mark's version of the fig-tree story before him [1980: 229]. However this argument becomes not cogent if we assume that Luke relies on fairly old non-Marcan traditions transferred to him. O'Neill settles for this theory of the transmission of synoptic traditions [1974-75: 273-285].

All these literary and linguistic traits lead to a conclusion that Luke, 13:6-9 and Mark 11:12-14, 20-21; Matt 21:18-20 have entirely different origins from the beginning [T. W. Manson: 1948: 274].[25]

4.7. Further, Mark 11:12-14 could be an authentic saying. The summary of E. Schwarz's argument is this: at the time, of the early church, in the path between Bethany and Jerusalem, there may have been a withered fig tree of which the early Christians made up a story that it would start to

---

[24] "Such an [parabolic] origin is hardly possible with any other miracle stories." Bultmann [1931: 231 (ET)].

[25] "Actually the two stories have nothing in common except the fact that the fig tree produces no fruit. They are so different that it is extremely unlikely that either could have arisen from the other." Goguel also notes that: "Hence the agreement between the two passages is too imperfect for us to regard it as in any way proved that there is a literary connexion between them." [1932: 241]. Branscomb also leaves the question of the relation between these two pericopes open [1937: 201]. Bartsch correctly argues that Luke did not find this pericope in his version or Mark [Bartsch, 1962: 259]. cf. Fitzmyer [1986: 1005].

bud again when their Lord came [1904: 83-84]. However Schwarz's argument is hardly convincing. Schwarz seems to rest upon a pure conjecture he, does not put forward any attesting text. Further, if the early church made up Mark 11:12-14, 20-21 to reflect the destruction of Israel they would at most have described Jesus as prophesying, not cursing, the withering tree, if it was meant to symbolize Israel. Mark 11: 12-14 hardly seems to stem from this alleged Christian legend. ὁ γὰρ καιρὸς οὐκ ἦν σύκων (v. 13)[26], ἀπὸ μακρόθεν (v. 13), would hardly appear in an alleged legend as claimed by Schwarz, or in a tradition made up by the early church. The early church would scarcely have portrayed Jesus as being foolish by approaching a fig tree at an odd time, especially when he was described as giving important teaching on the future with the parable of a fig tree (Mark 13:28).[27]

4.8.Τρία before ἔτη is not the Lucan style and could be a Semitism (cf. Mark 8:2; Luke 13:16) [Jeremias, 1980: 227; Wellhausen, 1904: 72]. Ποιήσῃ καρπὸν could be a Semitism [Black, 1967: 138-139]. Wellhausen thinks κἂν...μέλλον as Aramaism [1904: 72]. These linguistic features could support its authenticity.

4.9. Sayings which teach eschatological judgment in connection with a "fig tree" are attested in the multiple literary forms, prophecy (Mark 13:28-29; Matt 24:32-36; Luke 21:29-33), action narrative (Mark 11:12-14, 20-21; Matt 21:18-20), parable (Luke 13:6-9). Hence, this eschatological tone which is consistent with Jesus' authentic sayings could support the authenticity of this parable.

---

[26] Cranfield already expounds this point [1959: 355].

[27] Further Mark 13:28 seems to be a story about a living tree, not a story of a tree recovered from withering.

4.10. No hard evidence has been put forward concerning the secondary nature of this parable. Some scholars trace this parable back to Jesus with or without any additional reasons: Juelicher, 1899: 443; Montefiore, 1927, vol. 2: 500; Plummer, 1910: 337; Creed, 1953: 181; T. W. Manson, 1948: 275; Jerermias, 1962: 105[28] (ET); Davies, 1974: 355 n 54; Marshall, 1978: 552, 555: B. Meyer, 1979: 137-8, 165, 297; Schweizer, 1982: 220[29] (ET); Fitzmyer, 1986: 1005; Borg, 1987: 157, 168 n 30; Funk, Butts, Scott, 1989: Table 2; Stanton, 1989: 214-215; Evans, 1990: 548.

5.

5.1. The main thrust of this saying

Giving one more chance to produce fruit within a limited time clearly indicates the last warning for repentance. A last chance of repentance is given to the Jews, who are unrepentant. κἂν μὲν ποιήσῃ καρπὸν εἰς τὸ μέλλον and ἕως ὅτου imply the last opportunity. Manuring a vineyard is not mentioned in any passage in the O.T. Hence what the gardener proposes to do is something unusual, to take the last possible measure. This unusual action implies Jesus' desire to restore the unrepentant Jews. If the Jews reject even this call there is no more mercy,[30] the imminent judgment sweeps over them, εἰ δὲ μή γε, ἐκκόψεις αὐτήν.

5.2. The bearing on the forgiveness of sins

---

[28] Jeremias takes the absence of explicit application after this parable as one piece of evidence of its primitiveness and possible authenticity. cf. Bultmann [1931: 175 (ET)].

[29] Schweizer takes the present tense in v. 8 as pre-Lucan and probably a sign that it was a genuine saying of Jesus.

[30] W. Manson: "The meaning of this parable is that there is a limit to the divine patience with men." [1930: 163].

Sanders does not deal with authenticity of this parable. However he seems to agree with the authenticity of Luke 13:6-9. He notes that "there is no reason to reject the parables as such." [1985: 114-115]. But his point is elsewhere: these parables, although clear about judgment or selection, and hence about repentance, were targeted on the repentance of individuals, not the whole nation [1985: 114-116]. However Luke 13:6-9 seems to exemplify a parable targeted on all Israel as a final message of repentance. This passage is closely related to Luke 3:7-9; Matt 3:8-10 (cf. Matt 7:19), which stress judgment and national repentance. Further, the fig tree stands for Israel in the Old Testament and in Judaism (Hos 9:10; Jer 24; 29: 17), or the national crisis [Robin, 1961-61: 277, 281; Meyer, 1979: 165, 137-8]. Isa 5:7 "For the vineyard of the Lord of hosts is the house of Israel and the men of Judah are his pleasant plantings and he looked for justice, but behold, bloodshed; for righteousness, but behold, a cry", Joel 1:7 "It has laid waste my vines, and splintered my fig trees", Hos 9:10 "like grapes in the wilderness, I found Israel. Like the first fruit on the fig tree, in the first season, I saw your fathers" all depict Israel as a vineyard or a fig tree which faces judgment. Hos 2:12, Isa 34:4, Jer 5:17, 8:13, Jer 24; 29:17, m. Sotah 9:9 all have fig trees and speak of judgment and national repentance. Hence Jesus could call for the national repentance of Israel in this parable.

C. Did Jesus stress repentance and restitution in Luke 18:9-14?

1. The conjectured original text

Luke 18:10 ῎Ανθρωποι δύο ἀνέβησαν εἰς τὸ ἱερὸν προσεύξασθαι, ὁ εἷς Φαρισαῖος καὶ ὁ ἕτερος τελώνης 11 ὁ Φαρισαῖος σταθεὶς πρὸς ἑαυτὸν ταῦτα προσηύχετο, ὁ θεός εὐχαριστῶ σοί ὅτι οὐκ εἰμὶ ὥσπερ οἱ λοιποὶ τῶν ἀνθρώπων, ἅρπαγες ἄδικοι, μοιχοί, ἢ καὶ ὡς οὗτος ὁ τελώνης· 12 νηστεύω δὶς τοῦ σαββάτου, ἀποδεκατῶ πάντα ὅσα κτῶμαι 13 ὁ δὲ τελώνης μακρόθεν ἑστὼς οὐκ ἤθελεν οὐδὲ τοὺς ὀφθαλμοὺς ἐπᾶραι εἰς τὸν οὐρανόν, ἀλλ᾽ ἔτυπτεν τὸ στῆθος αὐτοῦ λέγων, ὁ θεός, ἱλάσθητί μοι τῷ ἁμαρτωλῷ 14a λέγω ὑμῖν, κατέβη οὗτος δεδικαιωμένος εἰς τὸν οἶκον αὐτοῦ παρ᾽ ἐκεῖνον.

2. Arguments concerning the excluded parts

v. 14b.ὅτι πᾶς ὁ ὑψῶν ἑαυτὸν ταπεινωθήσεται, ὁ δὲ ταπεινῶν ἑαυτὸν ὑψωθήσεται. This clause could be an independent saying of Jesus [T. W. Manson, 1948: 312] or an isolated wisdom saying [Fitzmyer, 1986: 1183; Winton, 1990:136, 166] placed here later.[31]

3. Arguments against 1

3. 1. Some scholars argue that this passage was made up by the early

---

[31] However some scholars see this verse as secondary. Montefiore [1927, vol. 2: 558]: "The tag at the end does not belong, to the parable." Linnemann reads v. 14b as an originally independent saying of Jesus [1964: 64 (ET)]. Uniquely Marshall argues that v. 14b "fits in well with the lesson of the parable ... " [1978: 678].

church [Fiedler, 1976: 229].[32] The following reasons were put forward.

a. Luke 18:10-14 is not an authentic parable, but a theological caricature [Schottroff, 1973: 446, 448-449, 451].

b. The behaviour of the Pharisee contains nothing to be criticized [Schottroff, 1973: 451-452; Fiedler, 1976: 230-232].[33]

c. Luke 18:14a is hardly square with Luke 18:10-13, hence secondary: v.14a would have caused a stumbling block to bearers [Schottroff, 1973:447-448; Fiedler, 1976: 230-232].

d. One of the reasons why Fiedler suspects the authenticity of this passage is that the tax collector does not show any sign that he is ready to make restitution or to quit his profession [1976: 232[34]].

4. Arguments against 3

4.1. (3.1) is hardly convincing. The Hellenistic church is unlikely to have made up this passage because of its strong cultic setting, prayer in the

---

32 Bultmann does not discuss the authenticity of this parable. He merely states that 14b (beginning ὅτι) does not belong to vv. 9-14a originally [1931: 178 (ET)]:"After the editorial preparation in v. 9 the passage begins as pure narrative; the point is formulated in v. 14, marked out by λέγω ὑμῖν, and an unattached saying is joined on to this by ὅτι (cp. Lk. 14.11; Matt. 23.12) and this latter is certainly secondary, especially in so far as it does not fit the story, as the Publican had not really humbled himself." cf. Fuchs [1960: 145].

33 "The Pharisee is made to appear odious in the parable. But is the consciousness of not desiring to commit sins, even the consciousness of freedom from sin, necessarily odious and abominable?" [Montefiore, 1927, vol. 2: 557].

34 Jeremias also argues that the tax collector should quit his profession to receive forgiveness [1962: 143 (ET); Linnemann, 1964: 60 (ET)].

temple, tithe, fasting and heavy Semitism. Likewise the Palestinian church would have been reluctant to make up v.12, νηστεύω δὶς τοῦ σαββάτου, ἀποδεκατῶ πάντα ὅσα κτῶμαι because some of the members of the Palestinian church were still fasting twice a week. Did. 8:1 has evidence that the early church still fasted although they shifted the day of fast from Monday and Thursday, as some pious do, to Wednesday and Friday. It is most likely that the Palestinian church still continued to offer tithes.[35] Thus the early church need hardly have criticized the fasting and tithing of this pious Pharisee.

4.2. The Aramaic formula (ὅτι οὐκ εἰμὶ ὥσπερ οἱ λοιποὶ) could support the authenticity (cf. 1QH 11:20, 31; III:19, 37; IV:5; VII:34; Jdt 8:25 (εὐχαριστήσωμεν); 2 Macc 1:11 (εὐχαριστοῦμεν αὐτῷ) [Fitzmyer, 1986: 1186]. A strong Semitism of this parable, εἷς...εἷς (ἕτερος) [BDF column No. 247] and ἤθελεν,[36] could support the authenticity of this saying.

4.3. (3.1.a) is a tendentious interpretation. Schottroff argues that Luke 18:9-14 is a caricature of a Pharisee and a tax collector, not a genuine parable [1973; 448-452]. The Pharisee and the tax collector represent the

---

[35] Hamel conjectures that to fill the need of the people who are wholly devoted to prayer a "special requirement must have appeared to the new churches as a form of tithing." [1990: 190]. Citing, Oppenheimer [1977: 45-51] Hamel argues that "Collections for the sages and Torah scholars also takes place at different intervals and in many forms." [1990: 190]. Sanders also notes "... payment of tithes did not cease with the destruction of the temple..." [1990: 46]. It is very likely that the early Palestinian Christians were still paying tithes. Even the dispora Jews were sending their tithes to Israel (cf. m. Yebam. 4.3; Josephus, *Jewish Antiquities* 14. 244).

[36] Black argues that the original meaning was "was not daring" which later was read into "was not willing" [1967: 253].

righteous and the wicked respectively [Schottroff, 1973: 448-452]. However, it seems like there is not any particular reason why Jesus could not speak this parable to the general Jewish people. Schottroff argues that Luke 18:9-14 is a caricature while a rabbinic parallel in b. Ber. 28b is not a caricature [1973: 451]. "All men except the praying person" were described as robbers or adulterers in Luke 18:9-14 while that is not the case in b. Ber. 28b: therefore the two accounts are not comparable [451]. Two stories are comparable only on an account of piety (b. Ber. 28b) and a caricature of piety (Luke 18:9-14) [451]. The underlying point of Schottroff is that Jesus would hardly have made up Luke 18:9-14 from b. Ber. 28b. However, Schottroff's argument seems to be forced. "I am not like other men" (ὥσπερ οἱ λοιποὶ τῶν ἀνθρώπων) in Luke 18:11 hardly refers to all men except the praying person. οἱ λοιποὶ τῶν ἀνθρώπων refers to some people who behave badly like the tax collector. The Pharisee in v. 11 is presented as the model of the righteous in caricature. Further Jesus was hardly restrained only to copy stories of his day. Rather b. Ber. 28b affirms that the idea and literary pattern of a parable like 18:9 14 was familiar in Judaism.

4.4. Schottroff's point is only partially right. The Pharisee portrayed here is hardly like a Pharisee at the time of Jesus [1973: 451]. No Jews would have criticized this type of pious Pharisee [1973: 451-452]. This parable hardly depicts an incident which could have happened, hence secondary [1973: 451-452].[37] Schottroff's assumption is that this parable portrays a typical Pharisee set up by the early church. That does not seem to be the case here. The Pharisee's Prayer portrayed in this parable is a rather

---

[37] Schottroff argues that the audience of this parable would have assumed that a Christianized Pharisee is portrayed here [1973: 452].

exceptional case.[38] Thus the Pharisee is not supposed to hold this repentant sinner in contempt (b. Ber. 34b).[39] Nevertheless this regrettable contempt could have happened because not all Pharisees held a uniform view in regard to other people.[40]

4.5. (3.1.b) Fiedler argues that at the time of Jesus the Pharisee would rather pray as the tax-collector does in Luke 18:9-14 [1976: 232]. However these unique descriptions of repentance support the authenticity. If the penitent tax collector's prayer "God be merciful to me a sinner" as well as his gesture "he smote upon his breast" are essentially Pharisaic [Abrahams, 1917: 571] the early church would hardly have framed this passage: their intention of the sharp contrast between two opposite characters, the Pharisee (a positive model of behaviour) and the tax collector (a negative model of behaviour), does not work. Hence the early church would hardly have depicted the tax collector praying by beating his breast if Pharisees usually did.

---

[38] Montefiore correctly points out the danger of seeing this Pharisee as the typical Pharisee. "But this is not to say that the Pharisee of the story is the usual or characteristic product of the Rabbinic religion. He is the characteristic caricature or perversion of that religion. And that is usually where the German Protestant theologians usually go wrong. They mix up and confuse characteristic product with characteristic caricature." [1927, vol. 2: 556].

[39] "In a place in which those who repent stand, those who are completely righteous cannot stand, as it is said, "peace to him that was far and to him that is near "(Isa 57:19)." (Neusner's translation). Abrahams argues that whether to study the law faithfully or not, judgment is the same if both direct their hearts to Heaven [1917: 57]. He cites b. Ber. 17a: "All the same is the one who does much and the one who does little, so long as a person directs his heart to heaven." (Neusner's translation) and b. Menah. 110a. But these two texts seem to be less relevant than b. Ber. 34b is.

[40] T. W. Manson [1948: 309-310]: "We shall probably be near the truth if we think of the parables as directed not against the entire body of Pharisees, but against a certain section of them."

4.6. Schottroff argues that πρὸς ἑαυτὸν, σταθεὶς are insertions because these words are superfluous explanation, and accordingly they do not stem from the "prayer" itself [1973: 449]. Contrary to her argument which perpetuates the feature of caricature πρὸς ἑαυτὸν, σταθεὶς are in sharp contrast to μακρόθεν ἑστὼς (v.13). οὐκ ἤθελεν οὐδὲ τοὺς ὀφθαλμοὺς, ἐπᾶραι εἰς τὸν οὐρανόν, μακρόθεν ἑστὼς describe this tax collector's genuine repentance. ἔτυπτεν τὸ στῆθος αὐτοῦ highlights this acute repentance. These two essential words realistically portray how two figures differ in their way of praying.

4.7. (3.1.c) is a sharp point, however hardly convincing. Fiedler argues that the decision to declare the tax collector, instead of the Pharisee, righteous is unjust (v. 14a). Schottroff argues that the Pharisee did nothing for which to be blamed in light of the Jewish people. However this Pharisee is not free from any blame. The Pharisee is said to pray standing away from other people. πρὸς ἑαυτὸν is the equivalent of the Aramaic *Le* [Torrey, 1933: 312] and it indicates that the Pharisee "taking his stand" [Black, 1967: 103, 299] or "taking a prominent position" [Jeremias, 1962: 140 (ET)].[41] Further this way of praying belongs to one of the attitudes against which Hillel warns in order to avoid overconfidence (M. Abot. 2.5). Accordingly, the argument that this Pharisee does nothing that rouses criticism seems to be an overstatement.

4.8. Fiedler and Schottroff argue that the decision puzzles the audience because the Pharisee is rejected in his upright piety while the tax collector is accepted in *his moral failure* [1976: 230-232; Schottroff, 1973: 446-

---

[41] Marshall is less sure of this interpretation [1978: 679].

452].[42] Linnemann also raises a question whether this unexpected decision results in the risk of transferring the parable to the level of moralizing [1964: 145 (ET)].[43] This distorted view arises because Schottroff and Fiedler focus on the question as to which of the two earn righteousness as a result of his prayers. When the focal point changes, an entirely different interpretation could arise. Luke 18:14a focuses on who prays in the right way, not on who of the two earns righteousness as a result of prayer.[44]

4.9. Fiedler argues that Jesus would hardly attack the Pharisee when he teaches the need to be receptive (Luke 15:11-32, Matt 20:1-15) and to love even the enemy [1976: 231]. As (4. 8) shows, Jesus does not attack the Pharisee in this saying. Moreover, love for the enemy does not contradict an earnest admonition to fellow compatriots to repent.

4.10. It must be noted that here Jesus does not attack all the Pharisees. Jesus could simply have portrayed a pious Pharisee who ends with a wrong attitude of prayer. Fiedler argues that Jesus would not have said this parable because even Hillel warns Jews against too much confidence in their righteousness (m. Aboth 2.5) [1976: 232]. Hardly all the Pharisees follow Hillel's admonition. It is a well known fact that Shammai contends with Hillel in many cases. Even the same Pharisaic group seems not to

---

42 Schottroff argues that interpretation supporting the authenticity of this parable ends up with either a moral disqualification of the entire Judaism [1973: 451-452]. She even argues that v. 14a would not have been comprehensible except within the early church [1973: 446-448]. Schottroff separates v. 14a (a revelatory speech) from vv. 10-13 (an argument speech) [1973: 456]. However v.14a needs not to be dubbed as a "revelatory speech". Jesus could have announced God's will as the O.T. prophets did.

43 "Before God who forgives him, the sinner, the Pharisee's order of precedence loses its meaning. " [Linnemann, 1964: 62 (ET)].

44 δεδικαιωμένος is relative and answers the question: who was right between two, who has prayed in the right way? [Wellhausen, 1904: 100].

follow one blanket practice because this kind of self-imposed piety does not seem to be required for the whole body of Pharisaism, rather a voluntary observance [T. W. Manson, 1948: 309, 311].[45]

4.11. Then why was v. 14a spoken? What was wrong with this Pharisee? There are two reasons. His pious behaviour uttered in prayer lost its momentum when he begins to treat the tax collector with contempt. One of the meanings of "fasting" (v. 12) is the supplication for the Israelites (Neh 1:4-6; Dan 9:3-19). The pious who fasted twice weekly did so for the sins of the people [Jeremias, 1962: 140 (ET)].[46] Hence the Pharisee is supposed to pray for the miserable sinner with compassion. Quite the contrary, the Pharisee jeered at the tax collector. Jesus could have pointed to this contemptuous attitude as arising from frivolous self complacency.

4.12. (3.1.d) is intriguing, but hardly a compelling argument. Fiedler draws his case from Montefiore's argument: "I am convinced that a repentant tax collector, who gave up his job, would have been regarded by the rabbis as a good penitent, and it would have been held that God would forgive him." [1930: 371].[47] But giving up the profession of tax collector is not mandatory. For restitution it would be enough to render the sin offering along with the guilt offering after returning what he has defrauded: "...it may be noted that quite obviously neither John nor Jesus demanded in principle that toll collectors should give up their profession."

---

[45] T. W. Manson [1948: 310], cited above, n 10.

[46] They felt themselves called to cast themselves into the breach which the sins of the broad mass of the people was always creating between God and Israel, in order that the atoning power of their fasting might turn away the wrath of God and protect the People from national catastrophe [Billerbeck, II: 243].

[47] Linnemann also assumes the "visible and effective, penance was necessary" [1964: 60 (ET)].

[Michel, 1969: 105 (ET)]. Montefiore refers to a particular case; if a tax collector quits his job he would certainly have been regarded as a forgiven man. Montefiore, does not appear to be saying that tax collector cannot be forgiven unless he quits his job. Montefiore admits that "I do not suppose that this, my view, could be rigorously proved and demonstrated by quotations. It is a question of feeling. He who has read much Rabbinic literature and is impartial, will, I think, agree with me." [1930: 371]. Montefiore's hunch seems to be too subjective to be persuasive as a general principle,

4.13. One of the reasons why Fiedler denies the authenticity of this parable is that making restitution could be hard because tax collectors could not remember all who were overtaxed [1976: 232]. Nonetheless making restitution would still have been possible. In such particular cases the unreturned money could have been used for public utilities (b. Qam. 94b-95a; t. B. Mes. 8.26; cf t. B. Qam. 10.14).[48] Afterwards the tax collector could continue his profession with clean hands. The tax collectors were not regarded as beyond repentance [Maccoby, 1988: 143]. They were still Jews, and hope remained that they would return to a worthy way of life. [Maccoby, 1988: 143].[49]

---

[48] b.B. Qum. 94b-95a: "Again, why was it said in the concluding clause that out of articles of which they do not know the owners they should make *public utilities*, and R. Hisda said that these should be wells, ditches and caves?" t. B. Mes. 8:26: "A. As to tax-farmers and tax collectors, doing penitence is difficult." B. They return [what they can do] to those whom they recognize. C. And of the rest [of the taxes they propose to hand back], they make use *for the public good*." (italics mine).

[49] The condemnation of the tax collector was not universal [Abrahams, 1917: 54]. Except for some wicked exceptions the tax collectors were not different from ordinary Jewish people [Maccoby, 1989a: 100-102], b. Sanh. 25b-26a favourably reports a tax collector who was revered for his community spirit and honesty: "R. Zera's father acted as tax collector for thirteen years. When the *Resh-Nahara* [a man

4.14. Further in this parable it is possible to assume that the tax collector was praying after having rendered the sin offering and making restitution. Prayers are often linked with the hours at which sacrifice was offered (Luke 1:10; Acts 3:1; Rev 8:3-4). No account attests that this tax-collector comes only for prayer.[50]

4.15. Whether δεδικαιωμένος means "to be acquitted" [Jeremias, 1962: 141 (ET)] or "declared righteous" [Schrenk, 1935: 215 (ET)], it could imply the preceding offering to the Temple and assume his present righteousness. The judicial connotation in Ezra 4:18 "to acquit someone" could also indicate the previous sacrifice. Accordingly δεδικαιωμένος (v. 4a) could imply that this tax collector has already rendered the sin and guilt offering after full restitution. Further δεδικαιωμένος stems from neither the Pauline [Bruce, 1952: 68; Jeremias, 1962: 141 (ET)] nor the Qumran literature [Braun, 1966, vol. 1: 92]. Thus v. 11 could have come from Jesus and could indicate a previous sacrifice (cf. Ps 51:1-5, 9; 1 QSb 4:22; 4 Ezra 12:7).

4.16. Also ἀνέβησαν εἰς τὸ ἱερὸν προσεύξασθαι (v. 10), whether it is a Lucan or pre-Lucan addition, does not exclude the possibility of the

---

making exorbitant demands in taxation] used to come to town, if he [R. Zera's father] saw him, Come my people, enter thy chamber. And when he saw the other inhabitants of the town he would say to them, The *Resh-Nahara* is coming to the city, and now he will slaughter the father in the presence of the son, and the son in the presence of the father. Before he died, he said: Take the thirteen ma'ahs that are tied in my sheets and return them to so and so, for I took them from him [by way of tax] and have no need for them."

[50] Only the seemingly secondary addition v. 9 states that the tax collector comes for prayer.

previous sin offering. ἱλάσθητί, which means "be merciful" in v.13 also has another cultic connotation "to be propitiated" [BAGD: 375; Buechsel, 1938: 315-317 (ET)]. Accordingly this word could hint at previous sin offerings, after making restitution, because the idea of propitiation lies in the background [Hill, 1967: 36],

4.17. Some scholars regard this parable as authentic with additional reasons: Jeremias, 1962: 140-144 (ET)[51]; Perrin, 1967: 122[52]; Braun, 1969: 111[53] (ET).[54]

5.

5.1. The main thrust of this saying

Every nation is founded upon the morality of its people. The rise and fall of the morality of a community indicates a proportional up and down of its strength. The collapse of this overall morality means the entire community becomes at stake. In this context nothing would have

---

51 Jeremias counts the strong Semitism and the Palestinian setting as arguments for authenticity.

52 Along with strong Semitism and the Palestinian setting Perrin counts "I tell you...a direct challenge of Jesus to his hostile contemporaries, as evidence of authenticity."

53 "Jesus shows therefore, that the tax-collector is accepted not because he has amended his ways or at least promised to amend them but because he knows that he is lost and *in his lostness he hopes* (as his prayer dramatically demonstrates, Luke 18:9-14)" (italics mine). Certainly this parable is authentic. But Braun's interpretation is hardly convincing. If that is the case the Pharisee is also entitled to hope for his salvation. The Pharisee hardly differs from the tax collector in respect of their hope.

54 Some scholars read this parable as authentic without any additional reasons [T. W Manson, 1948: 312; Linnemann, 1964: 58-64 (ET); Marshall, 1978; 678: Westholm, 1978: 141 n 11: Fitzmyer, 1986: 1185].

been more deplorable than to despise repentant sinners because the determination to make restitution could recede. Jesus sets out his mission in this context. Throughout his whole ministry he shows acute sensitivity to sin, He takes an initiative, to reach out to sinners and to bring them back. This spirit underlies this parable. He calls for a sympathetic attitude toward sinners to help them to live with clean hands. One of the crucial points in interpreting this parable is that of whether Jesus could criticize the interior attitude of the Pharisee. Sanders rightly argues that "Jesus did not focus on the interior attitudes of the righteous and the opposition to him did not spring from his criticism for self-righteousness." [1985: 281] However Jesus could have criticized the attitude of prayer of this Pharisee. Pharisees were thought to maintain the utmost piety, but yet they needed to correct their attitude toward the prayer of people who repented although they belonged to disgraceful professions.

5.2. The bearing of this saying on the forgiveness of sins

Sanders argues that "I would regard the parable of the Pharisee and the Tax collector (Luke 19.9-14), with its heavy accent on breast-beating and repentance, as a Lucan (or pre-Lucan) creation." [1985: 175, cf. 281]. Sanders merely cites Fiedler's conclusion while Fiedler only partially elaborates Schottroff's main points [1976: 228-233; 271; 1985: 385 n 6]. Because the arguments of Schottroff and Fiedler turn out to be unconvincing Sanders' case becomes flimsy. The result supports the opposite case: Jesus assumes that sinners repent in conjunction with fulfilling a due date obligation, making restitution. This parable hardly excused this responsibility. On the contrary perhaps this man's making restitution is implicitly assumed.[55]

---

[55] "...tax-collectors who cast themselves on the mercy of God are accepted by him rather than legalistic Pharisees (18:9-14); to be sure, this does not mean that tax-collectors are excused from making restitution for their extortion, as 19:1-10

D. Did Jesus assume Zacchaeus resolved to make restitution as a result of consorting with him (Luke 19:1-10)?

1. The conjectured original text

Luke 19:1 Καὶ εἰσελθὼν διήρχετο τὴν Ἰεριχώ. 2 καὶ ἰδοὺ ἀνὴρ
ὀνόματι καλούμενος Ζακχαῖος, καὶ αὐτὸς ἦν ἀρχιτελώνης καὶ
αὐτὸς πλούσιος· 3 καὶ ἐζήτει ἰδεῖν τὸν Ἰησοῦν τίς ἐστιν καὶ οὐκ
ἠδύνατο ἀπὸ τοῦ ὄχλου, ὅτι τῇ ἡλικίᾳ μικρὸς ἦν. 4 καὶ
προδραμὼν εἰς τὸ ἔμπροσθεν ἀνέβη ἐπὶ συκομορέαν ἵνα ἴδῃ
αὐτὸν ὅτι ἐκείνης ἤμελλεν διέρχεσθαι. 5. καὶ ὡς ἦλθεν ἐπὶ τὸν
τὸπον, ἀναβλέψας ὁ Ἰησοῦς εἶπεν πρὸς αὐτὸν, Ζακχαῖε,
σπεύσας κατάβηθι, σήμερον γὰρ ἐν τῷ οἴκῳ σου δεῖ με μεῖναι.
6 καὶ απεύσας κατέβη καὶ ὑπεδέξατο αὐτὸν χαίρων. 7 καὶ
ἰδόντες πάντες διεγόγγυζον λέγοντες ὅτι παρὰ ἁμαρτωλῷ ἀνδρὶ
εἰσῆλθεν καταλῦσαι. 8 σταθεὶς δὲ Ζακχαῖος εἶπεν πρὸς τὸν
κύριον, ἰδοὺ τὰ ἡμίσιά μου τῶν ὑπαρχόντων, κύριε, τοῖς πτωχοῖς
δίδωμι, καὶ εἴ τινός τι ἐσυκοφάντησα ἀποδίδωμι τετραπλοῦν. 9
εἶπεν δέ πρὸς αὐτὸν ὁ Ἰησοῦς ὅτι σήμερον σωτηρία τῷ οἴκῳ
τούτῳ ἐγένετο, καθότι καὶ αὐτὸς υἱὸς Ἀβραάμ ἐστιν·

2. Arguments concerning the authenticity of the excluded parts.

v.10 ἦλθεν γάρ ὁ υἱὸς τοῦ ἀνθρώπου ζητῆσαι καὶ σῶσαι τὸ ἀπολωλὸς] Jesus seems to finish his sayings usually with one conclusive remark instead of two. V.9 seems to be enough as a final comment about the decision of Zacchaeus. Hence it would be reasonable to regard v. 10 as an isolated saying [Marshall, 1978: 695, 699] placed in an odd place.

---

makes clear." [Marshall, 1978: 677].

3. Arguments against the authenticity of 1

3.1. Luke 19:1-7, 9 is an extended unitary, but manifestly imaginary, version of Mark 2:14 and 2:15-17 [Bultmann, 1931: 33-34, 62 (ET); Wellhausen, 1904: 104]. Because Mark 2:14; 15-17 is not authentic [Bultmann, 1931: 57, 64, 47, 331 (ET)] Luke 19:1-7, 9 becomes inauthentic.

3 2. Some scholars are more sceptical. The whole of Luke 19:1-9 was made up by the early church or by Luke [Fiedler, 1976: 129-135]. Fiedler, along with Bultmann, argues that even Mark 2:14-17 has no historicity [Fiedler: 130 n 400, 135 n 413]. Sanders, resting upon Fiedler, argues that "the story is so strongly marked by Lucan language and theology that one need not look for a prior story which has been reworked."; "Fiedler (ibid, pp.129-35, 271), correctly in my view, regards the story as a secondary construction." [1985: 391 n 111; 385 n 7; 175, 203]. Luke 19:1-9 is merely an anecdote which was transformed into a story of a religious person but which has no historicity [Fiedler: 130]. This passage belongs in the category of "conflict sayings" [Fiedler: 130, 133-134]. The setting of this story is artificial.

3.3. The name Ζακχαῖος is secondary [Fiedler, 128-130, 135]. This addition of names is a strong evidence of the development of a tradition [Sanders, 1969: 169-273, 275]. The name of place Ἰεριχώ is also secondary [Bultmann, 1931: 64 (ET); Fiedler: 129, 331-332 n 396].

3.4. Some scholars cast doubts on the authenticity on the basis of the multiple sources of this passage. Luke 19:3-6 was used as the scaffolding of Luke 19:7-9. Luke 19:3-6 was originally an independent tradition which was later connected to Luke 19:1-2 and Luke 19:7-10 [Fiedler: 130, 133-134].

3.5. The same non-unitary features appear in vv. 7-9. V. 8 is a secondary Lucan addition because it hinders the smooth connection between v. 7 and v. 9 [Bultmann, 1931: 33 (ET)]. Bultmann prefers the text πρὸς αὐτοὺς ("to them") to πρὸς αὐτὸν ("to him"). He rejects the meaning of πρὸς αὐτὸν "with reference to him" (v. 9) [1931: 33-34 (ET)]. If πρὸς αὐτὸν means "to him", v. 9 makes Jesus refer to Zacchaeus in the third person in a sentence addressed to him. If we omit πρὸς αὐτὸν it is still strange that Jesus refers to Zacchaeus in his presence as "he" (αὐτὸς). The easiest course is to read πρὸς αὐτοὺς and omit v. 8 as a later intrusion.[56]

3.6. Bultmann calls into question the authenticity of v. 8 from another perspective. V.8 is Lucan: "Jesus does not establish his relationship to Zacchaeus by appealing to his morality, as v. 8 seems to suppose, but on the simple fact that Zacchaeus is as much a Jew as the rest. The detailed introduction is far better matched with v. 9 as its point than with v. 8, and so we may hold Luke himself responsible for this latter verse; and its moral suits him." [Bultmann, 1931: 34 (ET)].

3.7. This passage fits the Lucan theological emphasis: Jesus consorted with the disreputable and led them to repentance and reformation [Sanders, 1985: 175, 203, 206]. Many words in this passage echo this Lucan theology [Fiedler, 132-135].

3.8. Zacchaeus was not commanded to follow Jesus in this passage. The

[56] "Analysis has already shown that apophthegms developed in the tradition when independent sayings were joined to an already existing situation, whether this were unitarily conceived or compounded of elements." [Bultmann, 1931: 34 (ET)]. "... or how some element peculiar to one evangelist, occasionally receives an addition, as in Lk. 19.8." [ibid].

absence of this command confirms that the story had its origin much later, "when "following" could be less easily symbolized by the physical act." [Bultmann, 1931: 34 (ET)].

4. The arguments against 3.

4.1. (3.1) seems to remain unconvincing. Luke 19:1-9 is hardly an expansion of Mark 2:13-17; Matt 9:9-13. These Matthean and Marcan passages seem to be paralleled rather in Luke 5:27-32. Luke 19:1-9 seems to portray an entirely different occasion. Except for the fact that a tax collector is the central figure in both of these passages, no clear evidence of expansion seems to stand out. Zacchaeus was not sitting in the tax office to be called. People did not murmur to his disciples over Jesus' fellowship with tax collectors. Zacchaeus' announcement is not paralleled in Matt and Mark. Jesus did not call Zacchaeus as a disciple.

4.2. Contrary to (3.2) the multiple attestation of Jesus' consorting with tax collectors in three gospels in narrative (Mark 2:14-17; Matt 9:9-13; Matt 11:19; Luke 7:34) and parable (Luke 18:9-14) could support the historicity of Jesus' consorting with tax collectors. This passage could be regarded as an independent unit. Even Bultmann assumes some sort of connection between Luke 19:1-9 and Mark 2:15-17 [1931: 34 (ET)].[57]

---

[57] Bultmann and Fiedler suspect Jericho as secondary: "On the other hand there are a few apophthegms that contain *specific references to place.*" [Bultmann, 1931: 64 (ET)]. "... Luke 19.1-10, which name Bethany and Jericho respectively. Since precise indications of place are obviously unsuited to the apophthegmatic style, we cannot avoid the question whether they are all secondary additions." [64]. Wellhausen suspects the historicity of Luke 19:lff upon the assumption that the Sycamore tree was only outside Jericho [1904: 103]. However the location of the tree, outside or inside Jericho, could hardly cast the historicity of Zacchaeus' action into doubt because he could climb the tree wherever it was. Grundmann argues that v, 2-7, 9 comes from the old basic material [1981: 358] (italics mine).

These passages could portray the historic encounter between Jesus and tax collectors. How could Sanders argue that Jesus approached truly wicked sinners and offered them forgiveness [1985: 210, 263, 326] while rejecting the authenticity of such passages on Jesus' consorting with sinners in Mark 2:14-17 and Luke 19:1-9? This story could be one of the various forms of Jesus' association with sinners [Easton, 1928: 122-127]. Fiedler seems to be too sceptical on the historicity of Jesus' consorting with tax collectors portrayed in the gospels. The early church could have reflected on their own life setting with the help of these pre-Gospel traditions.[58] It is hardly likely that the early church or Luke made up the entire passage from a vacuum.[59] There seems to be a scholarly consensus with a few exceptions that Jesus approached sinners in his public ministry. Hence it would be more reasonable to favour the historicity of those relevant passages.

4.3. Against (3.3) the early church need not have made up the specific setting Jericho.[60] Jericho would naturally be a place of important custom station for travellers passing from Judaea to the land east of the Jordan because of its geographical location at the passage of the Jordan [Dalman,

[58] Bultmann regards Luke 19:1-10 as one of biographical apophthegms, a story reflecting the situation of the early church. Fiedler argues that, once we exclude Jesus' consorting with Zacchaeus, this story becomes a "conflict" saying [1976: 130, 332].

[59] Jesus' consorting with tax-collectors is authentic saying of Jesus [Jeremias, 1971: 156 (ET); Trautmann, 1980: 155] or at least has a historical core [Merklein, 1981: 198 n 206]. Braun correctly points out that Jesus consorting with sinners (Mark 2:14-16; Luke 19:10) reflects the characteristic action of Jesus because Matt 11:19 (Jesus as the friend of tax collectors) is an *early tradition* not formulated by the community [1969: 114-115 (ED}; cf. 1957, vol. 2: 38 n 1].

[60] Merklein correctly points out that Jericho was not introduced for the stylistic embellishment of an Apophthegm [1981: 198].

1924: 4-5; 243-244 (ET)].[61] Jesus could have expressed his intention of resting in someone's house after crossing the hot land. This passage is preceded by the story of the healing of the leper which also took place in Jericho (18:35-43). These facts could confirm the likelihood of this episode.

4.4. This pericope comprises anecdotal details which are essential to an historic incident (name, place, occupation, condition, stature, activity).[62] Against Fiedler the name Ζακχαῖος hardly seems to have been inserted into this pericope later. Along with Ἰεριχώ, Ζακχαῖος could support its historicity.[63] Luke could have listed the pre-Lucan stories which have

---

[61] Creed [1953: 230]: "Jericho would naturally be an important customs station from its position at the passage of the Jordan from Judaea to the lands of E. of Jordan." Grundmann [1961: 359] shares the same view.

[62] Dibelius [1933: 51, 115, 118 (ET)].

[63] M. R. James [1953: 50, 51, 76-77] (Infancy Gospels). Here the name Zacchaeus (Zacchyas) appears as the teacher of Jesus of earlier days. Because anecdotal detail is often the sign of late material, this name can be regarded as a spurious one. However, this argument cannot be an absolute one because another name of tax collector Levi (Mark 2:14) or the name of Pharisee Simon (Luke 7:40) is recognized as the real name. Fiedler hinges his argument upon Schmidt [1964: 264, 331 n 396]. However Schmidt argues that the location Jericho matches well with the tradition explaining about a tax collector Zacchaeus [1964: 264]. Schmidt leaves the historicity of this passage as an open question [1964: 265]. Contrary to Fiedler assumes [129] the insertion of name seems not always the case because sometimes deliberate omission also happened [Metzger, 1970: 98-99]. Dibelius argues that: "The occasional naming of a man as the hero of a Legend does not make doubtful the historicity of the figure, even if it cannot be guaranteed in this way. This is true also of the story of Zacchaeus (Luke xix. 1-10), a *genuine personal legend* fully told." [1933: 118 (ET)]. "Many of the other Legends were only shaped out in special honour of holy persons, but, of course, have their basis in historical reality. I am thinking, for example, of the stories of Martha and Mary, or of Zacchaeus...." [1933: 293 (ET)]. Fiedler, noticing Dibelius' argument, states that great caution must be

the thematic connection with the name Jericho, Bartimaeus (Luke 18:35-43; Mark 10:46-52) and Zacchaeus (19:10), together at the end of his "travel narrative" (Luke 9:51-19:27). Thus the argument based upon the artificial setting of this story does not seem to be convincing.

4.5. Contrary to (3.4) the early church would hardly have needed to include the unnecessary description on Zacchaeus' height and his endeavour to see Jesus (vv. 3-6). Fiedler assumes that the final editor could freely have inserted some verse [1976: 133-134]. However, that seems hardly likely. The section vv.3-6 goes well with the other neighbouring verses. Vv. 3-6 is not just an embellishment. Why would the early church have included an isolated tradition which does not reflect their life setting? Without this part it becomes difficult to understand the following part v. 7ff. The flow of sentence becomes awkward when we omit v. 36. Zacchaeus suddenly came down from an unknown place (v. 6). How Jesus came to enter Zacchaeus house is unknown (v. 7). Hence it would be natural that vv. 3-6 belongs to the main body of this passage.[64] Fiedler's argument, an independent tradition about an unknown figure was inserted into the Zacchaeus story [1976: 134], seems to be very much an arbitrary hypothesis.

4.6. It is hardly likely that the early church inserted v. 8 between v. 7 and

---

observed in regarding this passage as a personal legend [1976: 135 (ET)].(italics mine)

64 "Luke xix, lff., the anecdotal traits told in regard to the publican are evidently the main thing—his small stature, the way in which he succeeded in seeing Jesus in spite of it, his reward and justification before Jesus." [Dibelius. 1933: 51 (ET)]. Fiedler argues that Dibelius' idea must be questioned because one could put this name to make up a legend of a person [1976: 130] συκομορέα and προτρέχειν (Luke 19:4; John 20:4) which occur only here could confirm its primitiveness and authenticity.

v. 9. Bultmann's argument (3.5) hinges upon the intrusion of the odd word πρὸς αὐτὸν which obscures the connection v. 7 and v. 9. However even his hypothesis does not resolve the fundamental intrinsic problem, the odd relationship between v. 7, 8, 9. Even if we assume that v. 7 was immediately followed by v. 9 in the original text a question still remains unanswered. The textual evidence supports πρὸς αὐτὸν (Aleph B etc. have this text; 2542 e d Persian Diatessaron omit this text) rather than πρὸς αὐτοὺς (R a b c f ff² i l s Latin vulg (4mss) Syr^harcl mg). Why did they put πρὸς αὐτὸν which causes the odd connection between two verses? Hence it would be unconvincing to ascribe the odd connection to the later insertion of v. 8. Whether the early church inserted v. 8 or not, they would hardly have used a πρὸς αὐτὸν (v. 9) that does go oddly with the preceding verse v. 7.

4.7. Jesus' response in v. 9. seems to refer correctly to the declaration of Zacchaeus. πρὸς αὐτὸν could point to Zacchaeus and to the crowd together at the same time.[65] When a person comments about another person before other people, the speaker speaks of the other person in the third person in order to draw the attention of the audience to the one of whom he wants to speak.[66] Accordingly it would be reasonable to argue that v. 7, 8, 9 are genuine sayings of Jesus, connected together from the beginning. V. 8 seems to belong to the main body of this passage; it does not hinder the continuity with the neighbouring verses.[67]

---

65 Fitzmyer [1996: 1225]: "...or better, to the crowd through him."

66 Marshall has already put forward the same argument [1978: 699]: "...it may mean about him." Schweizer [1982: 290 (ET)]: "It is not grammatically impossible; 20:19 (literally "told to them") probably includes the sense "referring to them.""

67 If we want to take off elements which hinder the smooth connection of entire passage, this hypothesis may be another easy way. The sudden appearance of people in v. 7 disrupts the natural connection between vv. 1-6 and v. 8-9. So v. 7 could be regarded as a gloss. The same judgment could go to v. 9. Then the original text could be what remains; vv. 1-6 and v. 8.

4.8. Even if we assume πρὸς αὐτοὺς that was the original text still the problem remains. Jesus' declaration would hardly have convinced the people gathered to regard Zacchaeus as a righteous person; tax collectors were hardly regarded as righteous at the time of Jesus (b. B. Qam 113a) [Abrahams, 1917: 54; Schuerer, 1973 (ET), vol. 1: 376].

4.9. The hypothesis (3.6) seems to be not convincing. The early church would hardly have made up v. 8 along with v. 10. V. 8 does not go along with v. 10; the portrayal of Zacchaeus' restitution in v. 8 could obscure Jesus' initiative of seeking and forgiving sinners in v. 10. If they made up v. 8 they would have been reluctant to compose v.10.[68] If the early church made up v. 10 they would have hardly needed to insert v. 8 which shifts the initiative of salvation from Jesus to Zacchaeus. V.10 stresses Jesus' initiative of salvation.[69]

4.10. If the early church made up this saying they would not have portrayed Zacchaeus as giving up only half of his property. The early church members seemed to have donated all they had to the church, not just a half (Acts 2:44-46; 5:1-5). Luke 19:1-9 seems to describe the

---

[68] Schweizer [1982: 290 (ET)]: "It is unlikely, however, that alongside vs. 10 he also composed vs. 8 and changed the meaning of v. 9." Fiedler argues that v. 8 reflects the Lucan theology well [1976: 133]. To support his hypothesis on the secondary nature of the entire passage Fiedler argues that v. 8 does not hinder the continuity with the neighbouring verses [135]. However Fiedler is aware of the difficulty of ascribing v. 7. 8, 9 to one editor Luke [134]. His assumption of Luke's flexibility in the edition (of the order and insertion) of some verses seems to be too arbitrary. Why would not Luke have ended with a passage free of odd connections?

[69] Further it may be a plausible hypothesis that v. 7 and v. 9 are inserted around v. 8. When following this theory all problems arising from textual complexities seem to resolve themselves. Jesus just entered Zacchaeus' house and Zacchaeus announced his decision of retribution and restitution.

situation at the time of Jesus not the time of the early church.

4.11. Even if this saying was made up by the early church, as some scholars claim, it shows they thought Jesus required restitution. This is early evidence. They would have not included the clause on restitution if they thought that Jesus suspended restitution.

4.12. It is unlikely that the Palestinian church made up v. 8 because of following reasons. The Palestinian church would not have written about the four fold restitution, which is far more than what the Jewish law requires in the case of an unwittingly committed robbery (Lev 6:1-7; cf. Exod 22:1, 2 Sam 12:6, Josephus *Jewish Antiquities* 16.3), unless they were willing to follow Zacchaeus' scale of restitution. Further such large restitution could have been borne only by the church community, not by individuals (cf. Acts 2:45-46).

4.13. Zacchaeus' decision to distribute his possessions and to repay those he had defrauded implies that he might have heard about the proclamation on repentance of John the Baptist (Luke 3:12). Zacchaeus could have declared that he would give half of his possessions as a token of obedience to the teaching of John the Baptist about sharing (Luke 3:11). He could have mulled over the possibility of retribution and restitution. He could have moved this speculation into decisive action at the time of Jesus' visit.

4.14. Bultmann's argument seems to be based upon his theological presupposition: human achievement works nothing for salvation. Contrary to Bultmann's hypothesis, Jesus could have intended to restore Zacchaeus' relationship to the community by appealing to his moral reform. Zacchaeus' Jewishness could not ensure his salvation. Jesus could call for a new Jewishness. Otherwise Jesus would not have called for the decision of repentance of his contemporaries along with the coming of the kingdom.

4.15. Bultmann's suspicion seems to rekindle the quest over the interpretation of the intention in Zacchaeus' declaration: was he offering evidence of what he had done in defence or was he expressing a resolve on future action? The two arguments are sharply different.

4.16. Zacchaeus' announcement seems to affirm his resolution to restore what he has defrauded.[70] Zacchaeus hardly made defence of his innocence.[71] interpreting Zacchaeus' declaration as a defence of his righteousness makes him boasting [Plummer, 1905: 435].

4.17. The argument that Zacchaeus defended his righteousness in v. 8

---

[70] Plummer, 1905: 434-435; Lagrange, 1939: Part 2: 116 (ET); Marshall, 1978: 697; Hamm, 1988: 432-433].

[71] Godet [1872: 217 (ET)]: "But if the pres. I give may certainly apply to a gift which Zaccheus [sic!] makes at the instant once for all, the pres. I restore fourfold seems rather to designate a rule of conduct already admitted and long practised by him. It is unnatural to apply it to a measure which would relate only to some special cases of injustice to be repaired in the future." But Godet affirms that Zacchaeus' Jewishness does not assure his salvation: that kind of idea contradicts Jesus' whole teaching [1872: 218 (ET)]. cf. Fitzmyer, 1986: 1221-1223, 1225: Mitchell, 1990: 153-176. In the most recent article on this debate Mitchell argues for the legitimacy of Zacchaeus' salvation in terms of his Jewishness: "Jesus offers Zacchaeus salvation because he is a believing Jew and not because he had a sudden change of heart." [1990: 154] "... Luke wanted to show how salvation came to a loyal Jew, a son of Abraham, without necessarily implying that Jesus saw him as a sinner." [1990: 154]. John the Baptist warns the Jews not to begin to say of themselves that they were children of Abraham (Luke 3:8). If Zacchaeus' salvation was guaranteed so perfectly Luke need not have portrayed Jesus' approach to him. Mitchell does not consider the point that Zacchaeus is hardly regarded as righteous enough to be called as the son of Abraham. Zacchaeus was a tax collector, a sinner.

seems unconvincing due to the following reason. A repeated distribution of the half of one's possessions would hardly have been likely.[72]

4.18. It is hardly likely that at the time of Jesus tax collectors were in general so meticulous to return defrauded taxes collected in Judaea. The strict demand from the Roman Empire would have led them to keep every penny.[73] The scale of charity and restitution is far beyond what is expected for charity: one-fifth was enough as charity and the requirement of the Law (Lev 6:5; not Exod 22:1 theft of a sheep).

4.19. Some scholars argue that Zacchaeus' status as a "sinner" is not clearly unlike other Lucan stories [Fitzmyer, 1986: 1223; Mitchell, 1990: 155]. However that argument does not seem to be convincing. Zacchaeus did not need to have asked for mercy because his sins were different from sins which caused disease which needed the declaration of God's forgiveness for healing (17:14; 18:38). Nor need he have expressed sorrow (Luke 15:21; 18:13). Zacchaeus' declaration of charity and restitution is tantamount to his full repentance. This solemn announcement could demonstrate his faith and sorrow and could be a full sign of repentance.

4.20. Does Zacchaeus' overgenerous restoration indicate his habitual compensation for inadvertent extortion [Fitzmyer, 1986: 1225; Mitchell, 1990: 154]? That is highly unlikely because this hypothesis could cut both

---

[72] Mitchell rekindles the debate. He argues that ὑπαρχόντα could include "income" [1990: 155]. Mitchell cites BAGD [838]: "...which belongs to someone, someone's property, possessions, means." However Mitchell admits "even if ὑπαρχόντα were stretched to include income, the word still embraced property" [1990: 155]. Hence Mitchell's argument seems to remain unconvincing.

[73] Schuerer [1973, vol. 1: 374]: "Whatever the revenue yielded in excess of that sum was their gain, but if the revenue fell short off the rental, they had to bear the loss."

ways. Overgenerosity could echo his long awaited action to correct the deliberate and likely overtaxation. Zacchaeus could not be overgenerous because he had himself to pay the uncollected taxes.

4.21. V. 8 hardly implies Zacchaeus' customary restitution.[74] The present tense of paragraph "I give it to the poor (v.8)" and "I restore it four-fold" are futuristic and express a resolve "here and now I give" (δίδωμι and ἀποδίδωμι).[75] Against Fitzmyer [1986: 1220-1221, 1225] ἀποδίδωμι hardly refers to Zacchaeus' habitual restoration. Zacchaeus' announcement of giving half of his assets to the poor could affirm that his decision was an unprecedented dramatic resolution. Hardly any man could give half of his property repeatedly.

4.22. The argument that Jesus could call Zacchaeus a righteous Jew without seeing any tangible sign of repentance seems to be an overstatement. Toll collectors (*Moccasin*) in particular could hardly have been regarded as righteous because of the pressure to reach the target amount [Jeremias, 1971: 110-111 (ET)]. They were regarded as more sinful than tax collectors.[76] Thus the Jews in his community would hardly have accepted him as a righteous Jew until he made full restitution in

---

[74] Fitzmyer [1986: 231]: "There is no need to understand it as futuristic pres., "I am giving as of now (in pledge).""

[75] Creed [1953: 231]: "The present tense describes here a present resolve, not as e.g. in xviii, 12, a present habit." Marshall [1978: 697]: "The today conforms the view that "give" and "restore" refer to a personal resolve and not to a past practice." "... his action is to be seen as an example of the sort of change in life that should follow upon the reception of salvation," which implies one single decisive action.

[76] A tax collector is unfit to act as witness. b. Sanh. 25b: "Tax collectors and publicans: "At first they thought that they collected no more than the legally imposed tax. But when its was seen that they overcharged, they were disqualified.""

repentance.

4.23. The scale of the distribution of his possessions and the restoration of defrauded tax (v.8) demonstrates clear sign of his repentance. Zacchaeus declared that he would return more than the general rule required.[77] Accordingly, the idea that Zacchaeus tried to assert his self-justification through his customary retribution would be quite inappropriate. Rather, the declaration of Zacchaeus illustrates the earnestness and sharpness of his repentance. Defence of his innocence is not what he is about here. So far as these arguments are concerned, this story confirms the consorting of Jesus with a sinner and the sharp repentance of a chief tax collector. Did Jesus vindicate Zacchaeus' righteousness in v. 9 [Mitchell, 1990: 159]? That is hardly likely. Jesus declared Zacchaeus' salvation only after v. 8.

4.24. (3.7) seems to be a Procrustian's bed not furnished by Luke. While this passage may include some of Luke's favourite words, many pre-Lucan words in this passage[78] could indicate its primitive nature. It is hardly likely that the hellenistic church or Luke entirely made up or expanded this story. (See also below)

4.25. Fiedler's argument seems to be based too much upon his

---

[77] Plummer [1905: 435]: "When the defrauder confessed and made voluntary restitution, the whole amount stolen, with a fifth added, was sufficient (Lev. vi. 5; Num. v. 7)." Derrett [1970: 285]: "It illustrates further Jesus' policy of relying upon the ability of the individual whose conscience has been touched to react appropriately, to know that he is forgiven, and to act in such a way to demonstrate or to guarantee that fact". Conzelmann [1960: 229 (FT)]: "There are certain descriptions which give a concrete example of the event of conversion, such as the story of Zacchaeus (Luke 19:lff)."

[78] Jeremias; 1980: 275-277; Fitzmyer, 1986: 1219.

presupposition on Lucan words and theology. He neglected many words that do not fit into his argument. If those words could have come from the pre-Easter tradition Fiedler would be shown to have forced Luke into a Procrustian bed.[79]

4.26. Was πλούσιος inserted after καὶ αὐτὸς as an additional explanation? Fiedler suspects πλούσιος as Lucan on the assumption that ἔχων κτήματα πολλά could have been altered to πλούσιος σφόδρα (Luke 18:23) [1976: 130-131, 135]. However this hypothesis seems to be unconvincing because Matthew uses both πλούσιος (Matt 19:23), in a seemingly authentic saying of Jesus, and ἔχων κτήματα πολλά (Matt 19:22). Fiedler cites Loewe who merely speculates whether Luke uses πλούσιος as the final key for the wealth theme [1974: 322-323]. Loewe does not claim this word as "Lucan". Fiedler is also aware of the opposite argument: πλούσιος was in the tradition Luke received [130, 332 n 401]. Moreover πλούσιος σφόδρα (Luke 18:23), ἔχων κτήματα πολλὰ (Luke 18:24) could support the historicity of Jesus' meeting with the rich. It is a well known fact that an ἀρχιτελώνης was rich. Further Luke's detestation of the rich (Luke 6:24) would hardly have motivated him to insert πλούσιος [Fiedler, 1976: 130].

---

[79] Fiedler argues that Lucan editing stands out in this passage. καὶ ἰδοὺ (ἀνὴρ ὀνόματι καλούμενος Ζακχαῖος) is Lucan; καὶ ἐγένετο — καὶ αὐτὸς is a variation of this scheme (cf. Mark 2:1, Luke 8:1) [1976: 129-131]. But Fiedler admits that καὶ ἰδοὺ γυνὴ (13:11) was used when a new person was introduced. Accordingly Fiedler's argument seems not quite convincing. Fiedler also argues that εἶπεν...ἐγένετο, αὐτὸς υἱὸς 'Αβραάμ and καὶ ὑπεδέξατο (αὐτὸν χαίρων) are Lucan [1976; 132-133]. However these hypotheses seem to be not convincing because Fiedler does not put forward any clear reasons.

4.27. Fiedler suspects double occurrence καὶ αὐτὸς as a piece of evidence of reconstruction [1976: 130-131, 135]. However Semitism seems to be the better answer. καὶ αὐτὸς ἦν ἀρχιτελώνης καὶ αὐτὸς πλούσιος (v. 2), ἔμπροσθεν (v. 4), σπεύσας κατάβηθι (v. 5) show the traces of Semitism [Black, 1967: 64, 83; W. L. Knox, 1957: 111-112].

4.28. Fiedler suspects the hapaxlegomenon in the New Testament ἀρχιτελώνης as Lucan [1976: 129, 131-132].[80] Josephus does not use this term [Michel, 1969: 98n 105]. The absence of any word in Josephus does not prove its spuriousness. ἀρχιποίμενος (1 Peter 5:4), ἀρχιτρίκλινος (John 2:8, 9) are also absent in Josephus [BAGD: 113]. By the same token the single use of Josephus' βασιλεῖα could hardly blacken the authenticity of numerous occurrences βασιλεῖα a in the New Testament. It is hardly likely that Luke has added ἀρχι to τελώνης. Accordingly Fiedler's suspicion, ἀρχιτελώνης may be the misinterpretation of Zacchaeus' profession seems to remain unconvincing [1976: 132].

4.29. Zacchaeus could have called Jesus with the title κύριε (v. 8). Jesus could be given this title (Matt 8:2, 6; 8: 8; 15:22; 17:15; 20:31; Luke 5:12; 7:6; 10:17; 10:40; 11:1; 12:41; 18:41).

---

[80] Fiedler argues from the hypothesis that the same type of possible pattern of the merger of ἄρχων and τῆς συναγωγῆς (Mark 5:22) could result in ἀρχισυναγώγος (cf. Luke 8:49; 13:14; Acts 13:15; 18:8, 17). The interpretation seems to lead to unnecessary confusion over the authority of words in the New Testament. Fiedler cites Loewe. However, Loewe regards this word as pre-Lucan, not Lucan: "Luke takes up and expands the figure of the publicans in his sources" [1974: 322]. "From the Marcan material Lk takes up the story of the call of a publican to discipleship (5:27-39; cf. Mark 2:13ff., Matt 9:9ff)" [Loewe, 1974: 321-322].

4.30. Fiedler argues that ἐζήτει ἰδεῖν τὸν Ἰησοῦν τίς ἐστιν (v. 3) elucidates the faith motive in an "anecdotal" narrative [133-134, 333]. However contrary to Fiedler suspects ἐζήτουν αὐτὸν εἰσενεγκεῖν καὶ θεῖναι αὐτὸν ἐνώπιον αὐτοῦ (Luke 5:18) and ἐπυνθάνετο τί εἴη τοῦτο (Luke 18:36) describes the desperate aspiration to be saved from their plight. Hence these passages could rather support the historicity of this episode. Zacchaeus was a Jew not a Christian. If he was portrayed as a Christian he would not have been portrayed as needing to make restitution.

4.31. Even after accepting many of Fiedler's arguments on the secondary text, the main elements of this text remains firm; it does not affect the main thrust of this story.[81]

4.32. One of important premises of Sanders on Lucan theology is this: "Jesus did not issue a call for repentance and that it was Luke who emphasized the reform of the wicked who accepted him" [1985: 206]. The similar argument that Luke deliberately put the word "repent" or "repentance" to stress his theology is not entirely correct. The absence of the word "repentance" in Luke 19:1-9 casts doubt about this premise.

4.33. On (3.7), it does not necessarily mean that every passage on repentance is expanded or created by Luke. Some Lucan passages on

---

[81] Fiedler claims the following words as Lucan without putting forward any evidence: διερχέαθαι, τόπον, συπέσας, κατάβηθι, ἤμελλεν, οὐκ ἠδύνατο, ἀναβαίνειν, ἀναβλέπω [1976:133]; δεῖ [Fiedler, 1976: 132: Conzelmann, 1957: 143 (ET); Loewe, 1974: 325]; χαῖρων [Fiedler, 1976: 132]. However the suspicion of these words as secondary would serve little purpose to attempt to defend Fiedler's argument.

repentance are regarded as genuine despite their single occurrences.[82]

4.34. Contrary to (3. 8) "following" was required only of Jesus' disciples [Bultmann 1931: 34 (ET)].[83] Jesus did not ask every repentant sinners to follow him. He left them to do what was necessary instead. Jesus, unlike Levi (Mark 2:14-17), did not call Zacchaeus to be one of his disciples.

4.35. There are many accounts where Jesus commands the would-be followers not to follow. These passages illustrate that not every person who met Jesus followed him. Further the need of restitution described in v. 8 could hardly have confirmed the origin of Luke 19:1-9 from the early church.

4.36. The fact that Zacchaeus did not, like Levi, "follow" Jesus, is hardly due to his being converted with his family, as Wellhausen mistakenly supposed from τῷ οἴκῳ τούτῳ in v. 9. The presupposition that every repentant sinner must have followed Jesus is wrong. Jesus called only twelve as his disciples. Thus the absence of Jesus' command for Zacchaeus to follow him hardly affects the authenticity.

4.37. The Jews despised tax collectors. Accordingly the Palestinian church would have been reluctant to call a tax collector with the name

[82] A sinful woman (Luke 7:36-50), the parable of barren fig Luke (Luke 13:6-9) and the pharisee and the tax collector (Luke 18:9-14) also refer to repentance without the word "repent" or "repentance". Further Sanders' assertion is not absolutely correct because Matt and Mark also emphasize repentance (cf Mark 1:15; Matt 4:17; Matt 11:20-24; Matt 12:38-42).

[83] "Bultmann's view that it is an expansion of the story of the Call of Levi, adapted to days when its was no longer possible simply to "follow Jesus" in the literal sense, is an interesting speculation, but has no evidence to support it" [W. L. Knox, 1957: 111-112].

"righteous" (Zacchaeus).

4.38. God's everlasting love, does not exclude God's demand of repentance. God loves even at the moment when a human being commits sins. But God waits for the repentance of sinners. Forgiveness cannot materialize unless sinners acknowledge their sins and repent.[84] It must be noted that "in Judaism, the stress on the possibility of repentance and the nature of God as forgiving is counterbalanced by the fact that repentance is left entirely to the sinner's own initiative." [Hagner, 1984: 200].[85] "Basic to the rabbinic viewpoint on repentance is human free will and man's inherent capability of repentance" [Hagner, 1984: 201].

4.39. Luke 19:1-9 could echo the tax-collector's repentance in Luke 18:9-

---

[84] W. L. Knox explains lucidly [1930: 35]: "*Penitence is the necessary condition of forgiveness.* Without penitence of some kind on the part of the sinner it is impossible for God to forgive the sinner." "God's forgiveness, which is simply the love of God manifesting itself towards the sinner who repents, is always waiting for him to repent. *But so long as man's soul remains obstinately closed against the love of God by his preference for evil rather than good, manifested in the fact that he is conscious of having sinned and yet refuses to repent, it is also closed by his own act against the love of God.*" (italics mine). Fiedler argues that what is required for the sinners is to receive God's grace in a "repentant willing" mind [1976: 135]. However a "repentant willing" mind still affirms the need of repentance.

[85] Hagner cites Abrahams and Montefiore. "There were in the Pharisaism of all ages a real anxiety to make the return of the sinners easy. It was inclined to leave the initiative to the sinner, except that it always maintained God's readiness to take the first step. Jesus in his attitude towards sin and sinners was more inclined to take the initiative." [Abrahams, 1917: 58]. "The honour paid to repentance, the desire shown by God that man should repent, God's willingness to receive the penitent, are all characteristics features of the Rabbinic religion. What is new and striking in the teaching of Jesus is that this process of repentance takes an active turn. Man is bidden, not merely to receive the penitent gladly, but to seek out the sinner, to try to redeem him, and *make* him penitent." [Montefiore, 1927, vol. 2: 249]. (italics mine)

14.

5 .

5.1. The main thrust of the saying

The essence of this story lies in the fact that Zacchaeus repented, and, in doing so, declared his intention to return fourfold to any he had defrauded, and to give half of his possessions to the poor (v. 9). This came about as a result of Jesus' visit to his family, which was a sign of companionship.This passage has a particular significance in its illustration of the voluntary repentance and restitution of a flagrant sinner. The Jewish people at the time of Jesus despised the tax-collector as wicked.[86] Accordingly Zacchaeus' alienation from his Jewish community could drive him to yearn for friendship and recognition. Quite unexpectedly Jesus called his name and proposed to stay in his house. Even though Jesus did not exhort him to repent of his wrongdoings Zacchaeus responded in gratitude with the sign of repentance; sharing of possessions beyond the level of charity and making restitution.[87] For tax collectors the sharing of their assets could have had a particular significance. That was

---

[86] Abrahams [1917: 54]: "The class was consequently the object of popular resentment.... The association in the Gospels of the two expressions in Publicans and Sinners is parallel to the combination of "publicans and robbers" in the Rabbinic literature. The "sinners" were thus not those who neglected the rules of ritual piety, but were persons of immoral life, men of proven dishonesty or followers of suspected and degrading occupations." Schuerer [1973 (ET), vol. 1: 376]: "There was plenty of scope for the arbitrariness and rapacity of the tax-collectors. The exploitation of such opportunities and the not infrequent overcharges made by those officials caused them, as a class, to be loathed by the people."

[87] From his experience, Jesus could know that his consorting could result in Zacchaeus' repentance [cf. W. L. Knox, 1957: 112].

the most cherished and last thing they could rely on.

Does Zacchaeus' response exclude every idea of performance as Fiedler argues [1976: 135]? Were the Jewish people, at the time of Zacchaeus ensured of their salvation irrespective of their moral reformation? That was highly unlikely. John the Baptist crushed the Jewish people's false complacency resting upon their ancestral relationship with Abraham. If that complacency were solid why did Jesus start his public ministry calling for repentance which required another dimension of Jewishness? Zacchaeus' Jewishness was not enough to ensure his salvation. His change reflected in his radical resolution could meet the demand. As a model case Zacchaeus' declaration illustrates the need of repentance and making restitution after having received Jesus' mercy.[88]

Although Zacchaeus does not follow Jesus as a disciple Luke 19:1-9 demonstrates the need of making restitution required of the repentant sinners.[89] Jesus initiated his consorting with a sinner Zacchaeus and

---

[88] Schweizer correctly explains that here Zacchaeus takes initiative [1982: 291 (ET)]. The early church would not have followed the Roman law because they used a Jewish expression "Abraham's sonship" (v. 9). Marshall explains Zacchaeus' decision as resolution: "That emphasis in the Gospel of Luke brings is the sharpness of the call to decision expressed by Jesus. What it might mean in practice is shown by the case of Zacchaeus (Luke 19:8)." [1970: 207]. Marshall assumes that the repentant tax collector make restitution after being forgiven by Jesus [1978: 677]: "...to be sure. this does not mean that tax-collectors are excused from making restitution for their extortion, as 19:1-10 makes clear." "... When Zacchaeus restores his ill gotten gains a responsibility from which he is not excused! — this follows his acceptance by Jesus and does not precede it." [1978: 681].

[89] Marshall correctly points out that Zacchaeus' retribution and restitution clearly expressed the meaning of discipleship in regard to wealth [1978: 694]. This argument goes against the argument of Sanders who assumes that Jesus' followers were not required to make restitution. Schweizer assumes that Zacchaeus needs to make restitution rigorously [1982: 292 (ET)]: "No more than in the discipleship

expected him to repent voluntarily. Zacchaeus' declaration on retribution of his possessions and restoration of the defrauded taxes could reflect Jesus' expectation.

5.2. The bearing of the saying and the forgiveness of sins

Zacchaeus' announcement that he would give half of his possessions to the poor would eventually make him to go to the temple. Rabbis command the Jews not to receive charity from the tax collectors money box since such is deemed got by robbery (B. Qam. 10.1). Thus Zacchaeus could only give it to the priests. This deposit, along with articles of which tax-collectors do not know, can later be devoted to public needs like wells (b. B. Qam. 94b-95a; Michel, 1969: 103 (ET)] Jeremias, 1971: 103 (ET)] on the advice of the temple treasurer [Buechler, 1928: 398].

Zacchaeus' declaration implies that he will eventually fulfil restitution and offer the guilt offering in the Temple. The reason why Jesus declares Zacchaeus' salvation is based upon Jesus' assumption. In conclusion, Jesus does ask repentant sinners and followers to make restitution.

Jesus did not have to become a national hero from leading sinners to repentance and restitution as a result of his consorting with them.[90] Tax

---

stories is the difficulty of his undertaking described, what it means as a high official known throughout the city, to go from door to door and admit cases of fraud, and later to pay the sums he has contracted for without resort to fraud or extortion." Michel argues that v. 9 means that restoration must be extended to this man because even a tax-collector is a Jew [1969: 104 (ET)].

[90] Sanders [1985: 203]: "If Jesus by eating with tax-collectors led them to repent, repay those whom they had robbed, and leave off practising their profession, he would have been a national hero." Sanders also argues that: "...it is difficult to show that Jesus was a spokesman for a return of the sinners to the community. The story

collectors' repentance and making restitution could hardly have triggered a sensation among the Jewish people who would have assumed sinners' repentance and restitution as necessary and natural. In this religious milieu Jesus would hardly have allowed flagrant sinners to follow him in the absence of repentance and restitution. Rather Jesus could have assumed their thorough fulfilment of what was expected of repentant sinners.

---

of Zacchaeus (Luke 19:1-9) brings home the curiosity of the reported charge that Jesus ate with tax collectors and sinners and promised them a place in the kingdom. This story was, as I proposed above, created by Luke (or possibly a pre-Lucan writer) to emphasize repentance and reform." [1985: 203].

CHAPTER VI

Conclusion in Light of a Close Examination of the Relevant Passages

I have examined Sanders' five theses in light of a close examination of the relevant passages. The result shows a very different picture from that which Sanders draws. Despite some refreshingly new arguments and interpretations on the public ministry of Jesus some of his arguments on repentance and restitution remain unconvincing. Therefore, I put forward the following arguments as my conclusion.

1. As Mark 1:15; Matt 6:12, Luke 11: 4b; Mark 8:12, Matt 12:39, 16:4, 12:41-42, Luke 11:31-32; Matt 23:37-39, Luke 13:34-35; Matt 10:5-15; Mark 6:7-13; Luke 10:2-12; 9:1-6; Matt 11:16-19a, Luke 7:31-34; Matt 11:21-23a, Luke 10:13-15; Luke 13:1-5; Matt 18:12-14, Luke 15:4-7 attest, Jesus and his disciples called for national repentance. This claim would have been particularly appealing to the Jewish people at the time of Jesus, who had longed for their independence from the dominion of the Roman Empire.

Along with John the Baptist who renewed the prophetic tradition dating back to the O.T., Jesus proclaimed his message in various literary forms: prophetic proclamations, parables, prayers, wisdom sayings. In order to spread his claim nationwide Jesus commanded his disciples to proclaim the imminent kingdom with an expectation that the Jewish people would positively respond to this call. In this sense Jesus was a prophet, a teacher of the coming Kingdom.

Contrary to Sanders' arguments, national repentance and individual repentance are hardly distinguishable. Individual repentance and national repentance are so closely tied together that it is almost impossible to separate them into separate entities. These two kinds of repentance hardly exclude each other. Jesus' call for repentance encompasses both individuals and the whole of Israel: massive individual repentance equals national repentance. Further, one person's repentance is closely related to the repentance of the entire people of a nation. One person's repentance, that of King David, leads God to decide not to punish seventy thousand Israelites, a national disaster (1 Chr 21:1-27).

2. Jesus clearly stressed repentance and puts conditions on redemption, Matt 5:23-24, 6:14, Mark 11:25; Matt 5:25-26, Luke 12:57-59; Matt 6:12, Luke 11:4b; Matt 18:12-14, Luke 15:4-7; Matt 18:23-35; Luke 13:6-9 support this argument.

Sanders describes Jesus as a Jew who barely acknowledges repentance. But this description seems too remote from the real Jesus. Jesus hardly appears as a Jew who passively acknowledges repentance. On the contrary Jesus' belief in repentance and turning to God seems to lead him to embark on a bold approach, reaching out to the people and stressing repentance.

Often people make mistakes by painting God as a figure who is only to forgive, never to judge or punish. But the God of the Jewish people, especially in the first century Palestine, was regarded as the God who punishes and judges people's sins rigorously.

Jesus put repentance as a condition of salvation. Sanders argues that "Jesus offered forgiveness (inclusion in the kingdom) before requiring reformation." [1985: 204]. This idea would have been hardly understandable to the first century Jewish people. Sanders almost attributes to Jesus a possible Christian way of thinking in post-Easter Christianity: forgiveness is already fulfilled at the cross. What was then required of the Jewish people was the repentance of their unbelief in the risen Christ. This idea can hardly be attributed to pre-Easter Judaism. It would very much be a forced interpretation to argue that Jesus had already acted upon ideas of the early Christianity.

3. Jesus does make repentance a condition for joining his band of disciples who respond to his call. Jesus does not teach his followers or repentant sinners what to do; he, could assume that they knew what they should do e.g., the fast on the Day of Atonement [1985: 207]. Matt 8:2-4; Mark 1:40-45; Luke 5:12-16; Matt 5:23-24; Matt 6:14; Mark 11:25; Matt 5:25-26; Luke 12:57-59; Luke 18:9-14; Luke 19:1-10 support this argument. Judaism was not a religion which insisted on imposing on repentant sinners obligations which are utterly impossible to fulfil. Those seemingly stringent obligations were not necessarily a burden for repentant sinners. In early Christianity this point seems to become less stressed than in the pre-Easter period.

It is difficult to imagine Jesus surrounded by a group of people who had never restored what they owed or resolved situations in which they have wronged other people when necessary.[1] Although it is not directly mentioned, Matt 9:9-13; Mark 2:14-17; Luke 5:27-32 could imply repentance and restitution. Matthew's response to Jesus call could indicate his compliance with the requirement of Jesus' demand stressed in his teaching and public proclamation. Jesus' followers would hardly have foregone the responsibility of making restitution. This is particularly likely because in Judaism and in the O.T., moral requirements and external requirements are integrated into one unitary requirement, the

---

[1] P. S. Alexander rightly concurs with two aspects of restitution, 'civil' and 'religious' (Lev 6:17) [1988: 50]. He affirms the need of fulfilling the obligation of making restitution: "The [Jewish] courts would have enforced the restitution to the aggrieved party." [51]. In this legal context Jesus would hardly have allowed his band of disciples to forgo the responsibility of making a 'civil' restitution. Jesus would hardly have wanted to have followers whom the Jewish court wanted to charge. Alexander argues that "the sacrifice in the Temple," the religious aspect of restitution, would effectively have been left to the individuals's conscience [51].

Torah. Jesus could have assumed that the repentant sinners knew what they should do. In particular, accounts of tax collectors illustrate their repentance and restitution implicitly and explicitly. All sorts of alleged constraints could hardly have discouraged repentant sinners' determination to fulfil their obligations, which give them joy and freedom from guilt. These practices seem to have been obeyed consistently throughout the time of the O.T, the N.T., and Rabbinic Judaism. Jesus' teaching on repentance and restitution could have arisen from his aspiration to see the full restoration of repentant sinners to the community to which they had previously belonged.

4. Jesus teaches that people destined for the kingdom should keep the highest moral standards. "Following Jesus" could mean keeping the highest moral standards. The stress on repentance, restitution, forgiveness and reconciliation is an important element in upholding the highest moral standards. Matt 5:23-24; 6:16 (Mark 11:25); Matt 5:25-26; Luke 12:57-59; Matt 6:12; Luke 11:4b; Matt 18:12-14; Luke 15:4-7; Luke 18:9-14; Luke 19:1-10 support this argument. The radical command to fulfil the requirements of repentance and restitution even by the temporary delay of offering (Matt 5:23-24) attests how keen Jesus was at upholding the morality of the people. The command to be reconciled even with the enemy by clearing everything which might cause even a slight chance of an adverse judgment in the coming future also stresses this point. The command to forgive when the offender repents and makes restitution (Matt 6:12; Luke 11:4) before the imminent Kingdom stresses radical repentance and restitution.

The coming of the kingdom hardly allows people to relax their ethical standards. The reverse seems to be the case. In a context in which the intensification of fulfilling the law was widespread, Jesus would rather have stressed that the people destined for the kingdom should keep the highest moral standards. This idea was inherited even by the early church (cf. 1 Thess 5:23-24). In the context of Judaism one of the most natural ways of upholding the highest moral standards would have been by stressing the requirement of the Law upon which the whole of Judaism was founded.

5. Jesus works and speaks forgiveness in an eschatological context. The eschatological overtones in Matt 5:23-24; 6:14; Mark 11:25; Matt 5:25-26; Luke 12:57-59; Matt 6:12; Luke 11:4b; Matt 10:5-15; Luke 10:2-12; 9:1-6; Matt 11:16-19a; Luke 7:31-34; Matt 11:21-23a; Luke 10:13-15; Matt 11:41-42; Luke 11:31-32; Matt 23:37-39; Luke 13:34-35; Luke 13:1-5; Luke 13:6-9 support this claim. The Jewish people's awareness of the imminent Kingdom as we see particularly in the people of the Qumran and Essene community, would have helped them to grasp the point of the message of Jesus and disciples. In this milieu, Jesus seems to have worked consistently to help people prepare for the coming kingdom.

BIBLIOGRAPHY AND SYSTEM OF REFERENCES

1. Text and Translations

A. Text of the New Testament

Aland, K. & Nestle, E.
1979 *Novum Testamentum Graece.* 26 ed. (1st ed. 1898). Stuttgart: Deutsche Bibelstiftung.

Aland, K.
1985 *Synopsis Quattor Evangeliorum.* 13th rev. ed. Stuttgart: Deutsche Bibelgesellschaft.

Legg, S. C. E.
1940 *Novum Testamentum Graece Matthae.* Oxford: Oxford University Press.

Von Soden.
1913 *Die Schriften des Neuen Testaments.* vol. 2. Goettingen: Vandenhoeck & Ruprecht.

B. The Dead Sea Scrolls

Lohse, E.
1971 *Die Texte Aus Qumran (Hebraeisch und Deutsch).* Muenchen: Koesel Verlag.

Maier, J.
1960 *Die Texte vom Toten Meer.* vol. 1. Muenchen and Basel: Ernst Reinhardt Verlag.

Vermes, G.
1987 *The Dead Sea Scrolls in English.* ET by G. Vermes, 3rd revised and augmented ed.(lst ed. 1962). Harmondsworth: Penguin Books.

C. Apocrypha and Pseudepigrapha

Charles, R. H.
1913 *The Apocrypha and Pseudepigrapha of the Old Testament.* vols 12. Oxford: Oxford University Press

Charlesworth, J. H.
1983 *The Old Testament Pseudepigrapha,* vols. 1-2. Apocalyptic Literature & Testaments. ed. by J. H. Charlesworth. New York: Doubleday & Company.

D. Rabbinic Literature

Braude, W.

1959 *Midrash on Psalms*. vol. 1 (Psalms 1-72). vol. 2 (Psalms 73-150). New Haven: Yale University Press.

Cohen, A.

1921 *The Babylonian Talmud: Tractate Beracoth*. ET by A. Cohen. Cambridge: Cambridge University Press.

Danby, H.

1933 *The Mishnah*. ET by B. Danby. Oxford: Oxford University Press.

Epstein, I.

1935-52 *The Babylonian Talmud*. ed. by I. Epstein. vols. 1-35. London: Soncino Press.

Freedman, H.

1939 *The Midrash I-11. Genesis I* (in two vols.). ET by M. Simon & H. Freedman. London: Soncino Press.

Goldin, J.

1955 *The Fathers according to Rabbi Nathan*. New Haven: Yale University Press.

Kadushin, M.

1987 *A Conceptual Commentary on Midrash Leviticus Rabbah: Value Concepts in Jewish Thought*. Atlanta: Scholars Press.

Lauterbach, J. Z.

1933 *Mekilta De-Rabbi Ishmael*. vols.1-3. ET by J. Z. Lauterbach. Philadelphia: The Jewish Publication Society of America.

Maimonides

The Book of Knowledge from the Mishnah Torah of Maimonides. ET by H. M. Russell & J. Weinberg. Edinburgh: Royal College of Physicians of Edinburgh, 1981.

Neusner, J.

1975 *A History of the Mishnaic Law of Purities*. vol. 7. Sifra Negaim. Leiden: E. J. Brill

1977-86 *The Tosefta*. vol. 1 (1986), 2 (1981), 3 (1979), 4 (1981), 5 (1979), 6 (1977). ET by J. Neusner and others. New York: Ktav Publishing House Inc.

1985 *Sifra the Rabbinic Commentary on Leviticus*. Atlanta: Scholars Press.

1985 *Genesis Rabbah*. vols. 1-3. Atlanta: Scholars Press.

1986 *The Fathers according to Rabbi Nathan*. ET by J. Neusner. Atlanta: Scholars Press.

1986 *Sifre to numbers*. vols. 1-2 (An American Translation and Explanation). Atlanta: Scholars Press.

Sifre to Deuteronomy. vols. 1-2. (An American Translation and Explanation). Atlanta: Scholars Press.

Saldarini, A. J.

1975 *The Fathers according to Rabbi Nathan*. Leiden: E. J. Brill.

Zahavy, T.
1989 *The Talmud of the Land of Israel.* (Jerusalem Talmud) vol. 1. Chicago; The University of Chicago Press.

E. Other Jewish Literature and Texts

Josephus *The Life. Against Apion. Jewish Antiquities.* vols. 1-10. Loeb Classical Library. ET by H. S. J. Thackeray & R. Marcus & A. Wikgren & L. H. Feldmann. Cambridge (Massachusetts) and London: Harvard University Press & Heinemann Publication Company, 1926-1965.

Philo *Works.* vols. 1-10. ET by F. H. Colson & G. H. Whitaker & J. W. Earp. Cambridge & London: Harvard University Press & Heinemann Publication Company, 1929-1962

F. Greek Literature

Plutarch *Lives.* vol. 7 (Alexander and Caesar). Loeb Classical Library. ET by B. Perrin. London: W. Heinemann, 1919.

Diogenes *Laertius.* ET by R. D. Hicks. London: W. Heinemann, 1929.

G. Early Christian Literature

Didache *The Apostolic Fathers. vol* 1: 303-333. ET by K. Lake. Cambridge & London: Harvard University Press & W. Heinemann Publication Company.

Justin M. *Iustinus: Dialogus.* ed. by E. J. Goodspeed. Goettingen: Vandenhoeck & Ruprecht, 1914.
Dialogue with Trypho. Justin Martyr's Dialog with Trypho in *The Fathers of Church.* ET by T.B. Falls. Washington: The Catholic University of America, 1977.
Ante Nicene Fathers. II. ed. A. Roberts and J. Donaldson. Edinburgh:T. T. Clark.

Origen *Contra Celsum.* ET by H. Chadwick. Cambridge: Cambridge University Press, 1965.

2. General

Abrahams, I.
1917 *Studies in Pharisaism and the Gospels.* First Series. Cambridge: Cambridge University Press.
1924 *Studies in Pharisaism and the Gospels.* Second Series. Cambridge: Cambridge University Press.

Alexander, P. S.
1983 "Rabbinic Judaism and the New Testament". *ZNW* 74: 237-246.

1986 "Review of E. P. Sanders' Jesus and Judaism". *JJS* 37: 103-106.

Allison, D. C.

1987 "Jesus and the Covenant: A Response to E. P. Sanders". *JSNT* 29: 57-78.

Ambrozic, A. M.

1972 "The Hidden Kingdom: A Redaction-Critical Study of the References to the Kingdom of God in Mark's Gospel". *CBQ Monograph Series.* 2. Washington D.C.: Catholic Biblical Association of America.

Anderson, H.

1976 *The Gospel of Mark.* London: Marshall, Morgan & Scott Publishing Ltd..

Ashby, G.

1988 *Sacrifice: its nature and purpose.* London: SCM Press.

Aune, D. E.

1983 *Prophecy in Early Christianity and the Ancient Mediterranean* World. Grand Rapids: Wm. B. Eerdmans Publishing Company.

Bammel, E.

1964 "Erwaegungen zur Eschatologie Jesus". *SE.* vol 3. Part II. TU 88. ed. F.L. Cross, Berlin: Akademische Verlag.

1984 "The Feeding of the Multitudes". Pp. 11-68 in *Jesus and the Politics of His Day.* ed. by E. Bammel & C. F. D. Moule. Cambridge: Cambridge University Press.

Barrett, C. K.

1947 *The Holy Spirit and Gospel Tradition.* London: SPCK.

Bartsch, H. W.

1962 "Die Verfluchung des Feigenbaums". *ZNW* 53: 256-260.

Baumbach, G.

1963 *Das Verstaendnis des Boesen in den synoptischen Evangelien.* Berlin: Evangelische Verlagsanstalt.

Bayer, H.

1986 *Jesus' Predictions of Vindication and Resurrection.* Tuebingen: J. C. B. Mohr (Paul Siebeck).

Beasley-Murray, G. R.

1954 *Jesus and the Future: The Local Background to the Gospel Documents.* London: The Macmillan Publishing Company.

1986 *Jesus and the Kingdom of God.* Exeter: The Paternoster Press.

Becker, J.

1972 *Johannes* der *Tauefer und Jesus von Nazareth.* Neukirchen: Neukirchener Verlag.

Best, E.

1976-77 "The Role of the Discipleship in Mark". *NTS* 23: 377-401.

1981 *Following* Jesus: *Discipleship in the Gospel of Mark.* Sheffield: JSOT Press.

1986 *Disciples and Discipleship.* Edinburgh: T. & T. Clark.

1990 *The Temptation and The Passion: The Markan Soteriology. 2nd* ed. (I st ed. 1965). Cambridge: Cambridge University Press.

Betz, O.

1965 *Was wissen wir von Jesus?* Stuttgart: Kreuz-Verlag. ET by M. Kohl *What do we know about* Jesus? London: SCM Press, 1967.

1990 *Jesus der Herr der Kirche.* Tuebingen: J. C. B. Mohr (P. Siebeck).

Billerbeck, P.

1922-61 *Kommentar Zum Neuen Testament. ed.* by P. Billerbeck. vols. 1 (1926), 2 (1924), 3 (1926), 4-1 (1929), 4-2 (1928). vol. 6 (I 96 1). ed. by J. Jeremias, and K. Adolph. Muenchen: C. H. Beck'sche Verlagsbuchhandlung.

Bishop, E. F. F.

1955 *Jesus of Palestine: The Local Background to the Gospel Documents.* London: Lutterworth Press.

Black, M.

1967 *An Aramaic Approach to the Gospels and Acts.* 3rd ed. (lst ed. 1946). Oxford: Oxford University Press.

Blinzler, J.

1958 "Die Niedermetzelung von Galilaeern durch Pilatus". *Nov T 2:* 24-49.

Bonner, H.

1927 "Traces of Thaumaturgic Technique in the Miracles." *HTR* 20: 171-181.

Borg, M. J.

1987 *Jesus: A New Vision.* San Francisco: Harper & Row Publishers.

Bornkamm, G.

1958 "Evangelien". Pp. 750-766 in *Die Religion in Geschichte und Gegenwart.* 3rd ed. vol. 2 (D-G). Tuebingen: J. C. B. Mohr (P. Siebeck).

1959 *Jesus von Nazareth.* Stuttgart: W. Kohlhammer Verlag. 3rd ed. (1st ed.1956). ET by I. & F. McLuskey & J. M. Robinson. *Jesus of Nazareth.* 2nd ed. London: Hodder and Stoughton, 1966.

Boring, E.

1982 *The Sayings of the Risen Jesus.* Cambridge: Cambridge University Press.

Bousset, W.

1906 *Jesus.* Halle: Gebauer-Schwetschke Verlag, 1904. ed. by W. D. Morrison. ET by J. P. Trevelyn. London: Williams & Norgate.

1913 *Kyrios Christos.* Goettingen: Vandenhoeck and Ruprecht. ET by J. Steeley *Kyrios Christos.* Nashville: Abingdon Press, 1970.

Branscomb, B. H.

1937 *The Gospel of Mark.* London: Hodder & Stoughton.

Braun, H.

1957 *Spaetjuedische-haeretischer und fruechristlicher Radikalismus: Jesus von Nazareth und die essenische Qumransekte.* vols. 1-2. Tuebingen:J. C. B. Mohr (Paul Siebeck).

1959 πλανάω *TDNT.* vol. 6: 228- 253.

1966 *Qumran und Das Neue Testament.* vol. 1. Tuebingen: J. C. B. Mohr (Paul Siebeck).

1969 *Jesus.* Stuttgart: Kreuz Verlag. ET by E. R. Kalin *Jesus of Nazareth.*

Philadelphia: Fortress Press, 1979.

Brooks, S. H.
1987 *Matthew's Community; the evidence of his special sayings material.* Sheffield: Sheffield Academic Press.

Bruce, F. F.
1952 "Justification by Faith in the non-Pauline Writings of the New Testament". EQ 24: 66-77.
1984 "Render to Caesar". Pp. 249-264 in *Jesus and the Politics of His Day.* ed. E. Bammel & C. F. D. Moule. Cambridge: Cambridge University Press.

Buechler, A.
1928 *Studies in Sin and Atonement in the Rabbinic Literature of the First Century.* Oxford: Oxford University Press.

Buechsel, F.
1933 γενεά, *TDNT.* vol. 1: 662-665.
1938 ἱλάσκομοι, ἱλάσκεσθαι *TDNT.* vol. 3: 300-301, 310-318.

Bultmann, R.
1926 *Jesus.* Berlin: Deutsche Bibliothek. ET. L P. Smith & E. Huntress *Jesus and the Word.* London: I. Nicholson & Watson Ltd., 1935.
1931 *Die Geschichte der synoptischen Tradition.* 2nd ed. Goettingen: Vandenhoeck & Ruprecht. ET by J. Marsh. With Supplement (Ergaenzungheft) published in 1962. *The History of the Synoptic Tradition.* Oxford: Basil Blackwell, 1972.
1948 *Theologie des Neuen Testaments.* vol. 1. Tuebingen: J. C. B. Mohr, ET by K. Grobel. *New Testament Theology.* vol. 1 London: SCM Press, 1951.
1949 *Das Urchristentum im Rahmen der antiken Religionen.* Zuerich: Artemis-Verlag. ET. by R. H. Fuller. *Primitive Christianity in its Contemporary Setting.* London & New York: Thames & Hudson, 1956.

Burney. C. F.
1925 *Poetry of Our Lord: An Examination of the Formal Elements of Hebrew Poetry in the Discourses of Jesus Christ.* Oxford: Oxford University Press.

Cabraja, I.
1985 *Der Gedanke der Umkehr bei den Synoptikern.* St. Ottilien: EOS Verlag.

Cadoux, C. J.
1940-42 "The Use of Hyperbole in Scripture". *ExpTim* 52: 378-381.
1941 *The Historic Mission of Jesus.* London: Lutterworth Press.

Caird, C. B.
1963 *Saint Luke.* London: Penguin Books.

Carmignac, J.
1969 *Recherches sur le "Notre Pere ".* Paris: Letouzey & Ane.
1974 "The Spiritual Wealth of the Lord's Prayer" in *Das Vaterunser Gemeinsames im Beten von Juden und Christen.* Freiburg im Briesgau: Verlag Herder. ed. by J. Petuchowski & M. Brocke. ET by

E. R. Petuchowski. *The Lord's Prayer and Jewish Liturgy*. London: Burns & Oates, 1978. Pp. 137-148.

Catchpole, D.
1978 "John the Baptist, Jesus and the Parable of the Tares". *SJT* 131: 557-570.

Cave, C. H.
1978-79 "The Leper: Mark 1.40-45". *NTS* 25: 245-250.

Charlesworth, J. H.
1982 "The Historical Jesus in Light of Writings Contemporaneous with Him". *ANRW* II 25 (1): 451-476.

Chilton, B.
1979 *God in Strength:Jesus'Announcement of the Kingdom*. Freistadt: F. Ploechl Verlag.
1988 "Jesus and the Repentance of E. P. Sanders". *TynBul* 39: 1-18.

Christ, F.
1970 *Jesus Sophia (Die Sophia-Christologie bei den Synoptikern)*. Zuerich: Zwingli Verlag.

Colpe, C.
1969 ὁ υἱός τοῦ ἀνθρώπου *TDNT*. vol. 8: 400-477.

Conzelmann, H.
1957 *Die Mitte der Zeit*. Goettingen: Vandenhoeck and Ruprecht. Tuebingen: J. C. B. Mohr (P. Siebeck). ET by G. Bussnel *The Theology of Luke*. London: Faber and Faber, 1960.
1968 *Grundriss der Theologie des Neuen Testament*. Muenchen: Christian Kaiser Verlag. 2nd ed. ET by J. Bowman *An Outline of the Theology of the New Testament*. London: SCM Press, 1969.

Cranfield, C. E. B.
1959 *The Gospel According to Saint Mark*. Cambridge: Cambridge University Press.

Creed. J. M.
1953 *The Gospel According to Luke*. 1st ed. 1930. London: The Macmillan Company.

Dalman, G.
1898 *Die Worte Jesu*. Leipzig: J. C. Hinrich's. ET by D. M. Kay. *The Sayings of Jesus*. Edinburgh: T. & T. Clark, 1902.
1924 *Orte und Wege Jesu*. 3rd ed. (2nd ed. 1921) Guetersloh: Bertelsmann. ET by P. P. Levertoff *Sacred Sites and Ways*. London: SPCK, 1935.

Davies, W. D.
1964 *The Setting of the Sermon on the Mount*. Cambridge: Cambridge University Press.
1966 *The Sermon on the Mount*. Cambridge: Cambridge University Press.
1974 *The Gospel and the Land*. Berkeley:University of California Press.
1988 *The Gospel According to Saint Matthew*. vol. 1. With D. C. Allison, Edinburgh: T. & T. Clark.

deBoer, M. C.
1988 "Thousand Talents? Matthew's Interpretation and Redaction of the People of the Unforgiving Servant (Mt 18:23-35)". *CBQ* 150 (No. 3): 214-232.
Deissmann, A.
1923 *Licht vom Osten.* Tuebingen: J. C. Mohr (P. Siebeck). *Light from the Ancient East.* ET by L. R. M. Strachan. London: Hodder & Stoughton, 1927.
Derrett, J. D. M.
1970 *Law in the New Testament.* London: Darton, Longmann & Todd.
1973 "Fig Trees in the New Testament". *HeyJ* 14: 249-265.
1979-80 "Fresh Light on the Lost Sheep and the Lost Coin". *NTS* 26: 36-60.
Dibelius, M.
1933 *Die Formgeschichte des Evangelium.* 2nd ed. (1st ed. 1919). Tuebingen: J. C. B. Mohr. ET by B. L. Woolf *From Tradition to Gospels.* London: I. Nicholson & Watson Ltd., 1934
Dobshuetz, E.
1927 *Vom Auslegen des Neuen Testaments.* Goettingen: Vandenhoeck & Ruprecht.
Dodd, C. H.
1930 "Jesus as Teacher and Prophet". in *Mysterium Christi.* ed. by G. K. A. Bell & A. Deissmann. London: Longman.
1936 *The Parables of the Kingdom.* London: Nisbet & Co. Ltd.
1971 *The Founder of Christianity.* London: Collins.
Drury, J.
1985 *The Parables in the Gospels.* London: SPCK.
Dunn, J. D. G .
1975 *Jesus and the Spirit.* London: SCM Press
1989 *Christology in the Making.* rev. ed. London: SCM Press.
Easton, B. S.
1928 *The Gospel before the Gospels.* London: George Allen & Unwin, Ltd.
Edwards, R. A.
1971 *The Sign of Jonah: in the Theology of the Evangelists and Q.* London: SCM Press.
Elliott, J. K
1971 "The Conclusion of the Pericope of the Healing of the Leper and Mark 1.45". *JTS* vol. 22: 153-157.
1978 "The Healing of the Leper in the Synoptic Parallels". *TZ* vol. 34: 175-176.
Evans, C. F.
1990 *Saint Luke.* London: SCM Press.
Fenton, J. C.
1963 *Saint Matthew.* Harmondsworth: Penguin Books Ltd.
1971 *What was Jesus' Message.* London: SPCK.
Fiedler, P.
1976 *Jesus und Suender.* Peter & Herbert Lang: Frankfurt am Main & Bern.

Finegan, J.
1969 *The Archaeology of the New Testament.* Princeton: Princeton Univ. Press.

Fitzmyer, J.
1981 *The Gospel according* to *Luke.* vol. 1 (Chap. 1-9). New York: Doubleday & Company Inc..
1986 *The Gospel according to Luke.* vol. 2 (Chap. 10-24). New York: Doubleday & Company Inc.

Flew, R. N.
1938 *Jesus and his Church: A Study of the Idea of the Ecclesia in the* N.T. London: The Epworth Press.

Flusser, D.
1986 "Sanders' Jesus and Judaism". *JQR 176* (No. 3): 246-252.
1988 *Judaism and the Origins of Christianity.* Jerusalem: The Magnes Press.

Foerster, W.
1964 *σώζω. TDNT.* vol. 7: 965-1024.

Ford, J. M.
1968 "The forgiveness clause in the Matthean Form of the Our Father". *ZNW* 59: 127-131.

Fridrichsen, A.
1925 *Le Probleme du Miracle dans Le Christianisme Primitif* Strasbourg: Faculty of Protestant Theology at the University Strasbourg. ET by R.A. Harrisville and J. S. Hanson on *The Problem of Miracle.* Minneapolis; Augusburg Publishing House, 1972.

Fuchs, E.
1959 "The Parable of the Unmerciful Servant (Mt 18:23-35)". *SE (TU* 73): 487-494.
1960 *Zur Frage nach dem historischen Jesus. Tuebingen:* J. C. B. Mohr (Siebeck). ET by A. Scobie *Studies of the historical Jesus.* London: SCM.Press, 1964.

Fuller, R. H.
1954 *The Mission and Achievement of Jesus.* London: SCM Press.
1965 *The Formation of new Testament Christology. London:* Lutterworth Press.

Funk, R.
1988 *The Parables of Jesus.* coauthor Butts, J. R.& Scott, B. B. Sonoma: Polebridge Press.

Gaechter, P.
1963 *Das Matthaeusevangelium.* Innsbruck, Wien, Muenchen: Tyroli-Verlag.

Gaston, L.
1970 *No Stone on Another.* Leiden: E. J. Brill.

Gerhardsson, B.
1961 *Memory and Manuscript: Oral tradition and Written Transmission in Rabbinic Judaism and Early Christianity.* Copenhagen: Ejnar Munksgaard. ET by E. J. Sharpe from the Swedish. Lund: C.W.K.

Gleerup, 1963.

Gnilka, J.
1978 *Das Evangelium nach Markus.* vols. 1-2. Zuerich: Benziger Verlag.
1986 *Matthaeusevangelium.* vol. 1. Freiburg: Herder Verlag.
1988 *Matthaeusevangelium.* vol. 2. Freiburg: Herder Verlag.

Godet, F.
1872 *Commentaire sur Le Evangile de Saint Luc.* Paris: Sandoz & Fishbacher. ET from 2nd French ed. by M. D. Cusin *The Gospel of St. Luke.* vol. 2. 4th ed. Edinburgh: T. & T. Clark, 1890.

Goldin, J.
1955 *The Fathers according to Rabbi Nathan.* New Haven: Yale University Press.

Goppelt, L.
1975 *Theologie des Neuen Testaments. vol.* 1. ed. by J. Roloff. Goettingen: Vandenhoeck & Ruprecht. ET by J. E. Alsup. *Theology of the New Testament.* Grand Rapids: W. B. Eerdmans Publishing Company, 1981.

Goguel, M.
1932 *La Vie de Jesus.* Paris: Payot. ET by. 0. Wyon *The Life of Jesus.* London: George Allen & Unwin Ltd..

Goulder, M. D.
1963 "The Composition of the Lord' Prayer". *JTS* 14: 32-45.
1974 *Midrash and Lection in Matthew.* London: SPCK.

Graesser, E.
1957 *Der Problem der Parusieverzoegerung in den synoptischen Evangelien und in der Apostelgeschichte.* Berlin: Verlag A. Toepelmann.

Green, H. B.
1975 *The Gospel according to Matthew.* Oxford: Oxford University Press.

Grundmann, W.
1968 *Das Evangelium nach Matthaeus.* Berlin: Evangelische Verlagsanstalt
1977 *Das Evangelium nach Markus.* 7th ed. (1st ed. 1959). Berlin.
1981 *Das Evangelium nach Lukas.* 8th ed. (1st ed. 1961). Berlin: Evangelische Verlagsanstalt.

Haenchen, E.
1951 "Matthaeus 23 ". *ZTHK* 48: 39-63.
1968 *Der Weg Jesu: Eine Erklaerung des Markus Evangelium und der kanonischen Parallelen.* 2nd ed. Berlin: A. Toepelmann Verlag.

Hahn, F.
1963 *Das Verstaendnis der Mission im neuen Testament.* Neukirchen-Vluyn: Neukirchener Verlag. ET by F. Clarke *Mission in the New Testament.* London; SCM Press, 1965.
1963 *Christologische Hoheitstitel.* Goettiengen: Vandenhoeck & Ruprecht.
1970 *Der* urchristliche Gottesdienst. Stuttgart: Verlag Katholisches Bibelwerk. ed. H. Haag & R. Kilian & W. Pesch. ET by D. E. Green, ed. by J. Reumann. *The Worship of the Early Church.* Philadelphia: Fortress Press, 1973.

Hagner, D. G.
1984 *The Jewish Reclamation of Jesus,* Grand Rapids: Zondervan Publishing House.

Hamel, G.
1990 *Poverty and Charity in Roman Palestine, First Three Centuries,* C. E. Berkeley: University of California Press.

Hamm, D.
1988 "Luke 19:8 Once again: Does Zacchaeus Defend or Resolve?" *JBL* 107 (No. 3): 431-437.

Hare, D. R. A.
1967 *The Theme of Jewish Persecution of Christians in the Gospel According to St. Matthew.* Cambridge: Cambridge University Press.
1985 "The Lives of the Prophets" in *The Old Testament Pseudepigrapha.* vol.2. ed. by J. H. Charlesworth. New York: Doubleday & Company, Inc..

Harnack, A.
1907 *Sprueche und Reden Jesu.* Leipzig. (1st ed. 1904). ET J. R. Wilkinson. *The Sayings of Jesus.* London: Williams & Norgate, 1908.
1908 *Die Mission und Ausbreitung des Christentum in den ersten drei Jahrhunderten.* vols. 1-2. ET by J. Moffat *The Mission of Christianity.* London: Williams & Norgate.

Harvey, A. E.
1982 *Jesus and the Constraints of History.* London: SCM Press.

Hauck, H.
1954 ὀφείλω, ὀφειλή, ὀφείλημα, ὀφειλέτη. *TDNT.* vol. 559-566

Hawkins, J. C.
1909 *Horae Synopticae.* Oxford: Oxford University Press.

Hemer, C. J.
1989 *The Book of Acts in the Setting of Hellenistic History.* Tuebingen: J. C. B. Mohr (P. Siebeck).

Hengel, M.
1961 *Die Zeloten (Untersuchungen zur juedischen Freiheitsbewegung in der Zeit von Herodes.* Bis 7 Chr).Leiden: E. J. Brill. Second improved and enlarged ed. 1976. ET by D. Smith. *Jesus and the Zealots.* Edinburgh: T. & T. Clark, 1989.
1968 *Nachfolge und Charisma.* Berlin: A. Toepelmann. ET by C. G. Creig. *The Charismatic Leader and his Followers.* Edinburgh: T.& T. Clark, 1981.
1971 *Gewalt und Gewaltlosigkeit: Zur "politischen Theologie" in neutestamentlicher Zeit.* Stuttgart: Calwer Verlag. ET by D. E. Green *Victory over Violence.* London: SPCK, 1975.
1983 Probleme des Markusevangelium in *Das Evangelium un die Evangelien* ed. P. Stuhlmacher. Tuebingen: J. C. B. Mohr (P. Siebeck). ET by J. Bowden. *Literary, Theological and Historical Problems in the Gospel of Mark.* Pp. 225-265 in *Studies in the Gospel of Mark.* London: SCM Press, 1985.

Hiers, R.H.
1973 *The historical Jesus and the kingdom of God.* Gainesville: University of Florida Press.

Hill, D.
1967 *Greek Words and Hebrew Meanings.* Cambridge: Cambridge University Press.

Hirsch, E.
1941 *Fruehgeschichte des Evangeliums.* vol. 1. *Die Berden des Markusevageliums.* 1st ed. Tuebingen: J. C. B. Mohr (P. Siebeck).
1951 *Fruehgeschichte des Evangeliums.* vol. 2. *Die Vorlagen des Lukas und das Sondergut des Matthaeus.* 2nd rev. ed. (1st ed. 1941). Tuebingen: J. C. B. Mohr.

Hoffmann, P.
1972 *Studien zur Theologie* der *Logienquelle.* Muenster: Verlag Aschendorff.

Hogg, J.
1824 *The Private Memoirs and Confessions of a Justified Sinner.* London: The Cresset Press, 1947.

Horsley, R.
1987 *Jesus and the Spiral of Violence.* San Francisco: Harper & Row.

Hultgren, A. J.
1979 *Jesus and His Adversaries.* Minneapolis: Augusburg Publishing House.

Huemmel, R.
1966 *Die Ausandersetzung zwischen Kirche und Judentum im Matthaeusevangelium.* Muenchen: Chr. Kaiser Verlag.

James, M. R.
1953 *The Apocryphal New Testament.* rev. ed. (1st ed. 1924). Oxford: Oxford University Press.

Jeremias, J.
1938 *'Ιωνᾶς. TDNT.* vol. 3: 408-410.
1953 "Kennzeichen der ipsissima vox Jesu". Pp. 86-93 in *Synoptische Studien* (Festschrift for A. Wilkenhauer). Muenchen: Karl Zink Verlag.
1956 *Jesu Verheissung Fuer Die Volker.* Stuttgart: W. Kohlhammer. ET by S. H. Hooke. *Jesus' Promise to the Nations.* Philadelphia: Fortress Press, 1967.
1962 *Die Gleichnisse Jesu.* 6th ed. Vandenhoeck & Ruprecht: Goettingen. ET by S. H. Hooke *The Parables of Jesus. London:* SCM Press, 1961.
1962a *Day Vater-Unser im Lichte der Neureren Forschung.* Stuttgart: Calver-Verlag. ET by J. Bowden *The Prayers of Jesus.* London: SCM Press, 1967. Pp. 82-107.
1966 *Abba. Studien zur neutestamentlichen Theologie und Zeitgeschichte.* 15-67 (Abba), 68-80 (Das tagliche Gebet im Leben), 145-152. Goettingen: Vandenhoeck & Ruprecht. ET by J. Bowden *The Prayers of Jesus.* London: SCM Press, 1967. Pp. 11-57, 58-66.

1971 *Neutestamentliche Theologie. I Teil (Die Verkuendigung Jesu).* Guetersloher: Guetersloher Verlaghaus Gerd Mohn. ET by J. Bowden. *New Testament Theology I: The proclamation of Jesus.* London: SCM Press, 1972.

1980 *Die Sprache des Lukasevangelium.* Goettingen: Vandenhoeck und Ruprecht.

Johnson, S. E.

1955 "Paul and the Manual of Discipline." *HTHR* 148: 157-166.

Juelicher, A.

1899 *Die Gleichnisreden Jevu.* vol. 2. Freiburg: Akademische Verlagsbuchhandlong. Tuebingen: J. C. B. Mohr (P. Siebeck).

Kaesemann, E.

1965 *Exegetische Versuche und Besinnungen.* 2nd ed, Goettingen: Vandenhoeck & Ruprecht. ET by W. J. Montague *New Testament Questions of Today.* London: SCM Press, 1969.

Kee, H. C.

1986 *Medicine, Miracle and Magic in New Testament Times.* Cambridge: Cambridge University Press.

Kilpatrick. G. D.

1946 *The Origins of the Gospel according to St. Matthew.* Oxford: Oxford University Press.

Klausner, J.

1922 *Jesus of Nazareth.* ET by H. Danby from the original Hebrew. New York: The Macmillan Company, 1925.

Klein, G.

1969 "Die Pruefung der Zeit (Lukas 12.54-56)". *ZTHK* 61: 373-390.

Kleist, J. A.

1957 *The Didache in Ancient Christian Writers.* vol. 6. London: Longmans, Greens & Company.

Kloppenborg, J. S.

1986 "The Function of Apocalyptic Language in Q." Pp. 224-235 in *SBL Seminar Papers.* ed. by K. H. Richards. Atlanta: Scholars Press.

Klostemann, E.

1926 *Das Markusevangelium.* 2nd newly rev. ed.Tuebingen: J. C. B. Mohr (P. Siebeck).

1927 *Das Matthaeusevangelium.* 2nd newly rev. ed.Tuebingen: J. C. B Mohr (P. Siebeck).

1929 *Das Lukasevangelium.* 2nd newly rev. ed. Tuebingen: J. C. B. Mohr (P. Siebeck).

Knox, W. L.

1930 *Penitence and Forgiveness.* London: SPCK.

1953 *The Sources of the Synoptic Gospels.* vol. 1 (St. Mark). ed. by H. Chadwick. Cambridge: Cambridge University Press.

1957 *The Sources of the Synoptic Gospels.* vol. 2. (St. Luke and St. Matthew). ed. by H. Chadwick. Cambridge: Cambridge University Press.

Koester. H.
1990 *Ancient Christian Gospels: Their Literary and Development.* London: SCM Press.

Kuhn, K. G.
1950 *Achtzehngebet und Vaterunser und der Reim.* Tuebingen: J. C. Mohr (P. Siebeck).

Kuemmel, W. G.
1956 *Verheissung und Erfuellung.* Zuerich: Zwingli-Verlag. 3rd and completed rev. ed. ET by D. M . Barton. *Promise and Fulfilment.* London: SCM Press, 1957.
1971 "Eschatological Expectation in the Proclamation of Jesus". Pp. 36-51 in *The Kingdom of God.* ed. by B. Chilton. ET by C. E. Carlston. London: SPCK, 1984.
1972 *Die Theologie des Neuen Testaments nach seinen Hauptzeugen.* Goettingen: Vandenhoeck & Ruprecht. ET by J. Steeley *The Theology of the New Testament.* London: SCM Press, 1974

Kuschke, A.
1950-51 "Das Idiom der "relativen Negation" im NT". *ZNW* 43 (1950-1951): 263.

Lachs, S. T.
1980 "Hebrew Elements in the Gospels and Acts". *JQR* 71. 31-39.

Lagrange, M. J.
1927 *Evangile selon Saint Luc.* 3rd ed. Paris: J. Gabalda Fditeur.
1938 *Evangile de Jesus Christ.* part 1-2. Westmonsterri. ET by Members of the English Dominican Province. London: Burns Oates & Washborne Ltd., 1947.

Lattery, C.
1941 " The Prophets and Sacrifice: A Study of Biblical Relativity". *JTS* 42: 155-165.

Linnemann, E.
1964 *Gleichnisse Jesu, Einfuehrung und Auslegung.* 3rd ed (1st ed. 1961). Goettingen: Vandenhoeck & Ruprecht. ET by J. Sturdy *Parables of Jesus.* London: SPCK, 1966.

Linton, O.
1965 "The Demand for a Sign from Heaven (Mark 8:11-12, and par)". *ST* 19: 112-129.
1975-6 "The Parable of the Children's Game". *NTS* 22: 159 -179.

Loewe, W. P.
1974 "Towards an Interpretation of Luke 19:1-10". *CBQ* 36: 321-331.

Lohmeyer, F.
1937 *Das Evangelium des Markus.* Goettingen: Vandenhoeck & Ruprecht.
1939 *Das Evangelium des Matthaeus.* Completed by G. Schumach. Goettingen: Vandenhoeck & Ruprecht.
1942 *Kultus und Evangelium.* Goettingen: Vandenhoeck & Ruprecht. ET by S. Todd. *Lord of the Temple.* Edinburgh and London: Oliver and Boyd, 1961.
1946 *Das Vater-Unser.* Goettingen: Vandenhoeck & Ruprecht. ET by J.

Bowden *The Lord's Prayer*. London: Collins, 1965.

Loisy, E.

1908 *Les Evangiles Synoptiques.* vols. 1-2. published by the author. Effonds: Montier-En-Der.

Luehrmann, D.

1969 *Die Redaktion der Logienquelle.* Neukirchen-Vluyn: Neukirchener Verlag.

1987 *Das Markusevangelium.* vol. 1. Tuebingen: J. C. B. Mohr (P. Siebeck).

Luz, U.

1985 *Das Evangelium nach Matthaeus. vol.* 1 (Ch. 1-7). Zuerich: Benziger Verlag. ET by 0. Linns. Edinburgh: T. & T. Clark, 1990.

Maccoby, H.

1988 *Early Rabbinic Writings.* Cambridge: Cambridge Univ. Press.

1989a *Judaism in the First Century,* London: Sheldon Press.

Maish, I.

1975 "Die Botschaft Jesu von der Gotteshertschaft". Pp. 27-42 in *Gegenwart und Kommendes Reich. ed.* by P. Fiedler und D. Zeller. Stuttgart: Katholisches Bibelwerk Verlag.

Manson, T. W.

1948 *The Sayings of Jesus,* 2nd ed. (a few notes on particular points and some additions were added to bibliography). 1st ed. published with works of H. D. A. Major & C. J. Wright *The Mission and Message of Jesus.* London: SCM Press, 1937.

1955 The Lord's Prayer. *BJRL* vol. 38. No. 1. Manchester: Manchester University Press.

1956 The Lord's Prayer. *BJRL* vol. 38. No. 2. Manchester: Manchester University Press.

1960 *Ethics and the Gospel.* London: SCM Press.

Manson, W.

1930 *The Gospel of Luke*. London: Hodder & Stoughton.

1943 *Jesus the Messiah.* London: Hodder & Stoughton.

Marshall, I. H.

1965-66 "The Synoptic Son of Man Sayings in Recent Discussion". *NTS* 12: 327-351.

1969 *Kept by the Power of God: A Study of Perseverance and Falling* Away, London: Epworth Press.

1970 *Luke: Historian & Theologian.* Exeter: The Paternoster Press.

1972-73 "Palestinian and Hellenistic Christianity: Some Critical Comments". *NTS* 19: 271-187.

1978 *Commentary on Luke.* Exeter: The Paternoster Press.

Marxen, W.

1956 *Der Evangelist Markus.* Goettingen:Vandenhoeck & Ruprecht. ET by J. Boyce, D. Juel, W. Poehlmann, R.A. Harrisville *Mark the Evangelist: Studies on the Redaction History of the Gospels.* Nashville: Abingdon Press, 1969.

McNeile, A. H.
1915 *The Gospel according to St. Matthew.* London: Macmillan & Company.
Merklein, H.
1981 *Die Gottesherrschaft als Handlungsprinzip (Untersuchung zur Ethik Jesu).* Wuerzburg: Echter Verlag.
Metzger, B. M.
1970 "Names for the Nameless in the New Testament. A Study in the Growth of Christian Tradition". Pp.79-99 in *Kyriakon. Festschrift for J. Quasten. vol.* 1. Muenster: Verlag Aschendorff.
Meyer, B.
1979 *The Aims of Jesus.* London: SCM Press.
1990 "Many (=All) are called, But Few (=not All) are chosen". *NTS* 136 (No. 1): 89-97.
Michel. O.
1969 Τελώνης *TDNT.* vol. 8: 88-105.
Michaelis, W. M.
1956 *Die Gleichnisse Jesue, Eine Einfuehrung.* 3rd ed. Hamburg; Furche Verlag.
Miller, R.
1988 "The Rejection of the Prophets in Q". *JBL* 107 (No. 2): 225-240.
Mitchell, A.C.
1990 "Zacchaeus Revisited: Luke 19:8 as a Defence" *Biblica* 71: 153-176.
Montefiore, C. G.
1927 *The Synoptic Gospels.* 1st ed. 1909. vols. 1-2. London: The Macmillan Publishing Company.
1930 *Rabbinic Literature and Gospel Teachings.* London: The Macmillan Publishing Company.
Moore, G. F.
1927 *Judaism in the First Centuries of the Christian Era.* vols. 1-3. Cambridge: Harvard University Press.
Morgan R. & Barton. J.
1988 *Biblical Interpretation.* Oxford: Oxford University Press.
Moule, C. F. D.
1978 "...As we forgive...: a Note on the Distinction between Deserts and Capacity in the Understanding of Forgiveness". Pp. 68-77 in *Donum Gentilicium.* ed. by E. Bammel, C. K. Barrett, & W. D. Davies. Oxford: Oxford University Press.
1981 *The Birth of the New Testament.* 3rd. rev. ed. (1st ed. 1962). London: A & C. Black.
Mueller, U. B.
1977 "Vision und Botschaft:Erwaegung zur prophetischen Struktur der Verkuendigung Jesu", *ZTHK* 174: 416-448.
Murphy-O'Connor, J.
1990 "John the Baptist and Jesus: History and Hypotheses". *NTS* 36: 359-374.

Mussner, F.
1959 "Der nicht erkannte Kairos (Matt 11: 16-19//Luke 7:31-35)". *Biblica* 40: 599-612.
1969 "Wege zum Selbstbewusstsein Jesu". BZ 12: 161-172.
1979 *Traktat ueber die Juden.* Muenchen: Koesel-Verlag. ET by L. Swidler *Tractate on the Jews.* London: SPCK; Philadelphia: Fortress Press, 1984.

Neale, D. A.
1991 *None but the Sinners: Religious Categories in the Gospel of Luke.* Sheffield: Sheffield University Press

Nineham, D.E.
1963 *The Gospel of Mark.* Harmondsworth; Penguin Books.

O'Neill, J. C.
1959 "The Six Amen Sayings in Luke". *JTS* 10: 1-9
1968-69 "The Silence of Jesus". *NTS* 15: 153-167.
1970 *The Theology of Acts in its Historical Setting.* rev. 2nd ed. (1st ed. 1961). London: SPCK.
1974-75 "The Synoptic Problem". *NTS* 21: 273-285.
1980 *Messiah: Six Lectures on the Ministry of Jesus.* Cambridge: Cochrane Press.

Oppenheimer, A.
1977 *The Am Ha-Aretz. (A study in the Social History of the Jewish People in the Hellenistic-Roman Period).* Leiden: E. J. Brill.

Peabody, D. B.
1987 "W. R. Farmer: A Bibliographical Essay". Pp. ix-xxxviii in *Jesus, the Gospels, and the Church* ed. by E. P. Sanders. Atlanta: Mercer University Press.

Perrin, N.
1963 *The Kingdom of God in the Teaching of Jesus.* London: SCM Press.
1967 *Rediscovering the Teaching of Jesus.* London: SCM Press.

Petersen, W. L.
1981 "The Parable of the Lost Sheep". *NovT* 23: 128-147.

Pesch, R.
1976 *Das Markusevangelium.* vol. 1. Freiburg, Basel, Wien: Herder Verlag.

Piper, R. A.
1989 *Wisdom in the Q Tradition: The aphoristic Teachings of Jesus.* Cambridge: Cambridge University Press.

Plummer, A,
1905 *St. Luke.* 4th ed. International Critical Commentary. Edinburgh: T.& T. Clark.
1909 *An Exegetical Commentary on the Gospel according to Matthew.* London: Elliott Stock.

Polag, A.
1979 *Fragmenta Q: Textheft Zur Logienquelle.* Neukirchener-Vluyn: Neukirchener Verlag.

Rasco, E.
1967 "Les Parables de Luc XV", in *De Jesus aux Evangiles. ed.* I. de la

Potterie. Paris: P. Lethieleux Editeur.

Rawlinson, A. E. J.
1927 *St. Mark.* 2nd ed. (lst ed. 1925). London: Methuen & Co. Ltd..

Reicke, B
1965 *Neutestatmentliche Zeitgeschichte.* Berlin: A. Toepelmann.

Rengstorf, K. H.
1933 ἀπόστολος *TDNT.* vol. 1: 398-447.
1964 σημεῖον *TDNT.* vol. 7: 200-269.

Robin, A. De Q.
1961-62 "The Cursing of the Fig Tree in Mark XI. A Hypothesis". *NTS* 8:276-281.

Robinson, J. M.
1959 *A New Quest of the Historical Jesus.* London; SCM Press.

Rowley, H. H.
1945-6 "The Unity of the Old Testament". *BJRL* 29: 326-358.
1950-1 "The Meaning of Sacrifice in the O.T.". *BJRL* 33: 74-1 10.

Sanders, E. P.
1968-9 "The Argument from Order and the Relationship Between Matthew and Luke". *NTS* 15: 249-261.
1969 *The Tendencies of the Synoptic Tradition.* Cambridge: Cambridge University Press.
1971 "Mark 10:17-31 and Parallels". Pp. 257-270 in *SBL* One hundred Seventh Annual Meeting Seminar Papers.
1972 "The Overlaps of Mark and Q and the Synoptic Problem". *NTS* 19: 453-465.
1977 *Paul and Palestinian Judaism.* London: SCM Press.
1983 *Paul, the Law, and the Jewish People.* London: SCM Press.
1983 "Jesus and the Sinners". *JSNT* 19:5 36.
1985 *Jesus and Judaism,* London: SCM Press.
1987 "Jesus and the Kingdom: The Restoration of Israel and the New People of God". Pp. 225-239 in *Jesus, the Gospels and the Church: Essays in honour of W. F. Farmer.* ed. by E. P. Sanders. Macon: Mercer University Press.
1987 *Studying the Synoptic Gospels.* London: SCM Press.
1990 *Jewish Law from Jesus to the time of Mishnah.* London: SCM Press
1991 *Paul.* Oxford: Oxford University Press.

Sanders, J. T.
1975 *Ethics in the New Testament.* London: SCM Press.

Schlatter, A.
1948 *Der* Evangelist Matthaeus. Stuttgart: Calwer Verlag.

Schmid, J.
1958 *Das Evangelium nach Markus.* Regensburg: Pustet Verlag. ET by K. Condon *The Gospel according to Mark.* Cork: The Mercier Press, 1968.
1960 *Das Evangelium nach Lukas.* Regensburg: Friedrich Pustet Verlag.

Schmidt, K. L.
1933 βασλεία *TDNT.* vol. 1: 574-593.

1964 *Der Rahmen der Geschichte: Literakritische untersuchungen zur aeltesten Jesusueberlieferung.* Darmstadt: Wissenschaftliche Buchgesellschaft.

Schmitt, G.
1978 "Das Zeichen des Jonah". *ZNW* 69 (1-2): 123-129.

Schnackenburg, R.
1963 *Gottes Herrschaft und Reich.* Freiburg: Herder Verlag. ET by J. Murray *God's Rule and Kingdom.* Nelson: Edinburgh-London.
1971 *Das Johannesevangelium.* vol. 2. Freiburg, Basel, Wien: Herder Verlag. ET by C. Hastings, F. McDonagh, D. Smith, R. Foley. *The Gospel According St. John.* vol. 2. New York: The Crossroad Publishing Company, 1990.
1985 *Matthaeusevangelium. vol.* 1 (1: 1-16:20). Wuerzburg: Echter Verlag.
1987 *Matthaeusevangelium.* vol. 2 (16:21-28:20). Wuerzburg: Echter Verlag.

Schniewind, J.
1954 *Das Evangelium nach Matthaeus.* Goettingen: Vandenhoeck & Ruprecht.

Schottroff, L.
1971 "Das Gleichnis von verlorenen Sohn". *ZThK* 69: 27-52
1973 "Die Erzaehlung von Pharisaeer und Zoellner als Beispiel fuer die Theologische Kunst des Ueberredens". Pp. 439-461 in *Neues Testament und Christliche Existenz.* ed. by H. D. Betz & L. Schottroff. Festschrift fuer H. Braun. Tuebingen: J. C. B. Mohr (P. Siebeck).

Schrage, W.
1982 *Ethik des Neuen Testaments.* ET by D. E. Green *The Ethics of the New Testament.* Edinburgh: T. & T. Clark, 1988.

Schrenk. G.
1935 δικαιόω. *TDNT.* vol. 2: 178-225.

Schuerer, E.
1973 *The History of the Jewish People in the Age of Jesus Christ (175 B.C.-A.D.133).* vol. 1 (1973), 2 (1979), 3.1 (1986), 3.2 (1987). A New English Version of *Geschichte des juedischen Volkes im Zeitatter Jesu Christ.* rev. & ed. by G. Vermes & F. Millar & M. Black. 2nd ed. Edinburgh: T. & T. Clark Ltd.

Schuermann, H.
1968 "Mt 10,5b-6 und die Vorgeschichte des synoptischen Aussendungsberichtes" Pp.137-149 in *Traditionsgeschichtliche Untersuchungen zu den synoptischen Evangelien.* Duesseldorf. Patmos Verlag.
1969 *Das Lukasevangelium.* vol. I (chap. 1: 1-9:50). Freiburg, Basel, Wien: Herder.

Schulz, S.
1972 *Die Spruchquelle Der Evangelisten.* Zuerich: Theologischer Verlag.

Schwarz, E.
1904 "Der Verfluchte Feigenbaum". *ZNW* 5: 80-84.

Schwarz, G.
1968-69 "Matthaeus VI.9-13/Lukas XI.2-4. Emendation und Rueckuebersetzung". *NTS* 15: 233-247.
1969 "Lukas xiii 1-5 Eine Emendation". *NovT* 11: 121-126.

Schweitzer, A.
1901 *Das Abendmahl: Das Messianitaets und Leidensgeheimnis.* Tuebingen: J. C. B. Mohr (P. Siebeck). ET by W. Lowrie *The Mystery of the kingdom of God.* London: Adam & Charles Black, 1914.
1951 *Reich Gottes und Christentum.* Tuebingen: J. C. B. Mohr (P. Siebeck). ed. by U. Neuenschwander. ET by L. A. Garrad. *The Kingdom of God and Primitive Christianity.* London: Adam & Charles Black, 1968.

Schweizer, E.
1955 *Erniedrigung und Erhoehung bei Jesus und seinen Nachfolgern.* Zuerich: Zwingli-Verlag. Trans. and revised edition of German work by the author. *Lordship and Discipleship.* London: SCM Press, 1968.
1967 *Das Evangelium nach Mark* Gottingen: Vandenhoeck & Ruprecht. ET by D. H. Madwig *The Good News according to Mark.* Atlanta: J. Knox Press, 1970.
1968 *Jesus Christus.* Munich: Siebenstern Verlag. ET by D. E. Green *Jesus.* London: SCM Press.
1973 *Das Evangelium nach Matthaeus.* Goettingen: Vandenhoeck & Ruprecht. ET by D. E. Green. *The Good News according to Matthew.* Atlanta: J. Knox Press, 1975.
1982 *Das Evangelium nach Lukas.* Goettingen: Vandenhoeck & Ruprecht. ET by D. E. Green. *The Good News according to Luke.* Atlanta: J. Knox Press, 1984.

Sherwin-White, A. N.
1963 *Roman Society and Roman Law in the New Testament. Oxford:* Oxford University Press,

Smith, B. T. D.
1937 *The Parables of the Synoptic Gospels.* Cambridge: Cambridge University Press.

Stanton, G. N.
1973 "On the Christology of Q". Pp. 27-42 in *Christ and Spirit in the New Testament.* ed. by B. Lindars & S. Smalley in honour of C. F. D. Moule. Cambridge: Cambridge University Press.
1989 *The Gospels and Jesus.* Oxford: Oxford University Press,

Stauffer, E.
1941 *Die Theologie des Neuen Testaments. Stuttgart:* W. Kohlhammer Verlag. ET by J. Marsh *New Testament Theology.* London: SCM Press, 1955.

Steck, O.
1967 *Israel und das gewaltsame Geschichte der Propheteten.* Neukirchen-

Vluyn: Neukirchener Verlag.
Stein, R. H.
1983 "The "Criteria" for Authenticity". *Gospel Perspectives. vol.* 1. ed. R. T. France & D. Wenham. Sheffield: Sheffield Press.
Strathmann, H.
1942 μαρτύριον. *TDNT.* vol. 4: 474-514.
Strecker, G.
1962 *Der Weg der Gerechtigkeit.* Goettingen: Vandenhoeck & Ruprecht.
1985 *Die Bergpredigt.* 2nd ed. Goettingen: Vandenhoeck & Ruprecht. ET by 0. C. Dean *The Sermon on the Mount.* Edinburgh: T. & T. Clark, 1988.
Suggs, M. J.
1970 *Wisdom, Christology, and Law in Matthew's Gospel.* Cambridge: Harvard University Press.
Swete, H. B.
1913 *The Gospel according to St. Mark,* London: The Macmillan Publishing Co..
Swinburne, R.
1989 *Reconciliation and Forgiveness.* Oxford: Oxford University Press.
Taylor, V.
1952 *The Gospel according to St. Mark.* London: The Macmillan Publishing Company.
Telford, W. R.
1980 *The Barren Temple and the Withered Tree.* Sheffield: Sheffield Academic Press.
Theissen, G.
1973 "Wanderradikalismus". *ZThK* 70: 245-270.
1974 *Urchristliche Wundergeschichten.* ET by F. McDonagh, The *Miracle Stories of the Early Christian Tradition.* Edinburgh: T. & T. Clark, 1983.
1977 *Soziologie der Jesusbewegung: Ein Beitrag zur Entstehung zum geschichte des Urchristentums.* Muenchen: Christian Kaiser Verlag. ET by J. Bowden, *The First Followers of Jesus.* London: SCM Press, 1978.
Thompson, G. H. P.
1972 *St. Luke (New Clarendon Bible).* Oxford: Oxford University Press.
Toedt, H. E.
1963 *Der Menschensohn in der synoptischen Ueberlieferung.* 2nd ed. Guetersloher Verlaghaus Gerd Mohn. ET by D. M. Barton *The Son of Man in the Synoptic Tradition.* London: SCM Press, 1965.
Torrey, C. C.
1933 *The Four Gospels (A New Translation).* London: Hodder & Stoughton.
Trautmann, M.
1980 *Zeichenhafte Handlungen Jesu (Ein Beitrag zur Frage nach den geschichtlichen Jesu).* Wuerzburg: Echter Verlag.

Trilling, W.
1965 *Das Evangelium nach Matthaeus.* vol. 1. Duesseldorf. Patmos-Verlag. ET by K. Smith *The Gospel according to St. Matthew.* London: Burns & Oats, 1969.
1975 *Das wahre Israel.* 3rd ed (lst ed. 1964). Leipzig: St. Benno.

Trocme E.
1963 *La Formation de l'Evangile selon Marc.* Paris: Presses Universitaires de France. ET by P. Gaughan. *The Formation of the Gospel according to Mark.* London: SPCK, 1975.
1972 *Jesus de Nazareth vu par les temains de sa vie.* Neuachtel-Delachausx et Niestle. *Jesus and His Contemporaries.* ET by R.A. Wilson. London: SCM Press, 1973.

Urbach. E.
1975 *The Sages: Their Concepts and Beliefs.* ET by I. Abrahams. Jerusalem: The Magnes Press.

Uro, R.
1987 *Sheep Among The Wolves: A Study on the Mission Instruction of Q.* Helsinki: Suomalainen Tiedeakatemia.

Vermes, G.
1967 "The Use of bar nash/bar nasha in Jewish Aramaic." Pp. 310-328 in M. Black *An Aramaic Approach to the Gospels and Acts.* 3rd ed. Oxford: Oxford University Press.
1973 *Jesus the Jew: A historian's reading of the Gospels. London:* Collins.
1981 *The Gospel of Jesus the Jew.* New Castle Upon Tyne: University of Newcastle Upon Tyne.

Via, D. O.
1967 *The Parables: Their literary and Existential Dimensions.* Philadelphia: Fortress Press.

Vielhauer, P.
1965 "Jesus und der Menschensohn". Pp. 92-140 in *Aufsaetze zum Neuen Testament* Muenchen: Chr. Kaiser Verlag.
1965 "Gottesreich und Menschensohn in der Verkuendigung Jesu". Pp. 141-198 in *Aufsaetze zum Neuen Testament.* Muenchen: Chr. Kaiser Verlag.

Voegtle, A.
1953 "Das Spruch vom Jonazeichen". Pp. 230-277 in *Synoptische Studien (Festschrift for A. Wilkenhauer)* ed. by J. Schmid and A. Voegtle. Muenich: Karl Zink Verlag.
1974 "The Lord's Prayer: A Prayer for Jews and Christians? " Pp. 93- 118 in *The Lord's Prayer and Jewish Liturgy.* Freiburg im Briesgau: Verlag Herder. ET by E. R. Petuchowski. ed. by J. Petuchowski & M. Brocke. London: Burns & Oates, 1978. sd

Watson, N.
1966-67 "Was Zacchaeus Really Reforming".*ExpT* 77: 282-285.

Weaver, D. J.
1990 *Matthew's Missionary Discourse.* Sheffield: Sheffield Academic Press.

Weder, H.
1978 *Die Gleichnisse Jesu als Metaphern.* Goettingen: Vandenhoeck & Ruprecht.
Weiser, A.
1971 *Die Knechtsgleichnisse Jesu der synoptischen Evangelien.* Muenchen: Koesel Verlag.
Weiss, J.
1892 *Die Predigt Jesus vom Reiche Gottes.* Goettingen: Vandenboeck & Ruprecht. ET by R. H. Hiers & D. L. Holland *The Proclamation of the Kingdom.* London: SCM Press, 1971.
1917 *Die Schriften des Neuen Testaments.* vol. 1. Goettingen: Vandenhoeck & Ruprecht.
Wellhausen, J.
1904 *Das Evangelium Lucae.* Berlin: Druck und Verlag von G. Reimer.
1909 *Das Evangelium Marci.* Berlin: Druck und Verlag von G. Reimer.
1911 *Einleitung in die Drei Ersten Evangelien.* Berlin: Druck und Verlag von G. Reimer.
1914 *Das Evangelium Matthaei.* Berlin: Druck und Verlag von G Reimer.
Westholm, S.
1979 *Jesus and the scribal Authority.* Lund: Gleerkup.
White, R.
1979 "Vindication for Zaccheus'?" *ExpT* 91: 21.
Who' Who editor.
1991 *Who's Who.* London: A & C Black.
Wilder, A.
1950 *Eschatology and Ethics in the Teaching of Jesus.* Rev. ed. Westport: Greenwood Press.
Wilkens, U.
1964 *σοφία, σοφός,σοφίζω. TDNT.* vol. 7: 465-476, 496-528.
Winton, A. P.
1979 *The Proverbs of Jesus (Issues of History and Rhetoric).* Sheffield: Sheffield Academic Press.
Wojciechowski, M.
1989 "The Touching of the Leper (Mark 1:40-45)". *BZ* 33: 114-119.
Wrede, W.
1901 *Das Messiasgeheimnis.* Goettingen: Vandenhoeck & Ruprecht. ET by C. E. G. Greig. *The Messianic Secret.* Cambridge and London: James Clarke & Co. Ltd.
Zeitlin, S.
1973-74 "Who were the Galileans: New Light on Josephus' Activities in Galilee". *JQR* vol. 64 (No. 1): 189-203.
Zeller, D.
1977 *Die weisheitliche Mahnsprueche bei den Synoptikern.* Wuerzburg: Echter Verlag.

INDEX